THE FAREWELL ANGEL

CARMEN MARTÍN GAITE was born in Salamanca in 1925. She published her first novel at the age of 29, and won the Premio Gijón. Her subsequent novels have won many awards. The publication of *Variable Cloud*, her first novel after 14 years, was a considerable event in Spain where it headed the bestseller lists for several weeks. The present novel won the Spanish National Prize for Literature.

MARGARET JULL COSTA translated *Variable Cloud*. She is also translator of works by Bernardo Atxaga and Javier Marías (including *A Heart so White* which won the Dublin International Impac Award). Her translation of Fernando Pessoa's *The Book of Disquiet* made her joint-winner of the Portuguese translation prize.

Carmen Martín Gaite

THE FAREWELL ANGEL

Translated from the Spanish
by Margaret Jull Costa

THE HARVILL PRESS
LONDON

First published in Spain with the title *La Reina de las Nieves* by
Editorial Anagrama, Barcelona, 1994

First published in Great Britain in 1999
by The Harvill Press,
2 Aztec Row, Berners Road
London N1 0PW

www.harvill-press.com

1 3 5 7 9 8 6 4 2

This edition has been translated with the financial assistance of the
Spanish Dirección General del Libro y Bibliotecas, Ministerio de Cultura

Carmen Martín Gaite asserts the moral right to be
identified as the author of this work

A CIP catalogue record for this book
is available from the British Library

ISBN 1 86046 357 6 (hbk)
ISBN 1 86046 358 4 (pbk)

Designed and typeset in Fournier at
Libanus Press, Marlborough, Wiltshire

Printed and bound in Great Britain by Butler & Tanner Ltd
at Selwood Printing, Burgess Hill

Contents

Translator's Note

The version of the Cavafy poem I use is by Rae Dalven, published in 1961 in *The Complete Poems of C. P. Cavafy*, (courtesy of the Estate of C. P. Cavafy and the Hogarth Press). The lines from Ibsen's *The Lady from the Sea* are an adaptation of Michael Meyer's translation published in *Ibsen Plays: Three*, Methuen, 1980.

I would like to thank Annella McDermott, Antonio Martín and Ben Sherriff for all their help and advice.

M.J.C.

Let go Hell; and your fall will
be broken by the roof of Heaven.

Djuna Barnes, Nightwood

For Hans Christian Andersen
without whose collaboration
this book would never have
been written.

And in memory of my daughter,
for the enthusiasm with which
she encouraged that
collaboration.

Preliminary note

This novel, for which I have been making notes since 1975, has had a very eventful evolution. I started writing it seriously in the spring of 1979 and worked on it assiduously until the end of 1984, especially in the autumn of that year, during a long stay in Chicago. I had gone to the University there as visiting professor and was staying on the seventeenth floor of the Blackstone, an old hotel with a revolving door. The window in my room looked out over Lake Michigan; I dragged my table over to the window and spent whole afternoons working there. I always associate *The Farewell Angel* with the cold, desolate view over that immense lake. I think I mentioned this literary project of mine in a couple of interviews I made at the time; the project was, I felt, at a sufficiently advanced stage and I planned to finish it on my return to Madrid.

However, for private and personal reasons, from January 1985 on, the very thought of the Snow Queen froze my heart, and I buried those notebooks seven leagues down, believing that I would never ever want to disinter them.

That wasn't what happened. After eight years, shortly after publishing *Variable Cloud*, in the void left by Sofía Montalvo and Mariana León, I experienced a sudden, sharp nostalgia for Leonardo Villalba, as you do when you seek refuge in a friend whom you've lost track of. And so the search began, even though it meant facing the unpredictable emotions that are likely with any re-encounter and which is almost always akin to opening up old wounds.

I started hunting for those notebooks – I could remember exactly what they looked like – and I couldn't find them anywhere. After three days spent rummaging in drawers, shelves and the boots of cars, my search was becoming ever more eager and passionate. By the time I finally found them, my feelings of anxiety had taught me how important the story still was to me; this was confirmed when I started reading the notebooks one July afternoon in Santander, and I decided never to abandon them again. I had forgotten how much of it I had written and how many notes I had taken for its continuation. Nevertheless, there was still plenty of work to be done on it and still many enigmas to be resolved. Almost without realizing it, I immersed myself in the task again and the plot came alive, for the simple reason that it wasn't dead.

I wanted to set all this down, albeit briefly, in order to forestall those people who always ask me: "And what are you working on now?", who might be surprised that I could have written such a complex and "peculiar" novel as this in only two years, off the top of my head. There is another reason too. The story is set firmly in the late 1970s, which is when I first started working on it. I feel it important to remind the reader of that, because neither nightclubs in Madrid, life in a remote village, nor a stay in a cell in Carabanchel prison are the same now as they were fifteen years ago. Fifteen years is a long time. They have to pass before you realize just how long.

Carmen Martín Gaite

PART ONE

I

The death of Rosa Figueroa

Almost every evening, at sunset, the lady from the big house, the Quinta Blanca, used to go for a walk as far as the lighthouse. No one ever went with her. She would walk along very erect, her gait slow and harmonious, as if she were absorbed in her own thoughts. Only when she passed through the village that lay halfway between the Quinta Blanca and the lighthouse would she occasionally look away from that remote point in the clouds which seemed to be her goal, in order to glance at one of the people staring at her and respond to their greeting with a brief, distant smile.

Although these forays of hers always had a certain odd, ritual quality about them, they also ended up being categorized amongst the other tasks, ceremonies and meteorological phenomena which, in any rural community, mark the flow of life from dawn to dusk and provide the threads from which day-to-day conversations are woven. Thus, whenever the lady failed to pass by as usual, the townspeople felt slightly nonplussed, just as if Don Ambrosio, for example, had failed to turn up for mass on Sunday without even bothering to offer an explanation. Her absence never went entirely undetected and it would cast a disquieting shadow over any farm work carried out at the end of the day, over the frugal suppers, over the return of the animals to their stables and over the lively chatter at the inn that stands at the bottom of the first steep slope of the hill leading up to the deserted lighthouse.

The inn also doubled as a shop selling cold meats, tools, china, candles and tobacco, and behind the same pine counter from which those goods were dispensed, they also prepared the coffee, cut up the cheese and served drinks to the regulars who gathered there, especially at nightfall. Some preferred to drink standing at the counter, either silently or chatting with their neighbours, with the innkeeper or with the women who came in to buy things or, on the pretext of fetching their husband home, simply to enjoy a little of the banter.

If one of the women who came looking for her husband did not find him standing near the counter, she would look across to another area on the right which was separated from the first by a screen adorned with various calendars, a fishing net and an old clock in an octagonal frame made out of blackened wood. It was a room furnished with narrow benches and two large scrubbed pine tables; here would gather the inveterate drinkers, slow and solemn, the obsessive players of card games and the dominoes addicts. Sooner or later, amongst the cigarette smoke and by the light of the long neon strip that bisected the ceiling, there would always be someone who, taking advantage of a pause in a game, would stare across at the window that looked out on to the road and say: "The lady from the Quinta Blanca didn't pass today." And after the silence that would inevitably follow that pronouncement, another man might add some comment on the weather, the way people do when they talk about the harvest; for example, he might say: "And it wasn't even raining today either." But their remarks rarely went further than that, because everything about her instilled in them a kind of respect.

Some years before, she had bought and renovated the Quinta Blanca, which had lain empty following the death of the previous owner. Since she moved in, hardly anyone – for fear of being dubbed fanciful – would have dared to flesh out the few known facts about her private life: that she had come from Brazil, where she had lost her husband – a rich landowner with no known connections with the village – that she had no children and that her husband (or she, or both) had maintained close, friendly relations (for business reasons perhaps) with the only son of Doña Inés Guitián who was buried there in the village cemetery, "the other lady", as some people had started to call her shortly after the new lady arrived to take possession of the abandoned house. The more daring of the village boys would sometimes scale the Quinta's thick, moss-covered walls, not so much in order to steal fruit from the orchard as to wander, with a mixture of fear and fascination, amongst the statues, arbours and box-lined labyrinths that filled the vast, neglected garden where the birds sang strange songs and where even the sight of a frog hopping, a snake slithering or a lizard scampering could make you feel oddly unsettled.

Doña Inés Guitián's son lived in Madrid, although it was also said that he travelled a lot; but ever since that now distant autumn afternoon when he came to attend his mother's funeral and to lock up the Quinta Blanca, he had not set foot in the house until some time after the present owner had renovated it and moved in, apparently for good.

It was after his first visit that whispered rumours started circulating in the village, fired by the imaginations of certain people with a taste for the sensual, the macabre or the marvellous. It is true that the traveller's behaviour on returning to the land of his fathers provided more than enough fuel for such rumours, especially bearing in mind that his visit was far from being the only one he would make to the lady of the Quinta Blanca and that he was rarely seen in the village during those visits – not frequent enough to seem routine, nor sporadic enough to be considered isolated exceptions – and that he had only ever once actually spoken to someone.

This encounter happened one April morning, almost as day was breaking, when he was leaving the Quinta and setting off briskly for the cemetery, bearing a bunch of freshly cut dahlias. An old village woman, who used to run errands for his late mother and tend the kitchen garden, would later tell how, on seeing him emerge at that early hour from the tall gate with its stone pillars topped with bronze vases, she had recognized him instantly and had made as if to throw herself into his arms, weeping.

"But he stopped me, he wouldn't let me. You know – that feeling you get when you have to draw back, as if you'd done the wrong thing. And he just stood there, looking all serious, not moving, as if he'd seen a ghost, although, to tell the truth, he was the one who looked like a ghost. He'd lost weight and his hair was thinning."

"But did you tell him you were Rosa?"

"I didn't have to. The moment he saw me, he said 'Hello, Rosa' and

asked after Ramón. When I told him that Ramón had died two winters
ago, he said 'Oh, I am sorry' and asked after Tola."

"And then what happened?"

"He looked even more serious, staring down at the ground, all
embarrassed, as if he couldn't wait to get away, and there we were, the
two of us, face to face, me in such a state that I nearly dropped
the bundle of firewood I was carrying on my head, remembering that
saint of a mother of his and asking after his son and wanting to know
how the child could be so ungrateful as not to have come back even
once to visit me, after all those hours he'd spent sitting on my knee and
all the stories I'd told him – that boy could never get his fill of stories,
and he always wanted to know if what I told him had really happened
and where and when."

"And what did he say about the boy?"

"Not much. Like I said, he hardly spoke. He pulled an odd face when
I mentioned his son and said that he didn't live with them any more, but
that he was fine – not much at all, really."

"Well, I don't know about him being fine. I've heard that he's been
mixed up in some very shady deals since he inherited that money from
his grandmother; being rich and spoiled is about the worst thing that
can happen to a young person, especially nowadays."

"That's what I heard too, though it's probably all lies, things people
have invented. He was such a sweet boy, and he certainly wasn't spoiled
by his mother, who never loved him; she never loved her mother-in-
law either, she never loved anyone here. She was like a block of ice that
woman. And she was obsessed with cleanliness, and germs, and boiling
everything, and about how in her country they did things this way or
that. It was as if she thought we were all savages. Honestly, when she
told me, that summer, not to kiss the boy because she'd noticed that I
smelled bad – well, that's something I won't forget as long as I live.
You see, that's why I say that the boy is an angel, because he was the
only one who defended me and who ran after me when he saw that
she'd made me cry: 'Don't cry, Rosa, come on, don't pay any attention
to her', clinging to my skirt he was, and his mother with a face like
thunder: 'I told you to come here right this instant', and him kicking

and punching when she tried to tear him away from me; and then he started shouting out that he liked the way I smelled and that he liked the smell of manure, and earth, and burning rubbish, and cows and that he didn't want any more eau-de-Cologne. You've no idea the hiding he got, right there in front of her husband and her mother-in-law. That's when I left."

"And what about them?"

"They were afraid of her, they always were. Well, she wouldn't try anything with Doña Inés – no one ever got the better of her – but she had her husband twisted round her little finger. Luckily, that was the last summer she came here. I'm sure it had something to do with what was said after I left, it must have been. They just stood there, frozen to the spot, speechless, like statues. She even stopped hitting the child. What I said was so unexpected, you see, even to me, it was like a river bursting its banks. Well, at least it served some purpose."

"But what did you say to her?"

"I said I didn't want to see her ever again, but I said it to her face, you know, straight out. I said: 'Someone's got to go, either you or Rosa Figueroa, and it looks like it'll have to be Rosa Figueroa,' and I took off my apron and I left. It was obvious I wasn't joking, because Doña Inés knows me – well, she did, I mean, poor woman, may she rest in peace, but it's just that whenever I mention her name it's as if I could still see her . . . Anyway, as I was saying, knowing what I'm like, she asked me to come round again a few days later, once they'd already left. I knew they'd gone, I'd seen them drive past in the morning, otherwise I wouldn't have been seen dead there; I told Ramón as much: 'I'd rather die of hunger,' I said. But the two of them left together and the boy stayed behind. And she never came back, so I know that something must have happened between mother-in-law and daughter-in-law. I never found out what, though; Doña Inés knew how to keep a secret. And she never told me off either. She just said to me: 'You've certainly got a temper, Rosa!', and I said to her: 'It's all we poor folk have got', and I set to peeling potatoes, and that was that."

"But her son came back, didn't he?"

"Not often. They used to spend the summers somewhere else and just left the boy with the grandmother from time to time. He was a bit delicate then, and the doctors had said that was the best thing for him. When autumn came around, sometimes it was his father who came to get him and sometimes it was the chauffeur, but I never saw hide nor hair of her again; it was as if she'd died."

"Do you think she's dead now?"

"No, woman! I saw her picture only the other day in one of those magazines that Antonia reads, the ones with all the photos of rich people's parties; she was wearing a very low-cut dress; she hasn't aged a bit. Her name's Gertrud, although they all called her something different, I can't quite remember what, because her name was hardly ever mentioned in the house again. Doña Inés didn't like to talk about her either way, and the boy found that odd; well, it *was* odd. He would pester his grandmother with questions, but she just ignored him. Then, when he grew up, he didn't talk about his mother either, for a while; he stopped asking questions and became more serious; but, goodness, when he was a little boy . . . He used to get out a big book of maps and open it out on the piano in the living room and show me the place where his mother came from, high up it was, a very cold place he said, although he'd never been there himself, and I always asked him why he hadn't. He used to get his grandmother to tell him stories about the place, and he'd invent his own too. He was ever so bright, with his big eyes wide open. Well, like I said, he was an angel. And he was so fond of my Tola!"

If she had time to do so before her listener escaped, old Rosa would round off her story by saying that when she met Doña Inés' son that morning with his bunch of dahlias, he hadn't been unfriendly exactly; it was more as if it bothered him to remember the past, as if he was sad and felt embarrassed that someone should see him looking sad. She said that, in the end, since she was still crying, he took a very fine, beautifully ironed handkerchief out of his top pocket and held it out to her, and she hardly dared unfold it and blow her nose on it because, unlike her, it smelled so good. It was at that point that she would mention the far-off scene – burned into her memory – in which the foreign woman obsessed with cleanliness and bad smells had beaten her son for having dared to make a declaration of principles different from her own. At other times, though, what she did was repeat the story again without realizing that she'd already told it, because old people do tend to lose the thread of what they're saying and confuse it with the thread of things they haven't yet said. And so, taking two steps forward and one step back, she would end up confessing that, in fact, it was the memory of that earlier scene that had finally made her decide to blow her nose frankly and almost lustily on the spotless handkerchief and soil it with tears and snot, and so take her revenge – better late than never! And she said that when the father of the boy-who-had-liked-the-smell-of-stables said goodbye to her, refusing to allow her to accompany him to the cemetery, she had tried to give him back the handkerchief, but he had said no, she should keep it as a souvenir. And when he said that, his voice had softened.

"'As a souvenir of all the things that will never come back, Rosa,' he said to me. And he looked at me really sadly, as if he was about to give me a kiss. But instead he rushed off as if the Devil was after him, without even saying goodbye. Ah, dear God, what a life!"

Whenever she retold her story of that encounter, each time enriched with new details and enlarged to include the various tangents that the subject suggested to her, Rosa would remove from her pocket the large batiste handkerchief with the initials E.V.G. embroidered on one corner and, with it, she would dry the tears that go to swell all the rivers whose waters never return. And when she went down to the village washing place to do the laundry, she would take special care when scrubbing the handkerchief on the smooth, curved stone, and would set it apart from all the other bits of clothing, although sometimes she didn't need to, because the handkerchief would be the only thing she took to wash, and that was why it was always so clean and well pressed whenever she took it out; Rosa's handkerchief was famous throughout the village. And she said that when she died they should cover her face with it, a last wish which, when she did finally leave this world some months later, was carried out with due respect and solemnity by her fellow villagers, and no one ever once even smiled when they remarked on it later. On the contrary, they spoke of it very seriously, because that was a village that prided itself on the ancient worship of all things enigmatic, immaterial and mysterious.

For rather similar reasons, no one found it odd either when, a few days after burying Rosa Figueroa, the village priest received a large sum of money from someone whose name he had undertaken never to reveal. The money was intended to cover any expense involved in sending the dead woman's only granddaughter to a home for the subnormal. The girl was slightly retarded, and when her parents emigrated to America, they had left her in the care of her grandparents and had gradually lost all interest in her.

Behind that money everyone saw the same hand that had given Rosa the handkerchief with which she had been buried. And that recognition – at first no more than a suspicion – became a certainty on the morning when an ambulance from the nearest town drove up and out stepped two men charged with taking Tola away; at first, she had cowered in a corner, with frightened eyes, her arms about the neck of her one cow, but then, convinced by the nurses' sweet, persuasive manners, she changed her mood entirely, and laughed and clapped as she left the hovel where she had spent all her twenty-seven years, and, once in the car, clutching her wretched little bundle of belongings in one hand, she waved cheerily to the people who had gathered to see her leave.

"Going away!" she shrilled. "Going away!"

More than one woman burst into tears when the ambulance disappeared round the first bend in the road, and, in the days that followed, the older people in the village spoke of how, when Tola was a little girl, she used to spend the summers playing with Doña Inés Guitián's grandson, the subject of those doubtful rumours that spoke of his involvement in various shady deals; according to the experts' calculations, he must be nearly thirty.

They also speculated, as was only natural, on the only likely explanation: that news of Rosa Figueroa's death must have reached her generous benefactor via the lady from the Quinta Blanca. The benefactor, by the way, did not return to the village for a long time or, rather, if he did, no one knew of it.

II

Prison cell by moonlight

When his cellmate was taken off to the prison hospital, Julián Expósito felt almost bereft, a feeling immediately superseded by a sense of guilt. Only the previous afternoon, he had been the one telling the guard on duty, nicknamed "Scumbag", of his concern about his cellmate's symptoms – amnesia and a complete divorce from reality – which grew more alarming with each passing day, and about the weird things he used to tell him. He said that he was almost beginning to feel afraid of sharing a cell with him, although he didn't go into the real reasons for that fear.

That night, Julián hadn't been able to get to sleep; he lay in the dark, remembering the glint of malignant glee in Scumbag's bulging eyes when he heard that information, and the convoluted questions he had asked him and the pally way he had offered him a packet of cigarettes, saying quietly: "Don't you worry, mate. If he *is* mad, we'll just have to lock him up." He had sharp pains in his stomach and felt terribly sick. He didn't want to make too much noise though, so as not to wake his cellmate whose eyes he had been trying to avoid for some days now. He lay very still, listening intently for noises coming from the other bed – not as yet tenuous enough to guarantee that the person lying there was asleep – and struggling to control the growing nausea brought on by his anxiety, until, finally, he broke out in a cold sweat and had to get up to vomit.

His cellmate had immediately turned on a torch, leapt out of bed and followed him into the small toilet, ignoring the peremptory gestures Julián made indicating that he wanted to be left alone. "I was much too short with him," Julián remembered later, "they were the kind of gestures you make to shoo away a fly, products of the same foul mood that made me throw up." But his cellmate took no notice. He held Julián's sweating forehead for as long as the spasms lasted and then, once Julián had lain down on his bed again with a bitter taste still in his mouth and his head pounding, he had placed a handkerchief soaked in cold water on his forehead and sat at the foot of the bed, as if waiting.

"Do you want the light on, or would you be better off in the dark?" he asked after a while.

"I don't mind. You go to bed now, go on. Leave me alone."

"I'm not in the least bit tired. If you prefer, I won't talk to you."

There was a silence. It was hardly surprising he didn't feel tired after that long nap, Julián had thought, but he didn't say anything. When he had come back in from the exercise yard, he had found his cellmate still asleep. That was when his conscience began to prick him, because he had just been talking to the guard, and the memory of those smiling, blackened teeth was in such marked contrast to the angelic expression of the man lying there asleep that he felt an utter heel. What could he be dreaming about that made him smile like that? The bloke had some very odd dreams. Sometimes he would write them down and at others he would tell them to him, and Julián was always the one who asked him to, even though he knew that he embroidered them with lies and fantasies formulated in his waking hours. He had to admit that when, as now, several days had gone by without his hearing that voice, the cell seemed to empty of air and time bobbed about in the ensuing void, as oppressive as a black cloud. He missed those perorations, even though he had often angrily interrupted them because they stopped him getting off to sleep, crammed as they were with strange words, crazy images, odd, tangential ideas; he couldn't possibly have dreamed all that, he must have invented it or read it in some book, but what did it matter when it was such fun.

"Are you feeling better?"

"A bit."

"Have you been drinking?"

"How could I have been? We've been together all day, apart from this afternoon when I went out into the exercise yard."

"You could probably do with a drink now. It might do you good."

"All right," Julián had said, beginning to be filled by a rather pleasant fatigue, an almost child-like abandon, lulled by his friend's imperturbable voice.

"Because he is my friend, I've never had a friend like him before," he thought with a sudden flash of insight that arose from a premonitory feeling that he was about to lose him.

Julián saw him get up, light a candle and leave the torch on the shelf made out of planks and bricks that he himself had made to put his books on. He was lithe and agile, almost feline; he had angular shoulders, narrow hips, long, straight legs and tanned skin. He was naked. He always slept in the nude, but he hardly seemed to sweat at all and he never smelled bad. He picked up his jeans from a chair and put them on, but not his shirt. It was a warm night in early September. He glanced at the moon through the tiny barred window and sighed. Then he crouched down to get the flask of whisky he kept underneath his bed amongst more books that he stored in a box he had stolen from the shop, and he brought it over along with two paper cups one inside the other. He separated the cups and checked to see that they were clean.

"I didn't know you were feeling ill. I thought you were asleep," he said, when he came back and sat down and poured out the whisky. "That's why I didn't speak to you, because sometimes you tell me that I get on your nerves a bit. Do you want a drop of water in it?"

"No, I'll have it straight."

They took their first sips in silence. The men in the cell next door were playing cards, and the occasional monosyllable would filter through the partition wall along with the intermittent click of the pebbles they used instead of money. Julián was sitting with his eyes fixed on the now dry damp-stains that the recent rains had left on the opposite wall on which the plaster was beginning to peel off in greasy patches; the other man was leaning slightly forwards with his arms resting on his knees, intently studying his bare feet; this was one of the positions he always adopted before launching into one of his perorations or before writing things down in his notebook. Behind him, next to an alarm clock, according to which it was one in the morning, the flickering light of the candle gleamed on his dark blond hair. One lock of hair fell over his forehead.

Suddenly, Julián saw him get up, as if impelled into action by a spring, and then stare in confusion at the rumpled bedclothes. He said nothing. Then he asked:

"Did I go out to the exercise yard today?"

Julián could not hold that urgent, searching look, which had caught him off guard; he lowered his eyes and merely shook his head, but in such a hesitant, half-hearted manner that his companion did not notice.

Why would he ask him that? He couldn't possibly tell him that when he left the exercise yard, he'd had a chat with the guard, he couldn't even mention it. He couldn't even change the story, adding a bit here and leaving out a bit there, as doubtless his friend did with his dreams. To do that, you have to know what you're about; not everyone can lie well and convincingly. Besides, he wouldn't let him get any further than that. "You mean you've been talking to Scumbag?" he would say. "You should never talk to that bloke, he's a complete and utter bastard. I mean, honestly, Julián, come on. The most you should do is spit on the ground whenever you walk past him."

Julián kept his head lowered as if he were actually hearing that reprimand, but also out of fear that the other might see in his eyes the confusion he was feeling. He never knew what to expect from him; for all he knew, he might even be capable of seeing the images aroused by his confused state of mind as they paraded past beneath his eyelids. Lying with his face slightly turned towards the floor, Julián could see again the afternoon sun shining on the clump of oleanders in the exercise yard, he could see Adolfo and Tupamaro sharing a joint as they leaned against the wall, he could see two people playing pelota, and the others, like a shifting stain, strolling about and talking; laughter, purposeless footsteps, eyes staring aimlessly up at the high wall topped with glittering glass, clouds unravelling, lazily changing shape like the curls of smoke from cigarettes, going nowhere, a dull rumble of cars driving along a road they couldn't see and which perhaps didn't lead anywhere either, the distant barking of a dog. And it seemed to him an idyllic picture, because at that point nothing had happened. Then came

the sound of clapping and all the prisoners had made their way reluctantly over to the gate. And there was Scumbag waiting for him with
his malicious smile. "Was it him who started walking alongside me
in the corridor, who offered me a cigarette and began drawing things
out of me; it's all his fault. He's a nasty bit of work, all right, a real
toe-rag." He kept stubbornly repeating this to himself, as if in a partial
attempt to shuffle off the load that kept his head bowed, because there
was now no escaping the significance of that scene, the memory of
which had brought on his recent fit of vomiting.

It wasn't the first time that someone had asked him about the Prof,
as some prisoners called his cellmate, and they always did so with the
same inquisitive air. They were intrigued that he never complained,
never got involved in gossip, that he wasn't hung-up about not being
part of a group; his enigmatic comments and that distant, superior air,
which they generally interpreted as pride, grated on them. Julián
shrugged and avoided such conversations, just as he had gradually
begun to flee his former cronies. He didn't know why, he just knew that
they bored him. Then one day, he found out that his friendship with the
Prof and the conversations they had – which were always broken off
with evident signs of annoyance whenever a third party joined in –
were giving rise to a series of jokes and rumours based on suspicions
of homosexuality. Artigas told him as much one suppertime; he was a
former cellmate of his on level 5, someone he used to see a lot. Julián
had been stunned.

"What are you trying to say, Daniel? Me, a fairy?"

And yet he couldn't just laugh it off, brutally, brazenly, mockingly,
as might have been expected of him when confronted by such a
rumour.

"But you know me," he said very seriously, feeling his heart beating
wildly despite himself. "You know me now and you knew me before,
outside. You know Teresa, you know the kids. How can you say that,
you of all people?"

"It's not me who's saying it, damn it, it's the others. That's why I'm
telling you, because we're friends, that's all."

"And why didn't you say anything before?"

"Did you expect me to say it in front of him? He's always there. When was I supposed to tell you?"

"But it's absurd. Surely you don't believe it!"

"Well, obviously I find it odd; like I told them, Julián's a good bloke, but deep down, I don't really care. At my age, I'm hardly going to be shocked by something that's as old as the hills, I mean, to each his own, I told them that too; it's none of my business."

Something very odd was happening to Julián. He was aware that his feeling of unease would simply vanish if he could only look Artigas in the eye and laughingly blurt out a few crude words; that would re-establish the banal relationship he had always had with him. But he saw too that he couldn't do it and he realized that Artigas had noticed that as well.

"It's absurd," he repeated in a low voice, looking worried, "absolutely absurd."

Artigas drank a spoonful of soup.

"It's all very well saying it's absurd, but it would be a bit sad if now, when they've given you time off for good behaviour and when you're just about to get out . . ."

The mention of his imminent freedom made Julián's face darken. For several months now, his wife had barely visited him. He had told Artigas as much. She had found a job in a tannery. The children were with their grandmother. And lately he had noticed that she seemed distinctly fed up.

"She seems odd, sort of impatient, do you know what I mean? More confident too. And she's always going on about all the things she's had to put up with because of me. But she doesn't cry when she says that; she doesn't cry like she used to, she says it really fiercely. And she's looking prettier too. She says she's worn out from working, and that's why she can't come, but she looks prettier. She won't let me complain about anything here either, she says she's had a much harder time of it than I have, that she's fed up with me complaining."

"Yes, women do get fed up, even though you don't expect them to, and it's our own fault," Artigas said sententiously. "We're always telling them not to be a drag, to stop meddling in our lives, but we don't really mean it, we just want to make them cry. It's a pretty lousy thing to do, really. Come on, your soup's getting cold."

Julián had lost his appetite. He remembered suddenly that he was forty years old; he thought about the rise in unemployment, how hard it was for an ex-con to find a place in society. All the newspapers said the same and they published endless surveys about this thorny and apparently insoluble problem. If he didn't have Teresa's unconditional support when he left prison, he was bound to re-offend. And when he thought that, he felt the paralysing, black wing of fear hovering over him, like an axe blow that changed inside him into a claw gripping his guts. It was an all-too-familiar feeling. Alongside that recognition, he felt a dull rancour growing against the person who had stirred it all up again, because he realized, with a mixture of guilt and surprise, that the feeling had been lying dormant, as if under the influence of some strange anaesthesia. It had been like that for three months more or less, ever since they had rewarded him for his good behaviour by moving him to a better cell. And was his record of good behaviour about to be sullied because of some totally unfounded rumours? Or *was* there some foundation? Was the fact that he was not entirely indifferent to news of those rumours merely a reflection of his fear of the possible consequences for him or was it because it placed before his eyes – albeit in a crude, distorting mirror – his relationship with that young man with his head in the clouds whose company was the only effective anti- dote he had ever known against fear, against the constant harping on his own guilt, and against the tedium of the days draining away down a black, hopeless sewer? At that very moment, while he was listening distractedly to Artigas' remarks, was he not overwhelmed by a desire to return to his cell, as if to a refuge? He stirred his soup without eating it, plunged in a sombre, dogged silence.

"So what is it with this bloke then?" Artigas asked, trying to pick up the original thread of the conversation.

Julián dropped his spoon into the plate, deliberately spattering the tablecloth. That made him feel better.

"What do you mean, what is it with him?" he said with a violence that even he felt was uncalled for.

17

They looked at each other. Artigas lowered his voice and said:

"What do you think I mean, for Christ's sake. Look, don't act dumb with me. Do you think he's a poofter or don't you? When you live with someone else you notice these things. At least in my experience you do. And don't shout at me, all right?"

"No, he's not a poofter. He's just mad, completely mad. They'll have to lock him up one day. That's all there is to it, nothing else."

From that day on, the betrayal – which culminated shortly afterwards with his tip-off to the guard with the bulging eyes – grew in Julián's mind, together with an urgent plan to struggle against the fascination he felt for his cellmate and a determination to put a stop to it with whatever weapons he had to hand, even though the knife might end up in his own back.

And that was exactly what was happening, even sooner than he had expected. Yes, here, as payment for his disloyalty, was the knife turning in his guts, just like when he used to go home after he'd been out boozing and be unable to find any clever way of blaming his subsequent hangover on Teresa, whose clear-eyed gaze he found utterly unbearable. It was the same now. However hard he tried, he could not see a dangerous madman in that bare-chested lad looking at him expectantly from the foot of his bed, nor could he in good faith say that he deserved to be admitted to the prison hospital.

He covered his face with his forearm while he listened to his cellmate reformulate the question more haltingly this time and in the veiled tones of a sleepwalker.

"I was with you in the exercise yard, wasn't I? Don't you remember? They called me to tell me that I had a visitor. I mean the exercise yard with the oleanders . . ."

"Of course, what other exercise yard is there? Don't be a fool. You weren't with me or with anyone else. What visitor are you talking about? You must have dreamed it. You haven't been out to the exercise yard today. Now leave me alone!"

He pressed his forearm harder down on his face. He thought he felt the other man get up, but he always moved so quietly that he couldn't be sure. He couldn't hear him moving about the cell. All he could hear was the occasional muffled word from the card players on the other side of the partition wall, and the tick tock of the alarm clock. After a while, he couldn't stand the silence any longer, he had to look. He gently removed his arm, letting it slide away, little by little, and when his hand was still covering his eyes, he half-opened his fingers, barely perceptibly, and peered out through the cracks.

He saw him standing with his back to him, in front of the barred window, surrounded by moonlight, as still as a waxwork. He waited, struggling between a desire to say something and a kind of paralysis that prevented him from doing so. Time passed. He desperately needed the other man to start talking; it frightened him to see him so still. At last, he thought he heard the softest of murmurs, something like a muttered prayer. He listened harder. "With your light you touch the farthermost hill . . ."

"Who the fuck are you talking to?" he exploded.

"No one," his friend said without turning round. "I was just looking at the moon. It's such a lovely night."

Julián saw himself being dragged unwillingly into a dance beneath the moon, amidst lights, gaudily painted metal and the smell of fried food. He was suddenly about the same age as his cellmate was now and Teresa was slightly younger; she looked like a little girl. He had just met her at an open-air dance in Alcobendas. They were playing that song, the one that goes: "The sun is tired of all its travelling, it's off and on its way," and she was singing it under her breath, her eyes half-closed. Then they started walking towards a clearing, their arms about each other's waist, beneath the full moon. She said: "What a lovely night!" and they stopped to kiss. How far off all that seemed. He needed to tell him; it would do him good, but he couldn't.

"I don't like the moon," he said. "It makes me nervous."

The other man still didn't turn round. Perhaps he was remembering a similar scene. When he first arrived, a girl with red hair used to come and visit him every Thursday. Then he stopped getting visits from anyone.

He was talking again now, but not about the girl, or about anything real. He was reciting the words slowly as if he were on the stage.

"With me it's quite the opposite. The moon calms me down, simply because it's so far away. When you can touch something, you stop believing in it. Besides, there are so many different ways you can look at it."

He had suddenly turned round and was staring at him. He caught him with his eyes uncovered.

"What do you mean different ways?"

"Well, you can think of it as being flat, or as a globe, or as if it were a hollow you could climb into. Just now I was looking at it as if it were a hollow; that's what I like most, because it draws me towards it, as if it were going to suck me in. Do you know the story about the woodman who was swallowed by the moon?"

"I'm not in the mood for stories tonight. I've got other things to think about."

That was the last thing Julián said in his attempt to remain on the defensive, but he could tell by the lack of conviction with which he said those words that he was losing ground. Besides, the other man was coming slowly over to him, smiling in that strange way of his.

"What things?" he asked. "What makes you think that those things aren't stories too? Tell me about them and you'll see. Everything's a story."

He didn't look at him as he spoke, as if he were alone. Now he had stopped by the shelf and was distractedly running his fingers over the books.

"What do I mean to him?" Julián said to himself. "Nothing most likely." And he looked at him with sudden resentment.

"We're not all good at telling stories," he muttered.

In the cell next door they heard loud guffaws, the scrape of a table being pushed to one side and then silence. It was four o'clock in the morning. They were obviously turning in for the night. Julián saw that the Prof had picked up a book and was leafing through it, sitting astride a chair, ignoring him. Or perhaps he was looking for some passage to read to him, as he had on other occasions. He saw him full face, his long legs sheathed in denim and those bare feet, one of which was touching the edge of the bed. Now the moonlight was making him feel even more uneasy. Julián had a lump in his throat. He reached out his arm and drank what was left of the whisky in his glass.

"Why did you say you'd had a visitor? There aren't any visitors at that time in the afternoon."

The Prof looked up from the book and gave him a surprised look.

"I thought you didn't feel like talking," he said.

"The moon's woken me up."

"I see."

There was a pause. Perhaps he was a bit annoyed with him and wanted to avenge himself by making him wait for the story. Or perhaps he was just playing for time in order to invent one.

"Well, you know," he began, "I was quite shocked to have a visitor too, and I said as much to you, but then isn't everything shocking, especially in our situation. We are so immeasurably different from everything around us . . ."

"Come on, get to the point. Tell me about the visit."

In his voice there was no longer the irritation of an adult trying to pick an argument or avoid one, there was only the frank impatience of a child. The Prof closed his book, leaving one finger between the pages as a marker.

"I was with you in the exercise yard when they came to call me into the visiting room because someone was asking for me. I thought it odd, but you thought it even odder, you got rather worked up about it actually. You even told me not to go, you said it would just upset me, and you grabbed my arm to hold me back. You said: 'The visiting room is a trap.'"

Julián was quite sure that he had said no such thing, but he stretched out luxuriously on the bed and realized that he could breathe easily again, without anxiety, as if he had just woken from a nightmare. What had really happened that afternoon in the exercise yard vanished, was wiped out. He much preferred the unexpectedly redemptive role he was playing in this scene. After all, it was the same scene. All he had to do was enter it.

"And you took no notice?" he asked.

"No. The fact is I thought you were right, but I wanted to go anyway. Then you laughed at me because I picked a sprig of oleander."

"Very romantic! And who had come to see you? Your girlfriend? The girl who used to visit you on Thursdays?"

The Prof had dropped the book on the floor and was sitting with his chin on his arms, resting on the back of the chair. He was staring into space with those green eyes of his, grown dark and very wide as if with the effort of remembering.

"No, no, of course not. It was another woman. I'd never seen her before."

"What did she say to you?"

"Well, that's the thing, you see, I can't remember. Wait, yes, she said something about my father, I think."

"How old was she?"

"No idea. She was all dressed in grey and was wearing a kind of veil. I couldn't see much of her face. But, of course, *that*'s who she was! It was the woman in the picture. Sometimes you get so confused you can't even understand the simplest things. She's the woman in the picture, yes, I've just this moment realized."

He had half-closed his eyes and was smiling abstractedly. Julián changed his position slightly and leaned instead on his elbow, trying not to make a sound. He was afraid that any loud noise might puncture the bubble of that process of remembering.

"What picture?" he asked almost in a whisper.

"That big engraving in my grandmother's house, the one above the piano. You can see a ship going down in the distance and there's a woman saying goodbye to it, waving a handkerchief. A marvellous woman. She's in half profile, her back against the rocks and over her face she's wearing a veil attached to a large hat. Once, I got up in the night, put on the light and climbed up on to the piano to get a better look at her and to find out if she was crying. She was covering her mouth with her left hand as if she didn't want to call out, but she wasn't crying; in fact, it was much more terrible than if she had been crying. I've never seen such desolation on a face, such a look of tragedy. Sometimes I would go into the living room when it was beginning to grow dark and I would sit crouched in a corner to keep her company, because I couldn't bear for her to be so alone, and I would talk to her softly as if to a girlfriend; I thought she was bound to notice, and she did notice, she did . . ."

"And it was the woman in the picture who came to visit you? Did you know her?"

"No, not personally. What was I saying?"

"That she talked to you about your father."

"Ah yes, my father. What could she have told me? It's gone now . . . be quiet . . . I said to her: 'I'm going to write it down.' I don't actually know if I did say that or not, but I know that I wanted to write it down – it's always the same, you have to write things down immediately, otherwise you get lazy and you say: 'Oh, it doesn't matter, how could I possibly forget something as important as that?' Because what she said to me was important . . . but I can't quite remember . . . Wait."

Julián was ready to wait as long as was necessary. He wasn't in a hurry, he wasn't sleepy, he had no more unpleasant thoughts in his head, and, however his friend's story ended, it wasn't going to involve him in any troublesome decisions. It was just like during the interval at the cinema. He suggested to him that he should roll a joint, because at other times, in similar situations, hash had helped him to postpone the collapse of his more extravagant fantasies. He suggested it in an affectionate tone of voice, pleased to be able to help him out, as he had in that dream when he tried to persuade him not to go and see the lady in grey. This time, though, the other man agreed to his suggestion gladly. He merely asked if his sickness had passed off, if smoking wouldn't make him feel worse. Julián said no, he really fancied a smoke, but thanked him for his concern. They were friends again.

There wasn't much hash left. They kept it in a hole in the toilet wall, hidden behind a loose tile. Julián waited with his eyes closed, enjoying listening and capturing the sounds of the different phases of that meticulous ritual, recording them in the camera obscura of his imagination. He became gradually infected by the peaceful deliberation with which the various stages of the ritual happened.

"Now he's carefully removing the tile. Now he's putting it back. He does things so well, so carefully. Now he's come out again. He's picking up the book that he dropped earlier on and he's putting it on the table. He places it there as if he was about to read it – he does so enjoy these preliminaries – only he's not going to read it, because now he's engaged on another task which I asked him to carry out. He shreds up the remains of a cigarette on top of the book. He removes the hash from its cellophane wrapping. He strikes a match and holds it near in order to soften it. He waves a small brown piece of hash over the flame. He's preparing it for me, in order to go on telling me stories. I've no idea whether the lady in grey will reappear in his story or not; with him you can never tell. Now he crumbles the hash between his fingertips and lets it fall on to the threads of tobacco; he mixes the two substances together; he plays with them like a child playing with sand. Then he picks up the cigarette paper, makes it into a kind of cone and fills it with the mixture, not wasting a single thread. Now he's started rolling it up. That's the thing he does best. His joints come out better than anyone else's: very smooth, no lumps. The bastard's really clever with his hands and he has such long, slender hands. A rich kid's hands, or an artist's, the hands of someone who has never done a day's hard labour. Some get the silver spoon, others get the wooden one; while I spent years locking horns with life, he was playing the piano beneath that painting of the lady with the veil, by a balcony that opened on to a big garden; even as a child he must have been a bit of a strange fish, with no friends, all wrapped up in cotton wool in a house like something out of a novel – I wonder if he just makes it all up? – with his grandmother telling him stories . . . he must be a bit of poofter, perhaps Artigas wasn't so wrong about that after all. But no, please, let's keep Artigas out of this, I don't want everything getting confused, I don't want to start feeling sick again, that belongs in another story, a very ugly story. And, please, let's keep quiet if Scumbag's ear appears at the door; I feel so good right now, Scumbag is the last thing we need. Don't be daft, Julián, you didn't even see Scumbag this afternoon, don't you remember? The person who came was the lady in grey. She actually stepped out of a painting, but what does it matter to you where she came from, the important thing is that she came. Now he's licking the sticky edge of the paper. I like it when he does that too, I almost like that part the best, he does it so delicately. He must have finished. Just be patient. He'll be lighting it and taking the first few puffs, now he's coming over. How peaceful it is! He may be just a lousy little rich boy, but I don't know how I stood it in here before I met him."

When he felt the touch of those long fingers passing him the joint, he opened his eyes to receive it and smiled up at the ceiling, voluptuously inhaling the smoke. Then he turned over and bent forwards a little to see where his companion was. He had brought his pillow over and placed it on the floor next to him. He discovered with a start that the hand that had given him the joint was resting on the bed and that, when he changed position, it was touching the unbuttoned jacket of his pyjamas. His breathing grew faster, but he didn't move. The hand didn't move either. It was simply there – trusting, passive, disquieting, like an animal that could as easily be asleep as alert, its intentions unknown to us. Of course, if he was a homosexual, he wasn't anything like the ones that Julián had met before: brazen, gesticulating, provocative. Once, out of pure boredom and desperation, half-drunk, he had given in slightly to the propositions of one of the gay men on level 5, but it turned his stomach to remember it. This was something completely different, though, different from anything. That's why he liked it. He took another deep drag on the joint and held it out in the air, without saying a word, without touching those fingers. The hand moved away from his pyjama jacket and disappeared, taking with it the glowing red tip. On the floor, the moon's rays were lying in parallel lines, alternating with the shadows cast by the bars.

"God, this is good," said Julián. "Fantastic. It doesn't seem possible that we're in prison, it seems a complete lie."

"It is a lie," the other said at once. "If it were true, we wouldn't be able to bear it."

"Sometimes I can't."

"That's because you keep thinking about getting out, making plans, remembering past mistakes; then, of course, it's hell, because you confuse what's inside with what's outside. But if you just concentrate on being here, without trying to work out what it is or why you're here, then it all just seems like an absurd lie and you start to feel OK, it doesn't get to you. Not outside though; outside, unfortunately, everything always seems all too true. And then when you come here you realize that that's a lie as well."

"What is?"

"Being out in the streets, freedom, all that."

"But why is it a lie?"

"Because you think you can have it all, that you can go where you like, make endless decisions for yourself; and then you can't, you can't rest, you spend all your time trying not to bump into the corners of other people, of time, of furniture, of machines, trying not to collide with things – it's like being on the dodgems at the fair. And you think you've gone where you wanted to go and that you've done what you felt like doing, but you haven't; you just lurch from one place to the next, avoiding corners and laws and phone calls, trying to choose between the thousand tempting alternatives offered you by this shifting world – how can it be simultaneously so fixed and so shifting? You feel it hovering unavoidably above you, forcing you to experience pleasures, feelings and hatreds which are like contaminated water; it pesters you with questions, pens you in with advice. What do you think? Where are we going? What time do you finish? Come on, hurry up, make up your mind; and then you switch off and you dream of living an adventure that goes against the grain and you declare yourself outside the law, all because of that, because you're running away from definitions, but then you drift into crime and you're redefined, whether you want it or not; you're a criminal and they're after you, so then you have to flee your pursuers, and you're back to square one again, and you simply can't fly away any more, no way. Until you land up here, that is, in this hole; you can rest then, because they've stopped chasing you. This is pure nothingness, pure absurdity, yes, the void, but from the void you can encompass anything, travel anywhere, because this place contains all other places. It's distilled them down, so that you can reclaim them with all their rough corners smoothed away."

Julián felt slightly dizzy, he couldn't keep up with that vertiginous flow of words. He needed to fix it somewhere, to draw some conclusion from it. He needed to keep his head above water, because he was drowning.

"So you don't want to get out of here, then?" he asked, bemused.

"You think you're getting out, but in fact you're going back in," came the answer. "You're back in the labyrinth of corners."

Julián closed his eyes. He could see a very long tiled corridor stretching endlessly out. He took a deep drag on the joint that the other man had passed back to him and then returned it. He tried to concentrate on that image of the corridor. Stagnant time, absolute passivity.

"A corridor," he said, "miles and miles of corridor stretching along the gallery, it's 196 tiles long, I've often counted them, and then two half-tiles by the gates, three-two-three-two-three. And there comes a point when, however hard you try to think about something real, the only thing in your head is that two-three rhythm that rises above any ideas you might have; you stop by the radiator, you light a cigarette – now what was I thinking about? nothing, you weren't thinking about anything, and you start walking again. The pelota court is thirty-two paces long, the basketball court is twenty-four paces long and twelve wide, the exercise yard, from door to door, is seventy, this cell is four by three and a half. And then there are the corners too, you keep bumping into the corners."

"Not the corners of time, not the corners of future plans; prison contains only as much time as your dreams, that's why it has a form and shape, that's why it's so white – it seems terribly white to me, does it to you? That's because it doesn't exist. It's the white of snow, of the moon, the white of nothingness; we have died already and we are remembering what happened before, observing it through a pane of glass and feeling nothing, as if we were looking out from the window of the ice palace that the Snow Queen dragged Kay off to. God, what a story! It's such a pity you don't like stories. Here you are, it's nearly finished."

Julián felt something like a warning pang. It wasn't just the joint that was nearly finished, it was something more. He made a gesture with his hand, brushing it aside.

"No, you finish it," he said. "My head's spinning. It's really got to me. It's probably because my stomach's empty."

He closed his eyes. There was a long silence. Along the tiled corridor he could now see coloured strings that tangled with each other and swelled in size until they were thick and sinuous as snakes, and bright tongues sprouted from their ends, tongues which, in turn, wrapped about each other, intertwined, enmeshed; they took on the shapes of bare-breasted women heaped together, writhing about, of lines of soldiers shouting, rifles at the ready, at a horizon of fire, of hanging carcasses of animals slit wide open, shapes that twisted and faded into splashes of mud and blood. He started to get palpitations and he lay quite still, waiting. He noticed that along with that joint and its last splutterings of verbiage, something important was taking place, he didn't know what: the vain salvos of a lost war, impossible to grasp, the death rattle of hope. He was beginning to feel sleepy, but he was sure he would have nightmares.

"Quiet," said the Prof suddenly.

Julián sat up, his heart in his mouth.

"What's wrong? Is someone coming?"

"No, it's just that I can see a marvellous place, and I can see it so clearly; it's like heaven, like returning to paradise. I haven't been there in ages!"

He had sat down on the ground, hugging his knees. Now he really did seem like a man deranged. It was a bit frightening seeing him like that.

"What place? What's it like?"

"Do you really want to come? Do you want to come with me?"

"Yes," said Julián faintly.

"Right then, just relax and forget about that long corridor, stop counting tiles. You'll see, it's spring and there's a bit of a wind, but it's not going to rain. You get there by a steep path edged with brambles and flowers: the path ends here. Stop. There are two hills covered in heather; you can hear the sea and smell it, but you can't yet see it. With the wind in our faces, we start to climb the steepest of the hills, the one to the right, until we reach the lighthouse. Look, can't you see the sea? Don't be afraid, only cowards stop at the lighthouse, follow me. Once beyond that point, you have to leap from rock to rock, because you

28

can't stop except to catch your breath, and the lapping waves cover everything. Sometimes it's like a soft rocking: boom-splash, and at others it's angry, fierce, exploding in great jets of foam down below, against the island of seagulls. There are hundreds of them, thousands, can't you hear them screaming, wa-wa-wa, some are clinging to the rock like flies, others are flying above it, lords and masters of the infinite space that opens out for them alone, haughty, confident, masters of the weather. And it's starting to grow dark, the lighthouse comes on, and the wild air pierces your clothes and tangles your hair; you can go a little further down still, although it's starting to get dangerous. Stop now. And look, look, look. Time has stopped. Let your eyes fly fearlessly. The sea is calling you to carry you far off, but stay here, on the edge, and keep looking. Don't move! You've made it. It's the beginning of the world. The end of the world. There is no time now. No corners. And if in this moment, when it is almost night, you stare very hard at the island of seagulls and you think about someone, even if they're far away, even if you're not sure that they exist, the message will have reached that person and it startles them – where did that voice come from? they say, who's calling me? They're bound to pick it up, assuming they exist, and even if they don't."

Julián didn't hear those last words. He had got stuck at "time-has-stopped", a white, undulating phrase that he saw fluttering above his head like a flock of seagulls, fourteen of them, each letter a seagull, and he felt his body become weightless, his lungs as spacious as caves swept by the sea, the rhythm of his blood calmer, boom-splash-boom-splash. He didn't want to know if that landscape really existed or if it was just an hallucination. But the sea had swept his lungs clean of snakes, of soldiers with rifles, of the tiled corridor, of pools of blood. It was as if someone had been singing him a lullaby, and he fell asleep without realizing it.

The other man did not. He stayed up until very late writing things down in his notebook. It was dawn by the time he went to bed.

The following morning they came to get him. He didn't know that they were taking him to the prison hospital. He didn't ask any questions. He picked up his things and unresistingly let himself be led away. His companion wasn't in the cell at the time. They did not say goodbye.

They never saw or heard anything about each other again, because the farewell note that Julián Expósito scribbled a few days later, when he left the prison, never reached his cellmate. He wrote it at the last moment, biting back tears, resting the scrap of paper on his suitcase, and he smuggled it in with a prisoner who was being admitted to the hospital after a period on hunger strike.

"Make sure you give it to him. He's been there a week. His name is Leo, Leonardo Villalba."

However, the young man died of heart failure before he had time to deliver the message. When the mother of the dead man collected his clothes afterwards, she found the message in the pocket of the trousers her son was wearing, along with a half-empty packet of cigarettes. It was a very small, crumpled bit of paper. She read it. It said: "Goodbye. I'm going out to bump against a few more corners. I'll never forget you. Forgive me." And she put it away, crying, because she thought it was intended for her.

III

The island of seagulls

On that early September afternoon, it looked like rain. The sun, riding amongst reefs of dense cloud, had been beating down since midday, one moment bestowing its capricious favours, the next threatening to withdraw them, and a group of indolent, disoriented summer visitors had abandoned the dubious pleasures of the beach for a seat in a tour bus. Included in the price of that visit to little-known corners of the area, and, according to the tour company guaranteed to provoke collective ecstasy, was a traditional afternoon snack of fried bread dunked in hot chocolate – a sweet finale to all the promised excitement – at one of the old hotels on the coast: the Pearl or the Mermaid or the Seagull. There, in the dining room with a panoramic view, the inert gaze of dozens of pairs of eyes would continue to founder on a monotonously churning sea that chose to conceal its secrets from the professional tourist.

The lady from the Quinta Blanca only heard the horn of the bus approaching from behind when the bus was almost on top of her, and on the narrow bend before the inn, she only just had time to step out of its path. She leaned as closely as she could into a roadside bramble bush and, from that position, watched with some distaste as the blue and silver hulk of the bus disappeared, its right flank almost brushing against her. Then she stood up and started slowly and carefully detaching her shawl which had become hooked on the brambles.

It was a ripe blackberry bush, and some of its more tender fruits had been crushed against her shawl and had left reddish marks on the pearl-grey background, as if anticipating the blood-red sunset that would soon be staining the fragile, rushing clouds. Then, once she had put the shawl around her shoulders again, she started picking the blackberries. She picked them carefully one by one, standing on tiptoe sometimes to reach those that were higher up, and savouring each fruit. Holding a few in the palm of her hand, she set off again towards the lighthouse. She was wearing a mauve dress and a straw hat decorated with a black ribbon and artificial cherries.

The path disappeared between two undulating hills thick with undergrowth and wild flowers, and the blue and silver bus, empty now, was parked there when the lady arrived. She exchanged a glance with the driver, who was standing at the door of the bus, smoking, looking bored, and then she strode up the hill on the right. She was singing to herself:

> Remember, dear child,
> remember this well,
> loves that have passed
> can never return, and
> there's no will in the world
> can make them stay . . .

The tourists had broken up into groups on the hillside, and the wind brought her scraps of their conversation mingled with the smell of the sea. Many of them had gone up as far as the lighthouse promontory and were taking photographs of each other. The woman headed in that direction too, but she didn't stop. When she got there, she walked straight past, not bothering to look at anyone, with the confident, expert step of someone who knows the terrain and knows where she's going. There was an expectant silence. The sea was very wild and the tourists were amazed at the spectacle of that woman in the straw hat intrepidly clambering across the rocks and down the cliff. One of them, a man with a neat blond beard, a university lecturer by the look of him, left his companions, leaned against the front wall of the lighthouse and looked down fascinated, as if he couldn't believe his eyes. In the end, he cried out in shock and alarm:

"Where are you going, madam? Come back! It's terribly dangerous!"

But the mauve and grey figure continued to leap from rock to rock without once turning round, concentrating hard on not losing her footing.

Some way down, so far down that the foam was already spattering her, there was a flat rock much larger than the others, and from there the descent became a sheer drop. It was very windy. The lady in the straw hat fastened the hat under her chin with a silk scarf that she was wearing round her neck, and stood, eyes half-closed, on that platform encrusted with cockles and mussels, letting herself be caressed by the salt air that tugged at her clothes and tousled her hair – an erect, defiant figure facing the sea that broke at her feet in milky whirlpools, like a figurehead on the keel of an ancient ship. Then she sat down on the rock and hugged her knees. The nostrils of her fine, straight nose trembled slightly, her eyes were lost on the far horizon, and a sad smile played on her lips. The seagulls drew arabesques above her head and then flew across to the island, only a short distance away, where they had their general headquarters. They flew over that bastion, eyes alert and wild, looking for a gap in the white carpet made up of hundreds of shifting silhouettes; they would drop down screaming, jostling each other, before lifting off again. The sky had clouded over and was lit by an unreal, bluish light – the eerie brightness that precedes a storm.

The woman took a letter from inside her dress, slowly unfolded it and started reading. The letter said:

"Dear Casilda,

I'm leaving for Chicago with Gertrud next week. We're going to spend some time at her sister's house. We have no option, really, since she's not getting any better here and she's taken against her psychiatrist almost as much as she has against me. I was talking to him a few days ago. He says that all Trud's conflicts stem from her refusal to talk about Leonardo or even to hear his name mentioned, and that that is what lies at the root of her aggression. And that only I can help her. What a surprise, eh? He was sounding me out to see if I had ever actually tried to help. He believes that by giving in to her blackmail, I am an accomplice in building the wall of silence that causes us both such pain and has such irreparable consequences. I realized that he thinks that I would make suitable analysis fodder too. Well, possibly, but it's too late to whip back the curtain and undo thirty years of mistakes. As usual,

I resorted to those skilful excuses with which I pretend to keep myself afloat and which are, in fact, plunging me into a bottomless pit. I'm reaching the limit of my strength, Casilda, and I need you as never before. Thinking has become a cul-de-sac, a useless torment that eats away at my health. The only light, the light that comes from you, doesn't warm me now either, because it shines from such a distant place, as if you were holding out a hand to me, but too high up for me to reach. How can you still hope that everything will sort itself out on its own? And yet I would like to be by your side and to be looking at you when you say that with blazing eyes, in that strange, poetic, illogical way of yours. As I told you last time, on the one hand, you drive me to despair, and on the other, you captivate me. You were always mad and I loved you for that because I envied you, because you used to – and still do – ride on your madness without losing hope, never falling into the temptation of changing horses. It would be absurd, at this point, for me to dare to doubt your generosity and loyalty towards me, but I know too that you – like Leonardo – despise me, although you have far more reason to do so. You belong to a different race, to that group of privileged, superior beings for whom solitude means freedom, not a prison sentence.

In my captive state, I invoke you as I would an elusive goddess, which is what you always were for me. But let me just say to you once more that in this whole sad story you have had the least unrewarding role. I don't know when I will see you again. Take care of yourself, my queen. I adore you,

Eugenio."

The lady from the Quinta Blanca folded the letter up again and held it for a while in her fist, like a damp handkerchief. She held it tight, thinking that the ink on certain words would probably be running as it mingled with the purple juice of the blackberries. Then she unclenched her hand and started tearing the paper up into tiny pieces that the wind immediately snatched up and carried off out to sea in a fluttering, capricious, whirling dance.

She started when she heard a grumbling voice behind her.

"And still they come! What do they expect to find? They don't even know. They come here in order to see what they can't see, always poking their nose in where nobody wants them, trying to take away with them what can't be taken away."

She turned round. It was the old man with the scar on his cheek whom she had often seen prowling around that part of the coast. The woman knew him by sight and, although they had never spoken to each other, a kind of complicity had grown up between them because each knew that they had been spotted by the other. He had just jumped down on to the rock behind her rock and he was standing frowning at the sea, trying to catch his breath after his indignant speech. Far off, they could hear the bus horn sounding.

"Do you want to come down here?" she asked, her face lit up by a smile that made her seem much younger. "You're going to slip if you're not careful. That rock's a bit wobbly. Wait a moment, I'll help you."

But by the time she had got up to hold out her hand to him, the old man had already leapt lightly down. He landed very close to her, and she had to steady him in her arms because she noticed him stagger slightly. He was small and gaunt. His clothes felt rough and smelled of woodsmoke. At that moment, the light in the lighthouse came on and the horn sounded again calling the tourists.

The lecturer with the blond beard was the last to leave his lookout post. He had got out a pair of binoculars and, still incredulous and amazed, he had them trained on those two eccentric people buffeted by the wind, like figures in a Romantic painting. Now they were happily ensconced next to each other, indifferent to the wild weather, to the fading light and the approaching storm, as if they were about to take tea in a cosy house, by a blazing fire.

"I can't believe it!" he muttered to himself. "They're mad!"

But he would have given anything to be transformed into a seagull and to fly above their heads and find out who they were, what they were talking about, when and how they had met. It was an impossible desire, but so strong that it made his pulse beat faster and kept him riveted to the spot, until a shrill female voice tore him from his thoughts:

"Come along, Gerald! We're leaving!"

He put his binoculars back in their case and the figures on the rock became distant and blurred, like figures in a dream. He sighed and reluctantly walked back towards his companions, some of whom were already climbing back onto the bus, submissive, bored, unaware of the marvel that had taken place. Halfway down the hill, having rejoined his wife, who was clutching his arm and complaining that she was cold, he felt the whole tedious summer and the imminent return to academic work hovering above him like a treacherous cloud of death. And he turned to look at the tall white lighthouse beneath the now dark clouds, as if bidding farewell to something irrecoverable. It was a sudden, secret revelation that he couldn't share with his wife or with anyone else; it was like when he used to hide away in his grandfather's library to read, only to have the book he had just started reading unceremoniously snatched from his hands. The horn sounded again, insistently this time.

"Thank God for that!" exclaimed the old man. "They're leaving. One of them even asked me how long the lighthouse has been without a keeper. As if I could just tell that story to the first person who asks me. And then those wretched cameras . . . They see everything through a camera lens and they're all pleased with themselves because they've captured it on film. But what have they captured? What do they take away with them? To tell the truth, I find them utterly unbearable."

The woman burst out laughing.

"Do you consider me a tourist too?" she asked.

They looked at each other. Set deep amongst the lines on his high-cheekboned face, the old man's eyes glowed so fiercely that she had to look away.

"No," he said gravely. "I don't imagine you think of me as one either."

The lady from the Quinta Blanca felt her heart beating very hard and her mouth was dry. She started picking cockles off the rock and opening them with a stone. They were cold and tasted of seaweed. They resisted being dragged from their shells.

"Have you lived here long?" she asked in a faint voice.

"I can't remember, dates don't mean much to me," he said. "Sometimes, when I go out to sea and I look back at the lighthouse, time becomes confused with eternity, with the waves and the clouds that never wonder why they keep moving, or what for, or since when. That's the thing about this place, it teaches you to live outside dates. But there'll be someone in the village who'll remember when I arrived; it must have been towards the end of the civil war. I came as a teacher, fleeing an unhappy love affair, and I knew the moment I got here that I would stay here for ever. Now, since I hardly speak to anyone any more, people who keep a count of time look at me suspiciously, as if I were a ghost. Ask anyone about Antonio Moura, they never liked me much; they'll tell you I'm crazy; they might even cross themselves. But the children aren't afraid of me. I'm always surrounded by children. I don't invite them to come, but I don't send them away either. They escape to my house, even though they get told off for it at home, and I show them maps and books and I tell them stories. Sometimes, I take them fishing too. I have a house behind that hill, near a little beach amongst the rocks, and a boat that I built myself, as I did the house. I don't need anyone. One evening, I'll die in that boat, in the beam of the lighthouse. That's how it should be. I'll fall asleep, telling myself a story that I can read in the water. And that will be that. It will be like handing over the last fragment to the sea, giving it back. It's the high tide that brings the stories. That's what Fabián always used to say."

Stuck to her skirt was a piece of the letter with the word "Eugenio" written diagonally across it. She rolled it between her fingers into a little ball and threw it as far as she could. Her eyes were shining.

"So you like stories, do you?" she said. "Why don't you tell me one?"

The old teacher took out a very worn tobacco pouch and, with a pleased look on his face, he started rolling a cigarette.

"You like them too, I can tell," he said. "The first time I saw you walking here, I knew that you would end up asking me for a story. But I was in no hurry. Do you want a true one or an invented one?"

The woman looked thoughtful. There was a glimmer of a smile on her face. Her voice trembled slightly, and she asked:

"Is there much difference do you think?"

"Not much," he said. "But the true stories tend to be more exotic."

37

"Tell me a true one, then," she said quietly.

And she folded her hands on her lap and half-closed her eyes. The sun was a dense ball of orange grapeshot with a sort of landscape across the middle, and it was about to set everything on fire as it fell.

"I'll tell you the story about the last lighthouse keeper who worked in this lighthouse," the old man began, having taken a first pull on his cigarette, which he had lit with a lighter. "Because before, as you'll know, even if only from novels, lighthouses didn't work automatically as they do now, a lighthouse was nothing without the man who lived inside it and tended it, the idea of a lighthouse without a lighthouse keeper would have seemed as absurd as a ship without a captain. At first, centuries ago, people used to light bonfires on the cliffs along the coast, 'There's another human being over there, warning me of some danger', the sailors would think when they saw that light out in the open. The Spanish word, *faro*, comes from Pharos, the name of an island at the entrance to the port of Alexandria, because that was where one of the first towers was erected around a fire in order to protect it. And countless others were built by the Phoenicians and the Romans, each one adding some new adornment to the invention. If I get on to that, though, we'll never finish, but as Fabián used to say: why worry about the ending, the important thing is to begin at the beginning, and although I'm not going to tell you everything now – because I'm not even sure you're that interested – I will just say that up until the use of metallic reflectors, improved later on by systems using clockwork and all kinds of other devices, the history of lighthouses is a fascinating one, lighthouses in their relation to men, and it's complicated too, a very long story, a story shaped by anonymous acts of heroism. Fabián knew everything there was to know about it, but he lived it too, he made it his own. That's why, when I talk about him, I have to begin by talking about lighthouses, because since I can no longer see him, when I want to remember him, like now, I can't imagine him other than by talking, for I can't see him if I remain silent; and if I close my eyes to listen to what he's saying, he's always talking about lighthouses from inside his own lighthouse, while he makes some putty or fills a crack or goes up the spiral staircase to clean the light or to check the speed or the rotation of some machine or writes his daily log or prepares tea for his granddaughter. He only comes to life again and I can only see him moving about when I manage to evoke his voice, something I can't always do. As I imagine you've already guessed, Fabián was the keeper of this lighthouse."

The woman had her eyes fixed on the island of seagulls.

"Yes," she said, "I had. And tell me, can you recall his voice as if you were hearing him now, at this very moment? Remembering a voice is one of the hardest things to do, don't you think, and one of the most mysterious too?"

"It is indeed," he agreed, "and there's no use trying to force it; the voice of someone absent comes when it wants to, in bursts, like smells. That's exactly it: when you breathe in a forgotten smell and recognize yourself in it, it hits you just like that and roots you to the spot. A moment ago, I could hear Fabián's voice in my head as clearly as if he were sitting here with us; but I can't now. When I hear your voice, I forget his."

"I'm sorry."

"Don't be, I wanted to hear your voice too. Don't imagine I like living solely off this cult of the dead. Although, of course, what else is there for me now?"

The woman noticed a bitter, weary, almost tearful note in Antonio Moura's voice, and she felt a pang when she thought how, one day, it would be hard to recall that voice too. The last remaining sliver of sun on the horizon suddenly plunged into the sea. Every now and then, the circling beams of light from the uninhabited lighthouse, controlled now by faceless machines, would linger on their faces.

"Did Fabián die a long time ago?" the woman asked.

Antonio Moura drew the back of his hand slowly across his eyes, as if he were wiping away sweat. Then he sighed and said:

"Those dates again! Yes, it must be a long time ago now. I remember that it was winter and they came to find me at the school because I was his best friend, and people were surprised when the lighthouse wasn't lit. They found him lying at the top of the spiral staircase. He'd had a heart attack. He hadn't seemed himself for some time; he had been weak, unwilling to talk. He would sigh and say what was the point of having studied so many things, what was the point of knowing stories, knowing about tinsmithing, herbal cures, bricklaying, electrics, drawing, if none of that helped him to find some peace in his soul. I would say to him: 'Don't die, master, vanquished by the weapons of mere melancholy,' but he would simply look straight through me. The fact is that he began to die long before that, when his granddaughter left and didn't come back, though he lived for quite some time without wanting to admit that to himself, because it went against his belief that man's only strength resides in learning to live alone. It would have been recognizing defeat. He had told me as much many times, as she was growing up: 'I must try to get used to not loving her so much, Antonio, I must give her a free rein, because she's sure to leave, and the last thing I want is for her to have regrets. She needs to go her own way. Birds were born to fly.' She said she was off in search of treasure. Poor Sila, her grandfather gave her wings and love broke them."

"Love does sometimes play some dirty tricks on you," said the lady from the Quinta Blanca.

"That's very true. Fabián liked the fact that his granddaughter was wild, free and rebellious. That was how he had dreamed she would be. And she certainly didn't disappoint him there. 'The sea brought her,' he used to say, 'like in the stories.' Good God, now I really can hear his voice."

The woman had glanced up suddenly and was vainly trying to look into the eyes of that averted face, absorbed in thought.

"The sea?" she asked.

"Yes, the sea brought her," the old man murmured, looking down at his mottled hands. "It was a very sad story, that's why she always liked sad stories so much when she was older. Forgive me, I'm telling it all out of order. Fabián was a widower with a daughter who was very pretty but a bit weak in the head. They say she was epileptic. One stormy night, an English ship was wrecked not far from here and the lighthouse keeper, as was his duty, went out to sea with other men to salvage some of the cargo and to help in the rescue of those who were injured. One of them, the captain, stayed at the lighthouse, and was nursed back to health with great care and affection. When he left, he said how sorry he was to go and that during his stay here he had lacked for absolutely nothing; only later on did we understand what he meant. Fabián and his daughter felt sad too. Fabián had carried out his job as lighthouse keeper to perfection, so much so that the local chief engineer, in accordance with reports he had received from the English captain, proposed offering him some recompense. However, as he said years later when he told me about it: 'Some recompense, eh, Antonio, and who could recompense me for my daughter?' For the girl, who would have been about fifteen then, soon realized that she was pregnant. That would have been the least of it; in this part of the world the children of single mothers grow as freely as the flowers on the heather and no one points the finger at them; the trouble was that, being weak, she died in childbirth. I never knew her. But Fabián said the little girl was the image of her mother, although much healthier and with a mind of her own. And as for intelligence, she was far brighter than her poor mother, and brighter than her own grandfather too, 'and that's saying something, Antonio, for as you know, her grandfather is a veritable sage like yourself,' and we would laugh as we watched her leaping from rock to rock. Yes, she was very bright, and extremely precocious. I couldn't teach her anything very much. When I came here as a teacher, she already knew how to read, and she was only three years old, and she was so mad keen on reading that if she had a book in her hands, there was no point in calling her, she would even forget to eat. She often used to come and sit down here, I can see her now; and she used to paint little pictures with a caption above them saying 'A souvenir of the lighthouse' and sell them to the tourists. The things she'd come out with. She was afraid of nothing – she'd even swim in the sea in the middle of winter, when the sea was at its roughest, because she was a wild creature, a well of passion. She too had her own sad tale to live, but that's another story."

He looked up and saw the still, grave profile of the woman, who was nodding slightly though she had her eyes fixed on the island dotted with white birds. The wind was getting stronger and her frail shoulders were trembling.

"Are you cold?" asked the old man, leaning forward solicitously. Without turning to look at him, she gave him a voluptuous smile.

"No, I'm fine," she whispered, half-closing her eyes. "It's just like reading a novel."

"Yes," said the old man, "a novel with an unhappy ending, those were the ones she liked best. Even as a little girl, she was always inventing stories with unhappy endings, so that she could sit crying and watching the waves, she said. But the strangest thing was the way that sentimentality fitted in with her wild, energetic nature. She reminded me of Ellida, the heroine of *The Lady from the Sea*. I gave it to her to read and she loved it. Do you know Ibsen's plays?"

"Yes, Ellida is the one who threw her ring into the sea in homage to a mysterious sailor. Or is that a different play? Then she got married, I think."

The old teacher looked at her in surprise.

"You talk about her as if you'd known her."

"Of course I knew her. That's the effect good stories have – you believe them. And what happened to Sila?"

"I don't know, she left when she was seventeen. According to a letter she wrote, she had gone off to demand an explanation from her father."

"But you said that hers was a novel with an unhappy ending. Do you know how it ended? Seventeen seems rather a young age in a woman to assume that a novel is over. I thought you liked novels."

The old man was looking at her, half-intrigued, half-incredulous.

"I like them very much, why do you ask?"

She burst out laughing and put an arm around his shoulder.

"Oh, nothing. We're at cross purposes. But it's your fault for comparing true stories with invented ones."

"You're quite right. Although not knowing how a true story ends keeps you more on tenterhooks."

"You can always invent an ending," she said affectionately. "Ask the sea what happened to the lighthouse keeper's granddaughter. Don't you ever talk to the sea?"

There was a silence lit by a flash of lightning and she felt his old body tremble beneath his rough clothes; then he unexpectedly bent over her lap to kiss the hand lying there.

"I will ask, my child," he said at last, in a voice heavy with emotion. "Although now I don't need to."

Those last words, spoken in a very low voice, were drowned out by a huge rumble of thunder. A few startled seagulls took flight and the lady from the Quinta Blanca sprang to her feet. You could hardly see a thing by then.

"We'd better go," she said. "It's nearly dark and the storm's about to break. It would be rash of us to stay here."

"Yes, indeed, very rash," said the old man, standing up with a sigh, as if he had woken from a sleep.

Then, getting to his feet, he stood looking at the sea and added with a smile:

"Sila didn't know the meaning of the word 'rash'. She used to swim over to that island and climb up and sit amongst the seagulls; I don't know how she dared, but she never came back with so much as a scratch. Well, that's not quite true, once when she jumped down, she twisted her ankle."

She didn't reply. Her face had grown suddenly dark, and she began to climb the cliff without looking back. The old man followed her. They climbed carefully, in silence, sometimes grasping each other round the waist to steady themselves against the force of the gale. Just before they reached the lighthouse promontory, heavy drops of rain had begun to fall; in a matter of moments they had become a violent rainstorm. Halfway down the hill, they paused for a few moments to say goodbye. Their two figures were lit by a flash of lightning. She was quite a lot taller than him.

"Thank you for your lovely story, Antonio Moura," she said in a calm voice. "You'll have to tell me the rest of it another day."

The old man was looking at her, entranced, his eyes squinting through the curtain of rain.

"Why would I need to do that, child?" he said with just the suggestion of a smile, yet he was crying.

The lady from the Quinta Blanca stooped and kissed him lightly on the cheek, then freed herself from his embrace and ran off without saying another word. A few yards on, she stopped and turned around. The rain was dripping off the brim of her hat and running down her face. There, absolutely still, stood the old teacher, steadfastly enduring the storm, his eyes fixed on her fleeing figure.

"God bless you, child, you've made me live again," he murmured to himself, as if he were praying.

But she couldn't hear what he was saying. She merely waved to him and shouted from a distance:

"Take care, Antonio! Where there's life, there's hope."

Then she started running again and disappeared down the hill, ignoring the brambles catching at her skirt.

She reached home soaked to the skin and that night she had a raging temperature.

I V

The girl with red hair

When Leonardo Villalba got out of prison, there was a girl waiting for him. She had red hair and she was pregnant. She went over to him and gave him a kiss.

"The car's over there," she said.

Leonardo followed her without saying anything. He wasn't sure if he wanted to follow her or if he even knew her very well. For example, he couldn't remember her name.

They walked out through the gate in the perimeter fence and reached the car, a dented, rather dirty, orange 2CV. It was an unpleasant, drizzly afternoon. The girl got in the driver's seat and opened the passenger door.

"Come on, get in. Why are you just standing there like that?" she said impatiently. "You can put your suitcase on the back seat."

Leonard obeyed rather limply, watched by her restless eyes. It felt cold in the car and there were crumpled newspapers and an empty cigarette packet on the floor. He sat hunched in his seat, looking through the window at the guard in one of the square towers on top of the prison wall. The guard wasn't moving, he looked like a puppet.

"You'd be more comfortable if you took your backpack off."

"It doesn't matter. I'm fine like this."

The car jolted into action. Her fingers had brushed his left thigh as she changed gear. They were painted with scarlet nail varnish slightly chipped around the edges.

"I'm assuming you're coming back with me. Javier wants to talk to you. Or did you have other plans?"

The car bumped along the pot-holed road. One of the springs in the seat was pressing into Leonardo's backpack. He noticed a wave of bitter saliva filling his mouth; he did his best not to give in to it.

"I don't know," he said. "I don't feel like thinking at all. In fact, I'd be very grateful if, just for the moment, you didn't ask me any questions."

The girl with red hair burst out laughing. Her laughter sounded dissonant, chilly. It came from outside and it remained outside, snaking about, blending in with other strident, alien sounds with more or less identifiable origins.

"Grateful, you? That's a good one! I didn't know the prison doctors could perform miracles."

The rain began beating harder on the dirty windscreen. Through the trails of water emerged the blurred figures of various workmen in safety helmets standing at the foot of a tall yellow crane lifting blocks of cement. It was very hard to grasp what possible relationship there could be between that scene and the scene being enacted inside the car, sheltered from the rain. And yet, although each was following its own course, both were taking place at the same time before Leonardo's inert gaze, turned now towards his companion's neat profile, fixed on the stubborn, unfamiliar fold of her lips.

"Listen," he said in a dull voice, "if you have something to say to me, I'd rather you came straight out with it, in as few words as possible. I'm not very well, you see, and I find it an effort to understand."

Her voice grew gentler.

"I know you're not well. I visited you a few times to ask how you were, and I brought you some food and clothes. Didn't they tell you?"

His face wore an expression of intense concentration. He closed his eyes.

"Yes," he said, "I think they did."

"And I could just as easily not have come back at all, I could just have forgotten your bloody name, after the way you treated me at first; it was a nasty shock, what with all the things I had to tell you, seeing you there with the same bored expression on your face, as if you couldn't wait for me to go. It's just as well I never said anything to

Javier about how badly you treated me, he'd have given me hell if he'd known. I think he's jealous, although he doesn't like to admit it."

"I don't know why you kept coming when you saw that I was bored," he said. "You must have wanted something from me. What?"

"I can't believe you're asking me that, Leonardo," she said, very upset. "What do you think I wanted? To see you and talk to you, because I felt awful about what happened. I wanted you to know that I didn't have anything to do with it, because sometimes you just don't take things in. I'd been warning you for some time to be careful, that they were using you, that you would be the one to pay for any break-ages, because I know them better than you do and it makes me angry to see them taking you for a fool. Do you remember that night in Goyo's house, a few days before they arrested you. I warned you then, didn't I? By the way, I'd left my pills at home that night and I'm positive that was the night I got pregnant, and that the baby is yours."

Leonardo was staring at the windscreen wipers that had just swung into action. He found it relaxing to watch that semicircular movement laboriously wiping away the raindrops. The voice of the girl with red hair was also describing a semicircle now, changing in inflection to become grave, almost pathetic.

"It was just one thing after another. I was a wreck, I really was. I spent every week just waiting for Thursday to come round, and it seemed like you were the only person in the world I wanted to talk to about what was happening to me. That's not because I don't love Javier – I get on really well with him and he takes a lot more notice of me than you ever did, but you know how he is about certain things: he's all for calling a spade a spade, for saying that two plus two always makes four, and you can't shift him, he's got no time for angst, he doesn't understand complicated feelings. But you do, don't tell me you don't; even when you don't say a word, even when you spend hours on end staring at the wall, you're different, Leo, you suffer. And you've never deliberately hurt anyone, not out of malice, I know that. I've done a lot of thinking these last few months. We were all very cruel to you, I was too. But you're just so difficult."

The rain was teeming down now, drenching building sites, rubbish tips, a vast scrapyard. The cars coming in the opposite direction disappeared amongst the raindrops. Now he could just make out a few tall buildings.

"As you can imagine," the girl went on, "for Javier, the only problem was getting enough money together for the trip to London, but apart from the fact that we didn't have any money until recently, when it was already too late, I wasn't in that much of a hurry. I know that must seem a rather strange reaction, but I wasn't sure that I wanted to have an abortion until I knew what you felt about it. I thought: 'What if the baby is Leo's? Because in that case, he's the one who has to make the decision', and I thought that because of what you said to me that evening in Tangiers, do you remember?"

The sentences ending in a question were the ones that most troubled Leonardo, and he shook his head. Tangiers was a place of brilliant, irrecoverable sunlight. Where was all that light now?

"Of course you do. Well, you told me that what you'd like most in the world was to have a child of your own, that you'd like the mother to give you the child and never ask for it back – it was in that little café where Mustapha used to play the *derbocka* – you said very seriously: 'I'd teach my child to be free', and I said you were mad, but the idea appealed to me too. I'd never heard a bloke say anything as strange or as romantic, I'd never known anyone like you. It was in August, shortly after I first met you, when you were still painting and you used to tell me your dreams, absurd like your paintings, but nice too. I felt that you were a very special friend to me. That was before we'd slept together."

Leonardo turned sharply towards his companion. For the first time, his eyes and face were lit by a glimmer of curiosity.

"I used to tell you about my dreams?" he asked. "Can you remember any?"

"Well, not very clearly, no," she said. "They weren't so much dreams as rather crazy stories. There was often a woman in them who you were never sure if she was your mother or your girlfriend; you used to call her the Snow Queen and I used to laugh at you. I'd say: 'You're mad, you are', but deep down I wanted to know what lay behind those fantasies; I was sure that something must have happened to you when you were a little boy."

Leonardo opened the window and stuck his head out. He needed to feel the rain on his skin, to feel the air outside.

"And you were different then, you weren't depressed like you are now, you had plans. What's wrong? Are you feeling sick?"

"A bit. I haven't had anything to eat. Have you got a cigarette?"

"No, the doctor won't let me smoke. We can stop at a bar if you like."

There was a pleasant silence, a pause in the discordant symphony binding together the world inside the car and the world outside. Leonardo leaned out of the window again. The bare slopes and building sites had given way to blocks of flats, metro stations and crossroads with signposts and traffic lights. His hair was dripping wet. The girl started talking again. He closed his eyes.

"There were so many things I wanted to say to you after they arrested you. You know I'm no good at writing, but I used to spend every night going over and over what I was going to ask you, putting it in order in my head; I thought it would help you to clarify things too, and by the time I got here on Thursdays, I knew it almost by heart, as if I'd written it in a letter. And for what? As soon as I sat down in the visiting room and you appeared behind that glass screen with all those little holes in it, I just felt lost, it was horrible, everything started to get all tangled up and I didn't know if you thought I was stupid, just plain cynical or what, because the worst thing wasn't that you hardly even spoke to me, the worst thing was that you looked at me as if you'd never seen me before in your entire life. Of course, now I understand that you weren't well. I found that out later. What's wrong? Why have you got your eyes closed?"

"Because being out in the streets makes me feel sick, makes me dizzy. Do you think you could possibly be quiet for a moment?"

They plunged into the maw of the city, crisscrossed by buses, ambulances, policemen, drills, flyovers, people carrying umbrellas that they closed in order to go into their houses, into the metro, into the bingo halls and into bars, just to break up the afternoon and to lead it gradually to its close. Leonardo, his eyes shut, was trying hard to think of the girl's litany beating against the wall of his silence as just one more element in the endless comings and goings of signs crowding the street, and trying to connect it with the queasy feeling in the pit of his stomach, as if he were tentatively conducting a ghost concerto whose chords might just calm him down if he could only stop feeling so responsible for them. Therein lay the secret, in distancing himself from the personal situation (from perplexity, hunger, nausea, cold) in order to connect the labyrinth outside with the provisional, unfamiliar topography of his own body. After all, wasn't everything just a system of concealed pipes bearing away waste water, gastric juices, gasoline, sweat, smoke, money, words, sewage, rubble? It was restful to imagine those waste pipes ceasing to function altogether; everything immediately grew less pressing, less important.

The girl with red hair had returned to her theme, but now she was speaking in a calmer tone of voice. She was talking about Javier again, trying to justify his actions: "He doesn't mind if you live with us, because deep down he knows it was his fault. We just want to help you." Leonardo noticed that one of his feet was going to sleep; he was simultaneously aware of the tingling sensation and of the jingle of that word: "Javier", which was repeated over and over; it slithered into his ear canal, Javier-Javier; backwards it sounded more innocuous, like a child's riddle, Vier-ja-vier-ja-vier-ja, it moved off, gradually fragmenting amongst the sounding car horns, then returned, a concerto bereft of meaning. The pins and needles in his foot became a cramp that crept up his leg.

"I've never lied to you, Leo, you have to admit that, and I have always made it quite clear to Javier that my friendship with you should be kept separate from any shady deals you two happen to get involved in and from who was or wasn't to blame for you getting caught. I've always taken your side, you know . . ."

Leonardo opened his eyes and bent over to rub his numb foot. He couldn't feel it, it was as if he had been bitten by some poisonous insect. He grabbed his foot with both hands and picked it up, revealing, beneath it, the old newspaper it had been covering; as he did so, twelve words leapt out at him from the trampled page and stabbed treacherously at his eyes, his side, his throat. He realized at once that the mortal bite now spreading throughout his body had come from the scorpion hidden beneath his foot. "Financier Eugenio Villalba Guitián and wife killed in car accident in Illinois." It was the headline on a news item lost amongst the amalgam of waste and rubbish that is washed in every day on the tide of the big city, twelve words crouching there, in ambush, creeping maliciously into his veins like bloodclots. He snatched up the newspaper, his hands shaking. The date was just above the article: 20 October.

". . . You've spent your whole life doing things that have never benefited you in any way," the alien voice was lecturing implacably on, "throwing away your money, your talent, your health, everything, just tossing it overboard . . ."

"Will you bloody well be quiet for a moment! What date is it today?" he howled, distraught.

The girl looked at him in amazement.

"The twenty-eighth," she said.

"Of October?"

"Yes, of course, of October. But what's wrong, Leo? What are you doing? Are you mad? We haven't even arrived yet . . ."

Looking white as a sheet, her companion had knelt down on the passenger seat and was removing his suitcase from the rear of the car. The look on his face was frightening.

"Stop at the traffic lights!" he shouted. "Stop here!"

"But why, Leonardo? Have I said something wrong? Aren't you feeling well?"

"Just leave me alone! Here! Pull up on the right! The lights are just about to change!"

The girl skidded to a halt, provoking protests from the car behind, and, without saying a word, suitcase in one hand and crumpled newspaper in the other, Leonardo jumped out before the car had completely stopped.

"Leonardo! Where are you going? Leonardo! Wait!"

He didn't look back. She watched him weaving in and out of the cars just before the lights turned green, she saw him reach the other side of the road and brandish the arm holding the newspaper in order to hail a taxi. She wound down her window and again shouted: "Leonardo!" as loudly as she could. She saw strange faces turn to look her, but not his. "Leonardo, Leo!" She saw him get into a taxi that carried him off in the opposite direction, she couldn't do a thing, she couldn't turn round to follow him, the lights had just changed, the cars behind were honking, and still she didn't move, her head out of the window, her eyes fixed on the vanishing taxi. "You're mad, completely mad," she said, utterly perplexed.

It was half past seven by the time she reached the small square in a modest area on the outskirts of the city and parked the car outside a house with square balconies that looked like drawers. It had stopped raining. She went into a bar next door and went up to the counter. Her legs felt like cotton wool. She had pains in her belly.

"Hi, Pepe."

The place smelled of fried squid. There were a lot of people standing at the bar looking at the television and keeping up a heated commentary on the football match being shown.

"Hi, Ángela. What's it to be, love?"

"A glass of brandy and a packet of Ducados."

"Your bloke was here a little while ago with that dark-haired girl. I think they're expecting you."

"Right. Did they go up?"

"Possibly. I don't honestly know."

She downed the brandy in one and paid for it.

"See you, Pepe, thanks."

In the lift, she lit a cigarette, the first for two months. She was beginning to get labour pains.

PART TWO
(From Leonardo's notebooks)

I

Attempts at order

Last night, very late, I thought I heard noises downstairs and I sat very still staring at the door. I knew I was alone, but I was equally certain that someone was about to come up and see me. And I waited and I wasn't afraid.

It's becoming more and more difficult for me to distinguish between fantasy and reality, and my arrival here has only confirmed how blurred that frontier is; the images from one camp cross over into the other as the mood takes them, so it doesn't really matter whether I dreamed it or imagined it. The only thing I knew, as surely as I now know that I have my pen in my hand, is that someone started climbing the stairs to this room, and when the door opened and my father appeared, I accepted it as perfectly natural.

He stood for a few moments at the door of his own study, taking everything in with his eyes, as if he were scrutinizing it from afar, and I felt rather worried as to how he would react to the mess I've made. I was especially worried that he would notice that I had at last managed to open the safe. But then he smiled, apparently neither embarrassed nor surprised.

He wasn't the man who died just recently; he was a younger version, the one who used to dream of my becoming a celebrated artist, writer, painter or, perhaps, musician. He was wearing a sports jacket and a white shirt open at the neck. He said simply:

"Leonardo, how lovely to have you back at last! Do you feel at home in here?"

I didn't say anything. I couldn't.

He closed the door, walked slowly over to the small bar in the corner and started preparing two cocktails, while I sat transfixed in my armchair, watching him. His gestures were those of someone who is in no hurry, who will never be in a hurry again. He had his back to me. He took his time before turning round. When he did, carrying a tray with two glasses on it, he didn't walk straight towards me.

"He's noticed," I thought, "or at least he soon will." And a strange, cold shiver ran down my spine.

He stopped by the desk from which I have removed all his fancy desk paraphernalia and which was now piled high with my notebooks and the books from my backpack, along with bundles of papers belonging to him which I haven't yet had time to look at, bulky envelopes, a few dollar bills, documents, files and photographs. Then, with the same calm demeanour, he turned his gaze on the iron-clad hole in the wall. It was empty, and the door was open, like a recently profaned tomb.

And then we looked at each other. He didn't look at me as a judge might look at a prisoner, and I didn't feel that I had to lower my eyes or resort to pretence. We simply looked at each other hard for the first time in our lives, establishing a kind of complicity between us.

"Well," he said, smiling. "I see you finally cracked the code – *flor de lis*. Was it difficult?"

I returned his smile.

"It was a bit. Especially the S, which it took me a while to get."

"Yes, I'm not surprised," he said, "it's a sinuous, subterranean letter. Can you think of some other adjective to define it? It has to begin with an S, otherwise it won't do."

His voice was suddenly that of my grandmother, inviting me to play the childhood game that begins: "Out of Havana sails a ship, laden with something beginning with . . ." and you have to think of words that begin with the chosen initial.

"Secret?" I suggested.

"Not bad. You're getting the idea. You have to pursue it along streets of shadow and of sleep, until you achieve sagacity."

He walked very slowly over to me, handed me one of the glasses and sat down opposite me.

"How's life been treating you, then? Tell me all about it. I don't imagine you're in any hurry."

His hair was still thick, black and glossy, newly washed, with almost no grey in it.

"Oh, please, Dad, let's just leave my recent life out of it!" I exclaimed impatiently. "We have to start at the beginning."

He sat looking out of the window and said in a grave, sweet, inscrutable voice that again reminded me of my grandmother.

"And where is the beginning?"

"Well, the beginning . . ."

And I began. That was it. All I can remember now is the feeling of plenitude at that moment when the brakes came off – the same brakes that now paralyse me – of finding a beginning amongst all the many possible beginnings, the ease with which I just started talking, and went on and on. My father's presence – I don't know when he left or if he was ever there – was replaced by the overwhelming rush of words which have vanished now, but which hurled themselves across the table, jumbling my papers up with his, and which grew and grew, demolishing walls, invading and spattering everything. My life was that tide of words, but at the same time, I was looking down on it from above, unmoved, with seagull eyes. I remember it as if I were seeing it now. But where did I begin?

Today I've been going through my notebooks of the last few years and it was like running my fingers over the scars left by the block I have about writing. In all of them, wildly inconsistent ravings and chaotic jottings alternate with the occasional blank space, after which my writing grows calmer and, for a few lines, until it gradually breaks down again, it maintains some attempt at order: the promise of a real beginning. Those moments – during which the need to break the circle of confusion seemed to me a matter of life or death – leap out at me from the page and make any notion I might have that things are now going to be different seem utterly illusory.

But my notebooks grip me with far more dangerous tentacles, by suggesting that I should identify with the wanderings and changes of address of the person writing them, whose evocation distracts me from what I'm looking for. Despite myself, they include me in scenes out of some silent movie taking place in Tangiers, in Amsterdam, in Verona, in prison, in the Boulevard Saint-Germain – isolated stories whose plots lack both grandeur and resolution. I see myself inside successive dreams, gesticulating in the company of shadowy figures, saying words I can't hear, pretending passions I don't feel, reliving the contact with anonymous bodies that cling on to me tenaciously, dragging me into humiliating or, quite simply, banal decisions, condemning me to enter places I would have preferred not to visit, constantly fleeing towards cities that never once said to me: stay!

And in all those places, my desire for flight bumps again and again against the corners of the scenery that is always there, that reappears with ever greater venom the more I try to suppress it. And it is the place from which I am fleeing: this room.

Re-reading those novel-ish beginnings, in which the boy-become-man returns to the castle of you-will-leave-and-never-come-back in order to demand an explanation from his father of all the things that were always so obscure, I suddenly reached a sentence which, like so many of my sentences, is addressed to the person who was thinking it while he was writing it, a lost "you". It was addressed to me too, to the person I am now. It took my breath away. It's a sentence written in a tremulous hand, in Tangiers, two years ago:

"Don't write any more, look at me and speak to me. Have you really come back? Have you actually dared to do that? Or are these just fragments of your dream?"

I got up, urged by that voice, and started feeling my way round the wood-panelled walls, the open safe, the window. I leaned out. From there I recognized the gravel path I had walked along in order to enter the ground floor, the oleanders in the small garden, the backs of the other houses.

"Yes, I'm home!" I shouted, as if I had just emerged from a nightmare. "I will never again get sidetracked along muddy paths. No more excuses. Today I will begin."

Then I closed all my notebooks and I put them in my backpack. I cleared the table of everything else. I'm not going to tackle my father's papers just now. I've put them back in the safe and replaced the painting that covers it. No one will interrupt me. I've taken the phone off the hook and night is beginning to fall. Even if someone were to knock at the door, I wouldn't open it. I feel alive, lucid, calm. And alone. This is a task I have to undertake alone. My father's definitive absence, the sight of his empty chair opposite me, is what distinguishes this beginning from all the others I once imagined.

But I don't want to go off along any more tangents. One thing at a time. I will begin with my arrival here. As he always used to say, all the best novels begin with an arrival.

II

The arrival

After the taxi disappeared, leaving me standing on the pavement with
my two pieces of luggage, I felt suddenly uncertain, slightly faint. It
had been more than seven years since I last went through the little iron
gate leading to the back of the house, and when I did, it was terrible;
I felt as if I were plunging into the void. I didn't fall quickly, though,
not straight down; as I fell, I kept getting snagged on awkward scenes
where I was the gesticulating protagonist and I would be hurled onto
the thorns of the next scene just as I was trying to come to terms with
the last one, to adapt to each individual scene, one by one.

"Why have I come back," I asked myself, "why?" I felt incapable of
stopping where I was and incapable of retreating, if only in my imagination, to situations where the atmosphere was less oppressive, and as
I left behind me the noises of the street and began to recognize different parts of the garden, I found myself torn between two contrary
impulses: one urged me forward on the strength of my newly abandoned inertia, the other warned me of the dangers that this might
involve and advised me to escape back into false adventures, to make
do with poor imitations of refuges in dimly remembered houses and
voices, in noisy clubs rife with drugs and money, where crazy plans are
hatched and fatal contacts made. In the end, I gave in to the first
impulse, though without much conviction, thinking: "Oh, what does it
matter? This is probably all just a dream as well!"

I managed to sort out the large downstairs room which, when I first
arrived, was crammed with motley objects: filing cabinets, dismantled
furniture, trunks full of curtains and old clothes, rolled-up carpets,
books, jars, cracked or otherwise defective curios – a little shepherdess
with no fingers, a harlequin without a nose; most intriguing of all was

a series of drawers of different sizes which, although they seemed to be there as witnesses to an attempt at establishing some sort of order, had clearly become part of the arbitrary geography of the place, having lost their character as landmarks in the thick of all that chaos, and now only underlined the failure of that attempt by displaying their own burdensome contents: an amalgam of plugs, screwdrivers, cables, lampshades, odd iron fittings, balls of string, light bulbs, keys, rolls of sticking plaster, and God knows what else. I refused point-blank to go upstairs – a decision made with the vehement mixture of insecurity and defiance that always fuels my most futile plans.

I was paralysed there, amongst all those objects exuding the acrid smell of must and camphor, and it seemed that the only remnant of willpower still capable of impinging on my lethargy was my reluctance to move from the first room I had set foot in – another choice made out of pure inertia, simply because, in the old days, whenever I arrived home late, I always used this entrance and not the front door – that and my refusal to make any attempt to explore the rest of the house. So, the first thing I did was to reinforce that "deal" with myself – so enthusiastically, in fact, that I managed to impale a chisel in the palm of my left hand – by barricading the door leading to the upper floors, fitting it with a large, keyless padlock, the first one I came across when scrabbling around in the drawers. Maybe I suspected that if I did set off in search of another room of a more suitable size, that would leave space for me to begin to doubt the importance of a task which, at that moment, was providing me with a necessary, indeed essential, stimulus to action.

The door had been recently painted, and the frame got rather chipped, since I attacked it from various angles, obsessively looking for a place where the wood would offer least resistance; in the end, though, the now slightly bent padlock held firm, standing out like a dark face against the white gloss.

Exhausted by my labours, I leaned against the wall, feeling the first painful throbbings of my injured hand. That was when I saw the tall, black man I had first glimpsed in the garden; he was standing on firm, straight legs in the middle of the room and was looking at me, absorbed, inscrutable. I couldn't tell if he perceived the look on my face as one of defiance or of perplexity; in fact, the look on my face derived from my need to find that out, rather than from any desire to learn what he might think of my behaviour, which seemed to leave him entirely unsurprised.

Feeling slightly dizzy, I dropped the hammer on the floor and watched him come over, pick it up and return it, together with the other tools, to the same drawer I had found them in. Then, still kneeling, he looked at me again.

"The mistress of the house was thinking of doing it up," he said, as though apologizing for the state the room was in.

He had a melodious voice, with just a trace of a Portuguese accent. I shrugged and murmured:

"When wasn't she?"

I didn't feel like asking him anything, but neither did I feel the unease I had experienced when I passed him in the garden, when it seemed to me that, far from being frightened, he had merely registered my fear of him. Now, while I watched him put the contents of the drawer into some semblance of order, place it on top of another drawer and push both back against the wall, I had to admit that his impassivity had the edge over mine, because, of the two of us, I was the real intruder.

"I know," he said, smiling, "she loved changing things around, it calmed her nerves."

I glanced across at the door, suddenly afraid that I might see her there issuing orders about the endless changes and alterations that had been a torment to me since childhood. Her plans carried with them an oppressive atmosphere that afflicted us all, for, whether we wanted to or not, we all got caught up in that frenzy of activity. The oddest thing was that the slightest headache, telephone call or even a shower of rain could give an unexpected slant to her mood and bring about an indefinite postponement of those plans, leaving the rest of us still infected by the unease incubating in those febrile expectations.

I looked about me. All around the room there were traces of her final burst of activity.

"I don't think anything calmed her nerves," I said.

But he didn't reply. He was standing some distance away and he suddenly looked exactly what he was: a black servant awaiting my orders, with no reason to meddle in anything. That master-servant relationship suited me fine; I didn't want any closer relationship.

I declined his offer to tidy up the whole room in which I was evidently preparing to install myself, and I would only allow him to help me shift the objects that were preventing me from reassembling my grand-mother's great iron bedstead, the various parts of which had to be painstakingly salvaged from amongst the welter of junk. It required time and patience, like a jigsaw puzzle; it seemed logical to me that it should be so difficult. It would be equally difficult to gather together all the fragments of my dreams – dreams in which this bed had occasionally appeared – to put them all together and find the key to the resulting plot.

I stopped work for a moment in order to remove from my backpack, which I had left leaning against the wall, a notebook with oilcloth covers that I had started in the prison hospital, and to make a note of the parallel between the rebuilding of dreams and of beds, a richly suggestive subject. Further ideas grew out of it and I sat down on the floor to write in more comfort. I filled several pages.

(By the way, I was re-reading those pages earlier and copying them out with a few corrections into the same notebook I'm using now, the yellow A4 ringbound one. I thought they might provide a way in, a beginning. Then I changed my mind. It's best to leave the notes as they were when I first set them down.)

I don't know how long I spent sitting on the floor beside my backpack; when I emerged from my thoughts, I recognized the scene about me with startled eyes. The black man was still putting together the various bits of the bed, as if my desertion of the task had not bothered him in the least. He had in his hand a large pair of scissors.

I got up to join him in the work again, with the feeling that I had fallen behind. The tacit permission I had given him to involve himself in my affairs was beginning to broaden out. But then, looking at him, I thought, who better than a stranger to help me put my grandmother's bed together; he does it better than a friend, because he does it from the

63

outside. The same thing happens in dreams. Often, a stranger appears who has been walking by our side, for how long we don't know, but whose main purpose seems to be to remain almost invisible, and sometimes he even hides or changes into someone else in order to throw us off the track. The same sort of secondary but fundamental beings that I subsequently found so often in novels and in films used to appear in my grandmother's stories too. They are witnesses who appear to be doing nothing, who pretend that they are just looking, but who might well be better informed than they seem to be.

He had sat down now and was snipping through the stitches made out of string sewn into some sacking which served as a kind of temporary cover for the bedhead. I had thrown myself into that work – the work that he was now undoing – with feverish, almost furious zeal, skinning my fingers on the rough sacking in the process, pricking myself with the blunt end of the stout needle, spending more than an hour kneeling on the floor. And then she came in and asked me loftily why I was doing that. We hadn't spoken for several days.

"Because I'm leaving," I said, "because I can't stand being here a day longer and I don't want anyone else to touch my grandmother's bed, do you understand?"

"Why don't you take it with you when you go then?" she exclaimed in a tight, angry voice. "I always thought it was just a piece of junk that had no place here anyway."

"Don't worry, I'll send for it as soon as I can."

That was our farewell and you always remember words of farewell, however sweet or bitter. I've never forgotten them all these years and, sometimes, in the different stopping-off places of my diaspora, that eternally postponed plan of returning to get my grandmother's bed would nag at me like a bit of unfinished business.

Now I was watching the fingers of the man holding the scissors, as if he were cutting the stitches on a wound, as if he were undoing an evil spell. When he had finished, he leaned the heavy bedhead against the wall and went to look for the foot of the bed that was on the other side of the room. That wasn't wrapped up – just one of the many tasks I have left incomplete in my life.

My head was bubbling with images that underlay and became a hieroglyph for the mere physical work of putting the bed together, an extremely unpleasant task that I would have been incapable of carrying out alone. As he nimbly lifted iron bars and siderails and gestured to me to pass him some tool or to help him drag the slatted base into place, I followed behind, my steps growing ever more hesitant and more dependent on his, the steps of a cabin boy in the wake of his captain. In the end, during the final stages of that task invented by me, I had to recognize that I was merely working to his orders.

When the bed was finally fully assembled in the middle of the room – each corner post topped by a golden ball and with a chubby little angel trumpeter gracing the pinnacle of the bedhead itself – I sat down on the mattress and started rolling a joint, while the black man carefully removed the tools blocking access to the back door and found a place for them in various corners. He hardly made a sound.

Then, wrapped in the sense of wellbeing brought on by the first effects of the hash, I noticed that he had completed his task and was leaning in the doorway that led out into the garden in an attitude of expectation and readiness, suggestive too of a certain voluptuous abandon. I was looking at him somewhat intrigued, as if in a dream.

"What on earth is he doing in the story, grandma? This is such a difficult story to understand!"

"We haven't even got to the really difficult bit yet," said my grand-mother. "The magpie was perched on the green lemon tree; with his beak he pecked the leaf, with the leaf he pecked the flower. Neither by day nor by night, neither by land nor by sea, neither naked nor clothed. Who am I?"

"Tell me more clearly, since you know everything, which is the really difficult bit?"

"You're too impatient for your own good, you are," said my grand-mother. "Let what is locked open of its own accord, but do not lock what is already open. Pin-pin, the peddlar does cry, tric-trac, he came into town, selling green lemons for half a crown. The really difficult thing to find out is who passed by here without being seen, who seemed to be here already and who was hiding."

"Are you referring to anyone in particular?"

"Now, come on," said my grandmother, "that's for you to find out. I will give my love an apple without e'er a core, I will give my love a house without e'er a door . . ."

"I know, I know, but this is different. You keep slipping away, don't hide, where are you?"

"Round and round, round about, if you haven't hidden yet, you'll soon be found out. You go and hide too."

"Where shall I hide? They always find me, grandma. Just when I think I'm really well hidden, they see me, they find me out; there aren't any good places left to hide in."

"Even if you hide in Pedro's house, where the doors are all locked, we'll cut them open with razor and knife, and, tris, tras, you'll be out in a trice."

I was rocking back and forth on her feet; she was holding my hands in hers, and as she recited in that singsong voice, she would sometimes lean her face towards me and then lean back; when she moved away from me she laughed, when she came close she didn't, she looked serious and a bit frightening, her face as still as the day that I saw her dead, the last time I went to the Quinta Blanca, the dead white Quinta, my dead white grandmother, but there was still a glimmer of laughter in that serious face, you could see it if you looked hard.

"Stop all these riddles, grandma, I don't understand them. Tell me a story instead."

"There's more to riddles than meets the eye, my child," said my grandmother, "why else would you remember them after all this time? There must be some reason."

"It must be because of the bed. I feel a bit sick and feverish actually."

"Do you?" said my grandmother. "Fever, fever, go away, don't come in my bed today. Let me see what you've done to that hand of yours, there's no point hiding it, let me see. You're bleeding."

"It's nothing. I did it padlocking a door."

"You see?" said my grandmother. "That's what you get for locking something that was open. You've got a real thing about doors, and yet you're always the first to burst in where you're not wanted, like

Bluebeard's wife. You really loved that story, that and the Snow Queen."

"Oh yes, it was marvellous. I still love that story. How did it begin?"

"Oh, you like it, all right," said my grandmother, "but you don't really understand it, because you haven't got the patience. You need a lot of patience if you want to understand something, you have to wait, utterly still, the way fishermen do, but you never stop. I've told you as much dozens of times."

I closed my eyes and the pain in my hand forced them open again. The whole room stretched out before me without corners or reference points, as if it were made of cotton wool. My eyes searched desperately, looking for something to fix on, and the black man was still there at the door that opened on to the now dark garden, like a totem standing guard. He remained there at his post, on the threshold separating inside from out. I took one last drag on my joint and I saw him approaching, bearing an ashtray. Our fingers met and we looked at each other.

"Your hand's bleeding," he said. "I'm going to look for some antiseptic."

Skirting the low bars of the bed and the packages scattered about on the floor, he headed for the place where I had installed the padlock that had been the cause of the accident. He ran his fingers along its upper edge, without forcing it, as if trying to see if it would give.

"Where's the key?" he asked at last.

"I don't know. I have no intention of ever opening it."

"Really? And am I not allowed to open it either?"

"You won't open it, because you can't," said my grandmother, "because you don't dare, because you ask what it isn't without understanding what it is. I have an ox who can plough the whole field round, hide what's in your hand where it can't be found."

"Stop!" I cried. "No, you can't open it either!"

With my hand, I batted away the crazy words of all the riddles; they lay face down and became a cloud of golden mosquitoes that flew up and formed a halo around the black man, a sprinkling of light that went from his shoulders to his hips. He had a slight tic when he blinked.

"Fine," he said, "but the antiseptic is in the upstairs bathroom. That bathroom over there has hardly been used lately. She was thinking of having it redecorated."

He said this with a lift of his chin, indicating another half-open door in the wall opposite, through which you could see signs of recent building work.

It's the landscape I will see from this ship when I open my eyes. The ship has changed direction and is no longer moving. Before, in the days of once upon a time, it used to set sail from a high-ceilinged bedroom through the windows of which came the smell of the sea. "On moonlit nights," my grandmother used to say, "you can come up on deck with me and I'll tell you stories about the stars." I would spring lightly aboard and she would make room for me, even if it was squally, even if I'd had a bad dream. Now the ship has run aground and there are no more voyages to be made.

To the right of the bathroom door, there was a carpenter's bench and, on the floor, amongst the shavings, there were several stacks of tiles, two sacks of cement and a bidet swathed in broad strips of brown paper with black lettering on it.

A shrill, surrealist landscape. I was beginning to feel sleepy, but the figure standing next to the padlocked door made me feel uncomfortable.

"What's the problem? Go round the garden and in through the front door."

To the left of the carpenter's bench, at the far end of the wall, was the square cavity left by the dumb waiter, the remains of an era when we used to have the dining room down here in the summer. Perhaps the dumb waiter no longer communicated with the kitchen. What a ludicrously complex archaeological task! I closed my eyes. I didn't want to ask if renovations were also underway upstairs, I didn't want to know anything about upstairs. I heard the black man go out into the garden.

"As you wish," he said.

III

Maurício Brito

I fell asleep and I changed into my mother. It's a dream, always camouflaged in different plots, that I've had ever since I was a child, ever since I first felt an ardent desire to get inside her body and her feelings, to find out whether she loved me or not, to understand what a woman thinks when she's getting herself ready in front of the mirror, when she's lying in bed but can't sleep, when she looks irritated when you come into the room because she was expecting someone else, when she looks at you without even seeing you; I wanted to find the place in her body where I could take the measure of her disquiets, I needed to know who or what she dreamed about. It's a curiosity I have never managed to assuage, rather like my childish desire to dismantle toys and clocks in order to find out how they worked.

I dreamed that I was arriving one moonlit night at the Quinta Blanca, now inhabited by different people. The garden was narrower and flanked by some peculiar kind of chicken house, with thorns on the wire fencing; the statues, however, were where they had always been and so I headed in that direction because everything else was somehow changed. As I approached, though, the statues grew in number. I stopped in front of one that was larger than all the others; I looked at it hard and I saw that it was stepping down from its pedestal. It was my mother. She gave me her hand, barely squeezing it, and started walking, taking longer strides than me, leaving me slightly behind. I saw her bare, white thighs and I tried to fit my steps to the rhythm of hers, knowing that, at any moment, I was about to become fused with her. At the same time, I was little Kay following the Snow Queen and knowing – in that confused yet obvious way that one does know things in dreams – that to save myself from danger, I had to remember the

69

story and tell it to someone else. When we were almost at the back of the house, she turned to look at me and put an arm around my shoulders. I noticed then a horrible coldness creeping up from my feet to my chest, numbing my limbs. I was turning to ice. I had to call out for help before my voice froze too.

I woke up drenched in sweat, and the black man was sitting on the edge of the bed. I had grabbed hold of his strong wrist like a drowning man a piece of wood, but it hurt so much that I immediately withdrew my hand, suppressing a cry of pain. At that moment, he stretched out his arm and turned on a reading lamp.

"Have you been here long?"

"For a while. I didn't want to wake you. They say you shouldn't wake someone up when they're having a nightmare, that you should leave them to work their own way out of it."

He was smiling, revealing a row of large, white teeth. I changed my position and shifted over towards the edge. Grandmother's mattresses always tended to dip a bit in the middle.

He had brought a bottle of antiseptic lotion and was unscrewing the top. Then he soaked a piece of cotton in the lotion. I sat up.

"Now then, would you mind showing me your hand?"

I held out my open palm. The cut was a deep one and it has, in fact, taken several days to heal completely. On contact with the antiseptic, whitish bubbles appeared around the edges of the cut. It really stung.

"Am I hurting you?"

"Yes, you are. Don't rub so hard."

"I have to make sure it's thoroughly clean," he said, gripping my wrist harder when he noticed me pulling away. "You've got dust in it from moving all this old junk around."

He washed the wound carefully and then bandaged my hand in spite of the fact that I said, rather half-heartedly, that it really wasn't worth it. Looking at his large pink nails, pale against his dark chocolate skin, I again experienced a certain excitement.

He picked up the various medicaments and placed them next to the reading lamp on the marble-topped bedside table which had appeared, as if by magic, to the right of the bed. That piece of furniture was another of the few things that had been brought here after my grandmother's death. The drawer was always full of unguents and strange implements of indeterminate use.

"Where did that bedside table come from?"

"I put it there just now, while you were asleep," he said. "It could be useful, don't you think?"

"Yes," I said, confused. "But where was it?"

He pointed to the wall opposite.

"Behind those pictures."

"I didn't hear you dragging it over here."

"I did it very slowly. And I brought you down this lamp as well. The light here's really bad."

There was a silence. He seemed to be waiting for me to tell him to leave, and I didn't dare ask him to stay. I would have had to confess too many things to him that I didn't want to confess even to myself. For example, that I was beginning to feel afraid of the night and of sleeping alone, that I felt suddenly terribly vulnerable. Cool air wafted in from the garden and a few birds were singing, surrendering to that ecstasy of chatter that precedes their silence and the definitive dark. No one knows where they hide themselves in order to sleep. I saw some sheets and blankets on the floor.

"Oh, and some bedclothes too," he added. "I assume you're going to sleep here."

"Yes, but it doesn't matter. I sleep any old how. Don't go to any bother."

"You sort it out for yourself then. I'm in a bit of a hurry now actually. Can you manage all right with your hand like that?"

"Yes, of course, don't worry."

"If there's nothing else . . . My name's Maurício Brito, at your service. I'm delighted to have met you."

Then he lowered his eyes sadly and added:

"And may I offer you my deepest sympathies."

He held out his hand to me and I shook it.

"But where are you going?" I mumbled, disconcerted.

I realized suddenly that, in that short space of time, the man had become a kind of anchor I could hold on to in order to begin my new life.

"The fact is my job here finished yesterday. I just came to pick up my things. But I'm very glad I met you. Something strange happened to me this afternoon. Don Ernesto had just left . . . you know who Don Ernesto is, don't you?"

"Yes, the administrator, a sewer rat."

Maurício burst out laughing.

"That's the one. Well, now he spends all his time in the late master's office talking on the phone, fiddling with keys and papers, putting things in order, taking messages – there are a lot of them, of course."

"Who are the messages from?"

"There are all kinds of messages," he said, after a slight pause. "Lots of different people phone, most of them local, but there are quite a few long-distance calls too. Some people have only just heard the news and want to know what happened, others are calling about business matters, and others . . ."

He stopped, like someone braking suddenly, for fear of touching on thorny problems.

"Others, what?"

"Others ask after you, of course – a lot of people, especially the notary. And there are a number of letters upstairs too, which Don Ernesto puts away. He works in the master's office every morning."

"Not for long he won't," I said sharply.

And as soon as I said that, I felt a strange anxiety. It was like declaring that I had come back to take charge of the house and to make all kinds of decisions about it. I couldn't bear it, and it made me angry that I should let myself get upset.

"Let's leave Don Ernesto in peace for the moment," I said, trying to sound calm. "What were you saying?"

"Just that I came by to pick up my things this afternoon and Don Ernesto seemed rather embarrassed. He said: 'Not off yet, Maurício?', as if he were afraid I might stay on here alone, although he knows me well enough and he knows how much the master cared for me. I was expecting a long-distance phone call and I told him so; then, finally, since he had to leave in a hurry, he said a rather reluctant goodbye and left. He asked me to leave the keys in the vase. Anyway, so as not to bother him, by the time the phone call came through, I had already taken my luggage out into the garden and was thinking of closing up downstairs, but I just kept hanging on and hanging on. It was because I was waiting for you – it *was* really, don't laugh; that's why I wasn't at all surprised when I saw you."

He fell silent, looking down at his knees. We could hear rock-and-roll music coming from next door.

"I'm not laughing," I said. "I get hunches like that sometimes too. But how did you know who I was?"

"From the way you behaved."

"I could have been a thief or an impostor. Do you know what an impostor is?"

"Yes, of course I do, they're always turning up in novels, but they never arrive at a house that doesn't belong to them, the way you did."

I was beginning to enjoy myself. I lit a cigarette and offered him one.

"How do impostors arrive, then? Sit down for a bit, you can't be in that much of a hurry."

He glanced at his watch and sat down at the foot of the bed. He was studying the end of his cigarette, as if thinking how best to reply.

"I don't know, it's just different," he said at last. "They're always full of explanations, precisely because they want to make it absolutely clear that the house is theirs. You can tell at once that they've carefully thought it all through beforehand so that no one will catch them out and denounce them; they're too cautious, too normal. No impostor would do the odd things you've done. Besides, I've seen a photo of you."

"Really? Where?"

"In a silver frame. You're on horseback. You were younger then, but it's obviously you."

He looked at his watch again. I felt almost as afraid to stop talking as to go on. I asked him how long he'd been at the house and if he was happy, and from then on, the conversation took the form of an interrogation, which doubtless made him feel rather uncomfortable. It had the same effect on me, because it removed us from the pleasant, unreal situation that we had momentarily enjoyed; and, to my regret, I was becoming someone who merely demands information. He said that he had spent three years at the house and that now he was returning to a previous post where he had worked for a long time before, for a lady who gave him almost nothing to do; he had come here three years ago because the pay was much better. On the other hand, he knew that my father had been very fond of him and was, in fact, the one who had first brought him here as a chauffeur. The last few months he had been carrying out the duties of a secretary or something of the sort. He told me all this very quickly and reluctantly, and, although his story was rather confused and contradictory, it was clear from what he said that it was my father who had insisted on keeping him on. I asked him what had happened to the other servants, because there had always been at least two. Now frankly embarrassed, Maurício stared down at the floor.

"Well," he said, "the mistress dismissed all the servants before leaving for Chicago. I stayed on alone, awaiting orders from the master."

"How come?"

"She left intending never to come back, to stay there for good. For once," he added sadly, "the poor woman didn't get a chance to change her mind."

"To stay there?" I asked, bemused. "Didn't you say that she was going to renovate the house?"

"Yes, but she forgot all about that. They had constant arguments during their last weeks here. That had been going on since the beginning of the year. The master couldn't bear it any longer. They had decided to separate. At least, so I believe."

I felt a burst of retrospective indignation.

"But that's absurd! Why did he go with her, then? It was obvious they couldn't separate, they were doomed to stay together, stopping each other's breath, strangling each other, even to the last it seems."

I hated myself for losing control like that in front of a stranger, but I couldn't help it.

"Well," said Maurício gravely, after a pause. "She was ill. You have to remember that. She was very ill."

Then, without my asking, he brought me up to date on some details of the accident. He told me that Aunt Ingrid had called him twice from Chicago to find out if I had turned up; he told me that they had both been cremated over there. Now he was the one spontaneously offering me information, as if he wanted to provoke in me some new reaction that would put an end to my silence. He gave me the names of the people who had phoned and, naturally, again mentioned Don Ernesto. I started to regret having come back; it exhausted me, that procession of vaguely remembered figures, like circling crows – "Poor Eugenio, poor Trud, and that awful son of theirs," the smiles, the sighs and the offers of help. According to Maurício, the notary, Don Octavio Andrade, was the person who most anxiously awaited my return. He had a pile of papers for me to sign. There was no turning back; whether I liked it or not, I had to get involved in a labyrinth of information and numbers that would impinge only very tangentially on my jigsaw puzzle. Land deals, shares, mortgages, life insurance, taxes, joint property, subrogations, investments – vague, rapacious words, slipping like worms into the hollow eye sockets of a skeleton.

"Don Ernesto always comes at nine. If you like, I could leave him a note upstairs to tell him you've arrived."

"No, please, I don't want to have to think about that right now. Forget it."

"It's just that he's going to find it odd seeing you here, it might give him a fright."

"Good!"

Maurício had stood up, but he still did not seem quite ready to leave. He hesitated. He obviously wanted to warn me about something else. He ended up confessing, after some beating about the bush, that, in the last few days, Don Ernesto had heard rumours that I might be in prison. I looked up and caught a knowing look in Maurício's eyes. I felt a moment of relief as I replied haughtily:

"Yes, it's true actually. I've just been let out. I spent seven months inside."

It was like breaking an evil spell only to fall immediately under another. Since getting to the house, I hadn't given a thought to my recent past. It had been wiped out as if it had never existed, but at the mention of those seven months, the image resurfaced of the pregnant girl who, only hours before, had gone to wait for me at the prison gate. If her suppositions were correct, I was about to become a father. It could be true or it could be a lie; I could just ignore it and forget about it. But a child who might be mine was about to come into the world, even if he grew up not knowing who I was.

I sat absorbed in thought, staring at the jumble of junk scattered about the room, except that I was no longer in that room, I was in a different, much smaller, more elongated room, more impersonal too. Just another hiding place like all the other hiding places where I have sought shelter amongst restless, hyped-up men and women with dark shadows under their eyes, all members of a fraternity of people doomed to drift. I suddenly remembered it very clearly. The room had a tiny window that looked out on to an inner courtyard and you could hear the noise of an ancient lift wheezing up and down. Opposite me, above a still unmade sofa bed, was a large poster of Mick Jagger. Goyo was feeling ill and had lain down there for a while; the others had woken him up when they had gone off in search of a consignment of heroin. They had left me alone with the girl with red hair, whose name was Ángela. I had started writing in my notebook, sitting on the floor, not even noticing that she had stayed behind. We had all smoked a lot of hash. I was writing very fast, with a terrible urgency; the writing is almost illegible, I was looking at it yesterday. They were the last notes I made before going to prison. I wrote that I couldn't go on like that, that it was my last chance to escape and start a new life, I scribbled down quotations from Walt Whitman, from Kafka, from Pavese – invocations to the sea; and emerging out of the word "sea", there's a scrawl at the bottom, like a snake. That's because she had come up behind me and put her arms around me, making me jump, I think I may even have cried out. She asked me if I still loved her and I said distractedly: "No". She was naked apart from a thin scarf around her neck. She took it off and started playing with it. First, she covered my face with it, like a veil, so that I couldn't see what I was writing. Then she put it round my wrists, which she tied behind me. "There, you're a prisoner," she said, "I've caught you, I've caught the mysterious monster." She pushed me over on to the floor, laughing, and started unbuttoning my shirt. "They won't be back for at least two hours," she said. Her breath troubled me, it smelled of whisky; it still troubles me now when I remember it. But I knew then that I was going under. Three days later they arrested me.

"And why did they arrest you?" asked Maurício. "Something to do with drugs?"

I looked up, surprised.

"Yes, how did you know?"

"Well, it's par for the course nowadays," he said in a neutral tone. "They don't put people in prison for politics any more."

"I was framed," I said rather lamely in my own defence. "Although, obviously, people can only frame you if you let them. I was an accomplice to what was happening to me. I knew that perfectly well. But it doesn't matter. It happens all the time. I have no intention of seeing those particular people ever again."

"And how come you were released just now? Because of your parents or because you'd finished your sentence?"

I stared at him, stunned. That perfectly logical question left me completely stumped. If I started thinking about it, if I pulled on the thread that it suggested to me, a lot of other similar questions would emerge and I would find myself tangled up in a skein that would obscure the object – already enigmatic in the extreme – of my real search.

"No . . . I mean, I don't actually know why they released me, or what for," I said, feeling suddenly weak.

I think that almost immediately after that, Maurício said goodbye. He was very sorry, he said, but he would miss his train if he didn't leave. He explained where he had left the keys for the front door in case I changed my mind and wanted to go upstairs.

"Besides, I think you should," he added, with a touch of authority in his voice, which, to my surprise, didn't bother me in the least. "You might have a bad night, you might even get a fever, because that wound could easily go septic. There's a cabinet crammed with tranquillizers and antibiotics in the bathroom that your mother, God rest her, used to use. It's next to her bedroom – she had it extended last year – and there's clean bed linen on the bed. There are things to eat in the kitchen too. If I was in your shoes, I wouldn't hesitate; it's a different world up there."

After all those months deprived of any kind of luxury, I imagined the pleasure of a hot bubble bath and a sensual tremor ran through me.

My mother's bedroom always smelled of flowers. She used to wear perfume by Dior.

"Thanks, Maurício. I'll see," I said doubtfully.

"I'd feel happier if you were upstairs," he said, holding out his hand.

I shook it mechanically and wished him luck.

"The same to you," he said. "And don't let things get to you too much. As my mistress always says, the day dawns even on the darkest night, if we let it. I can't wait to see her again. Goodbye, take care. I don't know where the time's gone. I'm going to miss my train if I'm not careful."

He half-turned and disappeared into the garden. My mind had become such a blank that it took me a while to realize that I was alone and that I shouldn't have let Maurício leave like that. I needed him urgently, but by the time I came to and ran out to call him, it was too late.

It was dark now and pouring with rain. I walked round the house. Beyond the small garden gate, cars were driving by, not many and not very fast; it's an area of detached houses some way from the centre. I pushed the gate open and went out on to the pavement, looking all around me. I could see no one. Suddenly, it occurred to me that he might have gone into the house to collect something and, although I couldn't see any lights on in the windows, I went up the five steps to the front door of the house and rang the doorbell several times. No one opened the door and the rain was getting heavier. I went back out on to the pavement and started shouting, looking up, cupping my mouth with my hands: "Maurício, Maurício!" I was answered by the barking of a dog in the next-door garden. I kept on shouting, my voice growing hoarser, until I heard a car pull up behind me, and I turned round.

A black Chrysler had stopped on the other side of the road and two women and a man, all elegantly dressed, had just that minute got out. They opened their umbrellas and looked at me, alarmed, distrustful, before going into one of the houses opposite. I started walking in the other direction and went up the first side road. I waited for a while, my heart pounding, before daring to reappear. I didn't want any of the neighbours to see me entering the house.

When I did, after all kinds of complicated precautions, I again felt in the grip of my status as suspect, of someone outside the law, and I re-experienced it with a bittersweet pain, letting myself be seduced by the distorting mirror of that identity which had so often brought me to the edge of delinquency.

Despite being soaked to the skin, I remained for a while longer prowling furtively through the garden in the shadows, wondering whether I could clamber over the back wall, recognizing places that had sometimes served me as a refuge when I was a child, imagining which of them might now provide me with a provisional hiding place if I suddenly heard the footsteps of a policeman alerted by the neighbours, approaching with his torch, a gun at his waist: "You're under arrest!" My childish imagination had often woven similar stories of persecution and capture; I always had the feeling that someone would unmask me.

When I noticed that my teeth were beginning to chatter, I went back into the room, closed the sliding doors, put the bar across it, and got out a blanket from the pile of bedclothes that Maurício had left on the floor. I took my clothes off, wrapped the blanket about me and lay down on my grandmother's bed. The dip in the mattress drew me back to its centre, and I lay there for a long time, not moving, looking up at the flaking ceiling, listening to the rain beating against the door. I turned off the light. I was beginning to feel feverish. The shape of the days to come began to be identified with the vague shapes around me and with the impalpable presence of those filling the rooms upstairs which I had refused to visit. They all flowed towards my father's study and out down the drain that was his safe. With my eyes closed, that geography of corridors, stairs, cavities and partition walls appeared on the inside of my eyelids with terrifying precision, and my mind was again filled by the surreal stories that my grandmother used to tell me, each with its implicit question, like a kind of hieroglyph. "Here's the cellar, here's the attic, here's the bedroom and the hall, here's the kitchen and the parlour, how many fingers can you see?"

The house up above me was pointing at me with a thousand black fingers like the muzzles of rifles, and what I found most frightening was that, suddenly, that house was mine. It was utterly useless fitting locks, destroying keys and playing at being Bluebeard, forbidding myself to go up there and inspect it all. It was mine and I had to take charge of it. That was why I had come, and I knew it. It was unavoidable; in the end, I would inevitably go upstairs.

"But not tonight, grandma, not yet," I said, snuggling into the folds of that soft, ancestral bed. "Let me stay here with you. If only I could cry, like I used to before the Snow Queen came. But I can't. How does the story begin? How does it go?"

I squeezed my eyes tight shut. I wanted to go back, to voyage back, to the early summers of the past, I needed to return to the kingdom of once upon a time, using that opening formula as a password. The summer was just beginning . . .

There was a flash of light inside me, like the glint of some long-buried jewel. All the birds of summer started to sing, flying up and down the sun's rays in order to welcome the still innocent boy who had just been deposited safe and sound at the Quinta Blanca by a chauffeur with an anonymous face, while his parents travelled off to unknown destinations.

"The summer was just beginning," I repeated joyfully, "the summer was just beginning."

IV

The kidnapping of Kay

The summer was just beginning; rays of golden sun played happily in the air, flooding with happiness the hearts of a boy and a girl for whom the arrival of the long summer days meant pure joy.

I had often drawn Hans Christian Andersen's two child protagonists in my notebooks; in my solitary condition as sickly little rich boy, I shared their joy at the arrival of summer. They were rather poor and lived next door to each other in houses connected by a flat roof; they had only to walk along a strip of roof to cross from window to window in order to tell each other stories and play trustingly together in the bosom of that flowering season which, as yet, presaged no misfortune. And when they couldn't walk across, they would look out and make signs to each other through the windows of their respective rooms.

Sometimes I would draw them like that, separate but looking and smiling at each other through their windows; at other times, I would depict them sitting together on their wooden stools, with a crowded backdrop of flowerpots, because the window boxes were already filled to overflowing with campanulas, azaleas, lilacs and rose trees, or, rather, I invented all those species to make it prettier. Before I knew how to read, my grandmother used to lend me the book of *The Snow Queen*, so that I could look at the pictures, and, although I can't actually remember, it's likely that one of the illustrations in the book may have given rise to the idea of my first drawing, but after that initial imitation – if imitation it was – my imagination added its own multiple variants. Above the boy's attic room and window, I always wrote a K, and above that of the girl, a G, both in mauve like Gerda's dress and Kay's shirt. He was barefoot and she wore little black slippers and striped stockings, that's how I imagined them; the little girl was blonde, of course, and he was dark. But what gave me the greatest pleasure, and what I took the most trouble over, was drawing the flowers in the pots behind them, an emblem of the happiness emanating from that mystical, fleeting summer; I drew heavily laden branches, densely drawn with volutes and spirals, in different shades of lilac, purple and mauve; the pencils in these colours always wore out fastest from so much sharpening and from outlining the petals that framed the smiling faces of Gerda and Kay.

"It's all very pretty," my grandmother would say when I showed it to her, "but you can hardly see the rose tree amongst all that tangle, and that's the most important bit, because roses were Gerda's favourite flowers. Don't you remember how, later on, it's the roses that remind her of home?"

And I would get angry and say no, the second part of the story was a lie.

"If that's what you want to think, fine, but don't press so hard with the pencil and don't put all that scribble round the flowers – let the rose tree stand out, all right? Besides, whoever saw a lilac-coloured rose tree?"

On other occasions, she would say that children were easy to draw and why didn't I try my hand at the Snow Queen.

The Snow Queen did not appear in any of the pictures in the book, and I never dared to draw her either, perhaps because I could see her so clearly in my head, as if I had known her all my life; she was part of those fears so palpably present that we prefer not to name them. She was very beautiful, but cold as ice, and when she came down to earth, the snowflakes began falling thick and fast, the roof tops became slippery and impassable, the flowers in the pots withered and, although the children had never yet seen her, she herself came at night to their window and engraved complicated patterns in the layers of frost on the glass panes: plants, birds, flowers, palaces, strange figures. Despite the cold outside, she probably took a long time over this, showing the same care and application as I did when I wielded my coloured pencils to draw that bright festival of flowers. But whilst my main aim was to let the sun shine through everything I painted, she, who was the sun's enemy, tried to erect barriers against the sun and to raise them up between the children of the sun too, by preventing them from sending forth their own tiny rays.

In fact, although they were sometimes allowed out in the square to play on Kay's sledge, as soon as the window panes were covered by those exquisite, labyrinthine images, the evenings at home became like a grim period of imprisonment for the children because they could no longer see each other or send each other signals. Then Kay would heat up a copper coin and press it against the glass until the frost drawings melted and disappeared; then he would look out through the hole and, at the other window, he would see an eye pressed to a circle made in the ice by exactly the same process. Kay knew that the eye belonged to Gerda because it shone like a star.

When my grandmother reached that point in the story, my eyes would fill with tears. That was before anyone had placed a splinter of glass in my eye and before I was kidnapped by the Snow Queen. My grandmother would stop and say:

"Don't be so silly, why are you crying?"

She nearly always told me these stories in the back garden, and I would sit looking up at the patches of sky you could see beyond the tall tree tops or down at the shifting shadows made by the leaves along the sandy paths and on the faces of the white statues bordering the paths, cold, mysterious faces that seemed to be listening to the mournful cry of the sea. One night, I discovered that when the moon fell on one of the statues in a certain way, it looked just like the Snow Queen, but, later, I never found it again in that same place, I wasn't even sure that I had seen it; they changed places in order to confuse me; it was all very vague, like a labyrinth. And Gerda and Kay were so far away. I felt imprisoned in that garden where nothing was what it seemed.

My grandmother would hand me a lace-edged handkerchief.

"Go on, blow your nose, and tell me what's the matter."

"Nothing, it's just that I'd like to warn the children and I can't. I'd like to send them a bird with a letter in its beak or something. If only they knew what was going to happen to them."

"Come along," said my grandmother, "if you cry, I won't go on reading. Why do you always ask me to read you the stories that make you cry the most?"

But I would beg her to go on, because I knew that even if she did only tell me the first part, what happened afterwards would happen anyway. The only possibility would have been if Gerda and Kay had not been so far away, separated from me by a thousand barriers of frost, and so could have heard me if I'd shouted to them: "Be careful. From now on, be very, very careful!" But the person has not yet been born who can warn us of the dangers that Fate brandishes aloft and then drops on us when she sees we are distracted. It's the same when an insect bites you at night and you wake up to find an itchy lump on your skin, but have no idea how it happened. Impotent to do anything, my heart in my mouth, I would watch the end of the happy time that Gerda and Kay were living through, both of them utterly unaware that it was coming to an end. And I would ask my grandmother to tell me that part very slowly, to make it last as long as possible, the part about the children looking at each other and smiling through the little circles filched from the frost, not knowing that a stage in their life was reaching its conclusion. And like me with my coloured pencils and the flowers, my grandmother would linger over her meticulous descriptions – always finding different metaphors – of the warm glow that came from Kay's eye when he looked at Gerda and the warm glow that came from hers when she looked back at him from her little circle, the glow of an undying star.

It was my grandmother who told me that the sudden changes that take place so mysteriously in certain people and freeze up all their tears, enthusiasm and affection are like the insect bites you get while you're asleep, that these things happen and you can do nothing about them, that it is not the fault of the bad person that they are bad; and she would smile when I asked her if, one day, the same thing would ever happen to me, without my realizing it. She would shake her head slowly and avoid the question, with the enigmatic smile of one who knows all secrets, but is not prepared to sell them to anyone cheaply.

"If what will ever happen to you?"

"The splinter of glass."

We both knew that it all depended on some vague coincidence and for reasons that remained unknowable; it was not something you could foresee, and you could only answer such a question by closing your eyes and pointing blindly, as when I used to point at the narrow roll of paper on which she would write all the different jobs I might do when I was older, stopping the roll at random, and whichever job it stopped at would be my future career.

"Maybe, maybe not, you do ask a lot of questions. Now, throw the stone up in the air, go on, close your eyes and choose a number between one and ten."

"Three."

The number I chose never coincided with the one my grandmother was thinking of. She would start humming.

"If you'd said seven, you would neither win nor lose, nor would you suffer as much as you're going to suffer . . . Oh, come on, you're not crying again, are you? Don't cry, silly, no one ever gets it right. Some people get the splinter of glass in their eye, and others don't."

"I've never seen *you* cry. Have you got it in your eye?"

She sat there staring into the distance, thinking.

"Who can say, child? It's been so many years since I cried!"

"How many years?"

"Since before your father was born. I used to cry a lot when I was single."

I always felt very uneasy when my grandmother alluded to a time before I had entered the world, especially since she was so reluctant to tell me any stories about the family. What I found hardest to imagine was that my father had run about in that same garden when he was a child. I was sure that none of the statues would recognize him now in that tall, serious gentleman who almost never visited because my mother didn't like old houses or remote villages where there is nothing to do. They travelled to different places with exotic names and sent me postcards which I kept in a large biscuit tin that I would get out at night. He would always write the postcard and she would merely add "Love" followed by her spiky signature. My mother intrigued me more than my father did, much more. I wondered why she had such cold, slender fingers, why sometimes she looked at me as if she were trying to read my thoughts or as if she were scolding me for something; I wondered when and how she had met my father, what they talked about on those journeys to which I was never a party; but it was pointless asking my grandmother anything about her; it was clear that they ignored each other as best they could and addressed each other only out of polite-ness. My mother was very pretty, very blonde and almost as tall as my father; she liked to wear pale colours; she was constantly changing servants, clothes and furniture; she spoke slowly and always seemed to be tired. She was obsessive about rules of hygiene and about manners. When I was ten years old and began to eat with them at table, I concen-trated on using my knife and fork as skilfully as possible and on making sure that they didn't see me looking at them out of the corner of my eye, whilst I suffered beneath the weight of their silences or of the opaque conversations that only ever seemed to touch on what we were eating. It was during one of those meals that I began to suspect that my parents did not love each other and to feel certain that the splinter of glass had already entered their eyes. But when? On which day did that happen? That was what most mattered to me, knowing when things had happened and how. Even when she recounted snippets of family history, my grandmother never put dates to events, never placed them in any kind of order so that I could understand them: she left it all swimming in an abstruse fog, what she said and what she didn't say, what really happened juxtaposed with something that was just a story, the past all mixed up with the future and with dreams – and there was that very particular way she had of telling things too, that peculiar tone of voice that left one simultaneously suspicious and thirsting for more. I wanted to know the when of everything so as not to lose myself, and yet I was lost in the fascinating tangle of my grandmother's stories, the only adult person of whom I dared ask any questions, even though she always answered them in such a mysterious way.

"Do you know what age I'll be when I get the splinter of glass in my eye? Tell me."

She would stroke my hair, tilt my chin and look at me with a witch-like expression on her face – which I found both comical and frightening – while she simultaneously traced slow circles in the air with her right hand.

"It will happen . . . it will happen . . . well, it will only happen long after I'm dead."

The trees in the garden stopped being a whirling blur, the sun slipped trustingly through the branches swaying in the breeze. I could see rainbow reflections in the air and could once more feel the ground firm and stable beneath my feet.

"That means never then, grandma, because you're never going to die."

My grandmother liked to hear me say that and whenever I did, she would give me a kiss.

The girl in the Hans Christian Andersen story also had a grandmother who told stories to her and her friend and lent them picture books. One afternoon, when they were looking at one of the books, Kay suddenly rubbed one eye and exclaimed in a frightened voice: "I've got something in my eye, it really hurts, it's like a needle of ice, and it hurts my heart too."

At that time, there was in the world a magic mirror which certain devils had made; when you looked into it you saw only bad, unpleasant things and forgot all about the good things. One night, gleefully counting up the tally of children who had turned bad that day by looking in the mirror, the devils were not careful enough when hanging it up on the nail where they usually left it. The mirror, which was very delicate, fell and shattered into a thousand pieces, as tiny as microscopic particles of dust, that flew through the atmosphere and spread throughout the world. If one of those particles got into someone's eye, they would start to see the bad side of everything; worse than that, it would then slip down into their heart, and the person would grow colder and colder until they became a piece of ice.

Gerda peered into Kay's eye, but she couldn't see anything, yet when she looked at him as she was trying to calm him down, he did not seem the same; he started tearing out pages from the book and throwing stones at the flowerpots, and when he saw Gerda's eyes filling with tears, he started laughing and saying that she looked really ugly when she cried and that the book was ugly too and that the flowers were horrible. From that day on, he was a changed boy. He pulled faces at Gerda's grandmother, made fun of the teacher in class and no longer enjoyed the company of his friend, Gerda, who struck him now as stupid, dull and very young; he spent all day in the street playing rough games with the other boys. He was the boldest of them all and they were all afraid of him.

Then came the saddest episode in the whole story, the one which, despite its cruel nature, I liked my grandmother to linger over, as with the scene of the two children looking at each other through the little circle on the window pane during the previous winter. Everything that happened now and, which, with the arrival of another winter, heralded the appearance of the Snow Queen, found an echo in some remote region of my heart, the same region into which I suspected the splinter of glass would one day slip and become ice, if it ever got in my eye. It seemed to me that the trees suddenly lost all their leaves, reaching out naked arms to a leaden sky; and when she took up the story after a brief pause, my grandmother's voice would take on the solemn tones of a rhapsodist. This now inexorable prelude to misfortune always opened with the same invariable words, just as the words in the opening paragraph of the story never changed either, nor would I have allowed her to change them, the paragraph where the writer described spring giving way to summer ("the summer was just beginning"). Those words were like a spell invoking happiness, these later words were a spell invoking perdition, and as my grandmother had told me many times, and as I understood perfectly well, you could not change the words of spells or prayers, because if they were said in any other way, they would lose their power.

Winter arrived with its cortège of storms; the trees grew bare, the flowers withered and the snow began to fall in astonishingly thick, white flakes, covering the black city like a white sheet.

There was another detail that never changed and which lent a special emphasis to those words, as did the story's opening lines: the fact that my grandmother read them or, rather, pretended to, because she must have known the story by heart, as I did. She would pick up the book with the grey covers – which she only consulted when she was reading those two passages – put on her glasses and find the page. When she had read the paragraph, she would take her glasses off again, carefully put them away in their case, close the book like someone closing a prayer book and leave it on her lap, or bend over to put it down on the grass.

From that moment on, the time it took for the Snow Queen to appear passed as tensely as the time spent at meals with my parents, except that I never quite knew if I wanted to make the time in the story shorter or to lengthen it out indefinitely. It was like waiting for sentence to be passed. Sometimes I would think: "I hope she never comes" and at others: "I hope she arrives now."

One afternoon, one of those very cold afternoons, Kay had unexpectedly gone up to visit his little friend, whom he had not seen for some time, and invited her to come out to play. He had his sledge with him, the same one that had given them so many hours of enjoyment the previous winter. They got on it and let themselves slide across the snow down a steep street that led to the square. I made that journey with my eyes closed, transfixed by a sense of sharp, wounding happiness, more intense than any I have experienced since. During the journey, Gerda sat behind Kay with her arms around his waist, and I shared with her the hope that the boy, of whom we could only see his back, would turn his head and smile at us with his familiar, friendly face, just so that we could recognize him and say: "He's the same boy". He could easily do it, he just had to turn towards us and put on the longed-for, unmistakeable expression that I had drawn in my notebooks (his lips, three parallel lines growing thinner and turning up at the corners); he must still know how to smile like that; what would it cost him to look at us and say: "I'm the same as I always was, the other boy was just a bad dream"; it could happen, and the hope that it would happen stirred my heart and the heart of the girl with her flushed cheeks and her hair tangled by the wind; we clung to each other as we sped down that white street towards the square, and I used that fleeting moment to murmur in her ear: "Don't worry. If the worst comes to the worst, I'll come with you and protect you; I'll be here even if Kay leaves."

But she couldn't hear me and I liked to think it was only because of the roaring wind.

When they reached the square, Kay abandoned Gerda and went to join his new friends, the older boys, who greeted him with shouts and waves of their berets. "Bye, Gerda," he said, waving his hand as he left her, "I'm off to play with my friends." We watched him disappear into that noisy swarm of boys who were trying to lash their sledges to horse-drawn carts. We still caught occasional glimpses of him, but then we lost sight of him completely. The sledges tied to the larger carts were laden with boys, clapping and shouting, clumps of gesticulating faces that rushed through the arches in the square, dragged along by the galloping horses, defying danger and speed. The carts were driven by village people, people whom they knew, who were off to work, and who agreed more or less willingly to drag in their wake that escort of naughty stowaways. When they reached the gates of the city, the boys would untie their sledges and return to the square to start the game again. But Kay was not amongst the other boys, as Gerda supposed, nor was he riding in any of those sledges. Although I could not see him either, I could no longer cling to that supposition because I knew only too well where he was and what was about to happen to him. But I watched Gerda standing underneath the arches, straining her eyes, watching the sledges travelling to and fro and I could not bring myself to tell her what I knew, I felt only pity for her – though what was the point? Sometimes, I would stop looking at Gerda and watch my grandmother's lips moving as she told me the story, and I would think that perhaps what lay behind her refusal to tell me all the family stories – which surely she remembered – was the same mixture of pain and impotence that I experienced in my silent pity for Gerda, my inability to help her, and, besides, what was the point? It might be the dismay provoked by poking vainly about in a wound, rather than any pleasure she might take in keeping secrets from me.

While his companions were playing, Kay had withdrawn to a solitary, ill-lit part of the square and was staring hard down the nearest side street, as if waiting for something. Then through the archway came a white-painted sledge, as bright as the snow it glided across.

A tall, majestic personage was driving it, wearing a white fur hat and cloak; the broad lapels of the cloak were turned up to hide the person's face. Immediately, without hesitation, Kay tied his little sledge to that larger, much more solid one. They took a turn about the square and then disappeared swiftly through the same arch where they had first joined forces. The white sledge crossed many city squares and streets and its strange driver turned round now and then to see if Kay was still there and nodded in the friendliest fashion, just as if they had always known each other. Those streets did not look the same as they normally did and when they reached the outskirts of the city and Kay wanted to untie his sledge because it was beginning to grow dark, the person pulling him along would not let him.

"Come on, little Kay, come on," said the figure in a grave voice, this time without turning round, "we have to go on."

That last phrase "we have to go on" was not spoken by the tall person all in white, nor was it spoken by my grandmother; I always added it mentally myself, spontaneously, because from that point on I could already sense my own complicity with evil. Once past the border where there was no turning back, I surrendered to the dark, malignant pleasure of allying myself to the fatalism of the situation. There was no option but to go on, to plunge off into strange, irrevocable distances.

They sped like arrows through the last of the city gates and out into the countryside. The snow began to thicken above their heads, falling in such huge, dense flakes that Kay could not see where the sledge was going. Terrified, he started shouting, but no one heard him, and the two sledges, indissolubly linked, continued travelling ever faster over the snow. As they went faster and faster, Kay's fear only grew. He tried to pray, but all he could think of were numbers, a flock of white numbers written in chalk on the school blackboard. He remembered his times table and started singing it out in a loud voice that no one else heard. He threw those numbers out into the air and they were left behind him in vague whirlpools. They beat against his face along with the snow, the flakes of which had grown so enormous that Kay even doubted that they really were snowflakes. They seemed more like dead, frozen birds.

"If you like, I won't go on," his grandmother would say, "I'll leave it there and we'll have some tea."

"No, go on," I would say, "don't stop, we have to go on."

"Well, don't look at me with those mad eyes," she would say, "you remind me of your father. He really loved this story too, when he was a little boy."

She seemed to do that on purpose, add those fleeting allusions to my father, right at the most crucial point, when I could not possibly divert myself from the course of the story in order to pursue the ghostly scraps of another story that she never told me. They were never more than that, scraps perpetually beating against my face pressed eagerly against forbidden doors, giant snowflakes bouncing off Kay's cheeks. How could anyone concentrate on any other figure but his, or on any other direction than that taken by those two sledges. Fancy mentioning my father at such a moment!

At last, they stopped in a deserted place and the person driving the white sledge stepped down. She was a tall, white woman, very beautiful. She held out to Kay a pair of long, pale hands and her eyes shone like stars in a clear night sky, but she was cold, cold as ice. She was the Snow Queen.

Some days we would arrive sooner than others at that barren landscape where, for the first time, Kay and the Snow Queen looked each other in the face. I would sigh with sadness, but with relief too. Nothing mattered any more. My heartbeat would slow, and I would listen to the rest of the story with a different sort of sorrow, a mixture of apathy and resignation. But regardless of whether that journey had been long or short, the lady in white always asked the same question:

"We travelled very fast, didn't we, Kay?"

Kay looked at her without saying a word. Of course, what could he say, how could you calculate how much time had passed, with the snowflakes beating against your face like dead birds? I had no idea either how I had reached the garden of statues, and my grandmother didn't want to tell me.

"But you're cold," added the Snow Queen. "Get under my fur cloak."

Kay obeyed and when he did, he felt as if he were sinking into a snowdrift; he started to tremble and his teeth began to chatter.

"Ah," she said. "I see you're still cold."

And that was when she kissed him. He was already stiff with cold, but the Snow Queen's kiss went deeper, straight to his heart. "I'm going turn into an icicle and die," was Kay's last thought while he yet had some notion of oddness, because he could still compare this situation with others whose memory had not yet been wiped out for ever. But this idea was as fleeting as a final flash of lightning. The lady in the white cloak kissed him once more and then Kay felt completely well again, because he did not feel anything. Everything was the same, everything was eternally white. He forgot about Gerda and the boys in the square, he forgot about summer, flowers, sums, his times table and the whole of his former existence, including his house and the steep little street that led up to it.

"I won't kiss you any more now," said the Snow Queen, "because if I did, you would die."

But Kay's heart was already as cold as death.

V

The flor de lis

Amongst the pictures that adorn the walls of the study, there is a nineteenth-century English engraving. As far as I can remember, it has always hung in the same place. It shows a lighthouse on a stormy night, and, in the distance, you can just see a ship going down. It's quite a large picture, framed in red velvet, and behind it is the safe.

Once, when I was a boy – I must have been about ten – I asked my father if that was where he kept his money.

"Yes," he said, "and other things that are worth much more than money."

I found his answer odd and I said as much. According to my grandmother, money was the only thing he cared about. He shrugged and, with what seemed to me a sad smile, he said:

"Your grandmother's never really understood me. What does she know about me?"

Those words awoke in me two contradictory emotions. On the one hand, I rejected the thought that anyone should dare to question my grandmother's wisdom, but, on the other, it was consoling to discover that, like me, he too felt misunderstood by his mother.

And suddenly, the smell of tobacco from the pipe he was smoking drew us together and cut us off from the rest of the world, like two shipwreck victims warming our hands at a feeble, makeshift bonfire.

"Do you hide your secrets in that box then?" I asked.

"Some of them," he said, "but not all."

"And do you show them to Mama?"

He blinked and looked away. The question seemed to have caught him off guard.

"Well," he said, "you know what she's like."

94

"No, I don't! What is she like?"

"I mean she's not very curious. She's not interested in my secrets or in anyone else's."

"And is that good or bad?"

"I couldn't say, son, it's just the way she is."

At that time, although it had taken a lot of tantrums before I accepted it, I had just begun to realize that people never give a child a straight answer, and the child is therefore forced to grow up amidst many unresolved riddles. That iron box hidden behind the painting was a visible symbol of all the closed doors that appear in stories.

"Why have you put all your secrets behind a picture of a lighthouse?" I asked on a sudden impulse. "Does that mean something?"

It was an ingenuous question, but I saw at once that it had pierced some chink in my father's armour. His look of distress and his angry, shaken voice betrayed that fact.

"For God's sake, Leonardo, you do talk some rubbish! I think your grandmother's turning your head with all her fairy tales, ghost stories and witches! What sort of a question is that? I like that engraving. I bought it in Chicago in an antique shop, years ago, and I could have put it anywhere, but I chose to put it there, that's all. All right?"

I fell silent, looking at him. It was the first time I had caught him out, although how, I didn't quite know, and I was savouring the results of my marksmanship. So he wasn't invulnerable.

"Why are you looking at me like that?" he asked in an angry voice.

I remained perfectly calm, just as I did when my mother exploded at him, or at me or at one of the servants, in a totally arbitrary fashion. It might frighten me a bit, but it made me feel superior too.

"That's how you look at Mama when she gets angry for no reason, but I haven't said anything to make you angry."

I kept my eyes fixed on his face as I said this, and I realized that he was struggling to calm himself. Finally, he thought he had managed it.

"I'm not angry," he said in a normal voice. "It's just that I can't abide stupid questions."

"But you've told me before that it's stupid not to ask questions, that you have to ask questions in order to find things out."

"It doesn't matter, just leave it. Do you want to see the safe?" he said, getting up.

"Okay."

It was a sort of consolation prize. On another occasion, he would not have done so. He did it to erase the memory of his loss of self-control, to throw me off the track. But I had picked up a new scrap of information, one of many that I was storing away without quite knowing why. Landscapes with lighthouses in them left both my father and myself far from indifferent. That was what I was thinking as I followed him to the locked safe. He picked me up and stood me on the stool that he placed in front of the safe so that I could see it close to, while I listened to his rather too meticulous explanations. The serene, neutral voice in which he explained everything to me was in too sharp a contrast to his recent upset to make me forget it.

The engraving of the lighthouse slid to the left on near-invisible rails fitted into the wooden wall. The striplight situated above the picture, however, remained fixed, illuminating the rectangular iron box that was now revealed, with its little wheel in the middle, like a bulging, mysterious eye etched with lines and signs. He told me that although safes were mass-produced in the same factory, they were all different because each one had a combination known only to its owner.

It was the first time I had heard the word "combination" in that context. My father, who had wanted to be a writer when he was a young man, enjoyed providing me with detailed explanations about the meaning of words. In the case of the safe, it meant a particular combination of the letters printed on the wheel, turned sometimes to the right and sometimes to the left. Then, when you had done that, you turned a little key in the lock below and the safe door opened.

I recognized that I was being presented here with an exceptional opportunity and I sharpened all my wits so as to make the most of it. I remembered the story about how Puss-in-Boots had managed to get into the ogre's castle by using his cunning, by doubting the ogre's words.

"How very odd, Papa; if I wasn't seeing it with my own eyes, I wouldn't believe it," I said with feigned candour.

"Really? But what could be easier? Would you like to see how it works?"

His voice was jovial, almost grateful. I had provoked his fatherly pride; he trusted me.

"Yes, if you wouldn't mind."

"Why should I mind?"

I watched attentively as he gave me a rapid, expert demonstration, manipulating the wheel – twice to the right and once to the left. I didn't manage to see which letters he stopped at, but there were three. He immediately took out his key ring, chose the smallest key, put it in the lock and the reinforced door swung open.

"Abracadabra!" he said. "And there you are!"

At the back, I could see the bundles of white papers which I have, at last, begun to read this very afternoon. It was only a glimpse. When he closed it again, he made sure to turn the wheel so that there was no trace of the last letter it had stopped at. It was one of the letters towards the end of the alphabet, perhaps the S, the R or the T.

"There you are," he repeated. "Now do you believe it?"

"Yes, it's amazing," I said.

"Well, that's all there is to it. Now we slide the painting back into position, and it's just as if nothing had happened."

That was always how it was, it was always as if nothing had happened, always that same impenetrable door banged shut on any urgent questions. In the background of the engraving, once more lit by the light, a ship was foundering amongst the waves.

My father was feeling pleasantly relaxed now. He sat down again and lit his pipe. I asked him if he wanted me to go, but he said no. I realized, with the obscure, but acute perception with which children sense they are approaching a dangerous frontier, that I could easily lose everything by asking him some direct or inopportune question. My grandmother had gradually been teaching me the art of beating about the bush. I sat down on the floor by his side. My mother had gone to play pinochle at the house of some friends, and they'd had an argument because he had refused to go with her. The telephone rang, and I was afraid it might be her. It wasn't, though; it was a business call, something which would only momentarily interrupt the possibility of continuing the conversation.

"You're very quiet," my father said when he put down the phone. "What are you thinking about?"

"I don't know. I was just looking round the room. When I'm older, I'd like to have a room like this."

He tousled my hair with his hand; he almost never touched me affectionately like that.

"Well, when you do, I hope you make better use of it than I have," he said.

He sat there looking out of the window and, suddenly, it was as if I wasn't there in the room with him. It was a good moment to approach without his noticing, the way you do when you want to catch a lizard.

"It's fun that business with the combination. Does the owner of the safe have to invent it himself?"

"Yes, of course. It's secret."

"Yes, but how do you come up with one? I don't think I could."

Puss-in-Boots' cunning again proved successful.

"Why not?" he said. "Why would a big word-game fan like you not be able to think of one? You could start by playing around with the initials of the people you love, and you might discover that they give you the name of a flower and, read backwards, the name of a river, I don't know, something like that."

"I see," I said. "Like one of grandma's riddles."

And immediately changing the subject, I started talking about how funny those riddles were, so that he wouldn't realize that I had absorbed and memorized those bits of information. A flower which, when spelled backwards, gives the name of a river. He had provided that as an example, but you couldn't possibly invent a strange example like that on the spur of the moment.

Later, when I went to my room, after spending some more time with him, looking at a book about ships, I felt I was in possession of an important secret, and I was proud of having got it out of him without arousing his suspicions. It was a furtive, clandestine pleasure, like the pleasure you might get from cleanly stealing someone's wallet.

We didn't talk about the safe again until a few nights ago when he appeared to me in my dreams after I had already opened it.

The truth is that I opened it almost straight away, with very little effort. I immediately recognized the little key on the key ring that Don Ernesto handed over to me, and, as for guessing the combination, I was almost certain that I had guessed it some time before, although I had never had occasion to prove or disprove my theory. I remembered that he had stopped the wheel three times, which meant that the flower must have three letters, and all three-letter words have a vowel in the middle. Rejecting the A, the O, the U and the E, which would not remind my father of any of his loved ones, I immediately opted for the I, for my grandmother, Inés. Further thinking suggested as an hypothesis the Spanish for fleur de lys: "flor de lis", which, when read in reverse, becomes a river, the river Sil. The word, therefore, also contained my initial. But what about the S? No one in the family had a name beginning with S. That discouraged me.

A few days ago, once Don Ernesto had left, and I had tried the combination and the iron door had opened, I stood there absolutely still, almost overwhelmed, looking at the papers, not daring to touch them. And I felt the S hovering above my head like a question mark. The S is my father's secret. Today, I have more of a basis in fact for my suspicions, but I'll talk about that later. It's a jigsaw puzzle that cannot be solved quickly.

At the moment, I'm amazed at my own perseverance and at its beneficial effects. Writing like this, unhurriedly, and with a certain pretence at style, as I have been doing, has eased my anxiety and become an occupation that has no particular aim, because its aim is implicit in itself. I knew at once, ever since I decided not to stay downstairs, that I would discard anything that might be an obstacle to this work of personal research. The greatest threat was Don Ernesto for whom I was waiting in this very study the morning after my arrival, very early, since I had hardly slept. As Maurício had predicted, the painful throbbing from the wound in my hand got steadily worse and was making me feverish. So, towards dawn, I wrapped a blanket around me and walked through the garden, picked up the keys from the vase in the porch and came up here in search of some medicine, a hot drink and a bit more comfort. Don Ernesto's alarm when he failed to find the keys in their usual place made him ring the doorbell so wildly that he woke me up, because I had fallen asleep, face down, on the desk in the study, determined not to go to bed until I had sorted things out with him. Swathed in an old dressing gown of my father's, I went down to the hall and opened the front door. His shock at seeing me, even greater than either I or Maurício had expected, made my icy tone still icier, a consequence perhaps of having spent the night thinking about the Snow Queen. On the other hand, my recent humiliations in prison – forgotten until then – probably revived a dormant thirst for cruelty. Suddenly, I was the one laying down conditions, I was the one casting disdainful looks and refusing to give an account of my conduct. I simply asked him for all the keys to the house ("my house," I said) and told him bluntly that, for the moment, I needed to be alone, that I found all company oppressive.

"Especially yours," I added, looking him in the eye.

His eyes reminded me of a certain hypocritical prison guard who had had me admitted to the infirmary without explanation, and who was incapable of holding my gaze whenever I made any kind of protest to him.

It seemed impossible to me that I was actually saying those things and, at the same time, I was sharply aware of my haggard, insomniac, unshaven appearance which made my insolence seem even bolder and more scandalous. My temperature had shot up by then and I saw him as if in a haze, but I think he was actually shaking with fear. He's very short and wears glasses. He kept glancing at my bandaged hand.

"What's wrong, Leo? You haven't been drinking or anything, have you? Are you all right?"

"I'm in my right mind, if that's what you mean. And I'm in my own house too. You can leave me your phone number and I'll call you if I need to clear up any problems. But you can leave now and, in future, please don't address me as 'tú'. I'm the master here, and don't you forget it."

The throbbing in my hand intensified with each blow delivered by those recently uttered words; a cry for shelter from my own body, an antidote against the secret threats implicit in such a bold declaration of principles. "We have to go on," said Kay inside me, his teeth chattering.

Don Ernesto got very upset, and in contrite, servile tones insisted that we must have a long conversation as soon as possible. I cut him short. He has left the keys, his phone number and a lot of letters and papers that I have promised him I will look at. He went up to the study to collect his things and I followed him, not letting him out of my sight for a moment. Then, in total silence, I accompanied him to the front door.

When he finally left, I went back upstairs and had a hot bath in my mother's sunken, oval bathtub, the kind that you have to go down two steps to get into. In her bedroom, with its pink wallpaper, everything is new and discreetly elegant. Most of the room is taken up by a four-poster bed. The armchairs, bedspread, curtains and carpet are in matching tones of pearl grey. Two large abstract paintings hang on the walls.

I opened the fitted wardrobe and breathed in a strong smell of her. She always used the same Dior perfume. In fact, I saw the half-empty bottle on one of the shelves, next to her handkerchiefs and tights and the leather box in which she kept her costume jewellery. I rummaged around in her underwear, looking for a pair of those men's silk pyjamas she used to sleep in – she was very tall. I chose a white pair, put them on and got into bed shivering.

I could not say how long I slept or how many times I woke up, went down to the kitchen to heat up some milk or went into my father's study. On one of those trips, I took the phone off the hook and on another I opened the safe. It must have been shortly after that that he appeared to me and we talked about the *flor de lis*.

Anyway, I can't really say how many hours passed, I've never been very good at keeping track of time. Now, though, my hand is no longer bandaged and I am no longer delirious and I realize how much work I have ahead of me. For the first time in my life, I'm looking forward to the task and I'm ready to tackle it sensibly.

Sometimes, I deal with the problems set out in the papers Don Ernesto left me, at others, I look at the papers hidden behind the lighthouse. Out of that mixture of past and present emerges a new, timeless furrow: my own writing.

VI

Leap into the void

I didn't see the photo until after I'd read several of the letters in the green file, which left me in a state of near shock, and at a moment when – lost in the undergrowth – I had paused to recap, because I was beginning to feel dizzy. "Can a woman like that really exist? Could she ever have existed? Where did he meet her? What was she like?"

The photograph was in a small envelope, in between the folds of two pieces of flimsy paper. I could feel how thick it was. Then, very slowly, I took it out, as if I were developing it as I did so. It had a white serrated edge and the central figure was in black and white. I was gripped by a devastating sense of disorientation and enchantment, by a fear of losing all spatial reference points, because the figure in the photograph was flying. That's what I saw: a woman flying. She was holding her arms up, brandishing something white, perhaps the clothes she was pulling up over her head at the very instant that she leapt. She was barefoot, and her body was covered only by a sort of skintight slip. She had long, lithe legs, but very little bust – the body of an adolescent. She had been caught in half-profile and she was laughing, with her hair blown about by the wind.

As I managed to tear my astonished eyes away from that figure and study her surroundings, as if to orientate myself and to find out if it wasn't perhaps just some kind of collage, any suspicion that it might not be real was shattered – that pleasant redoubt destroyed. It took my breath away to recognize a landscape that is not in the least fictitious, that forms part of my innermost soul, a substratum that appears again and again in my dreams, a place that is mine alone. What crack had that allegory of freedom slipped through, displacing me as the inhabitant of that very real geography? There was no doubt about it: those were the rocks below the lighthouse, the scene of my first planned acts of rebellion, where I had nurtured so many insubstantial longings for adventure and where, peering into the abyss, I first began to idealize Kay's fate.

And you? Who are you? What are you doing there, you fool, filling a space that no one invited you to share? How dare you? There was shock and envy, anger and admiration in my reproaches. For that wild creature was leaping off the rocks down on to the fringe of damp sand that surrounds the island of seagulls when the tide is at its lowest ebb. Some of the gulls had taken flight, others were looking up, waiting impassively for that extraordinary landing. It was a dangerous leap which I would never have attempted, not even in my moments of greatest exultation.

And who was the person who had followed her there to take the picture, to capture that unique moment? When? And why?

I turned the photo over. "Sila, August 1943", I read. It was my father's writing, without a shadow of a doubt.

I placed my arms on the table and stayed there for a while with my head resting on them, touching the scattered papers, crumpling them up, even voluptuously sniffing them.

Some of the papers are brief, urgent notes, and very few bear any address. They belong to different periods, but you can hardly tell, and it doesn't really matter. The female name that pierces the mists of the secret has emerged at last from the capital S with which the letters always end, the same consonant found in the "flor de lis". Sila, the child-woman who leaps through the air and talks like a philosopher; Sila wielding the negative, I don't want, make no mistake, you couldn't understand, don't ask me so many questions, I've already told you "no" – elusive, obstinate, defiant; Sila, goddess of the sea, rejecting the voices that attempt to channel that battering sea towards sensible, predictable goals.

"And what if I do belong to the sea, what if the sea does fetch me and carry me and know me and holds no fear for me? Don't trust me, Eugenio, I'm warning you, and don't blame me for my high tides or my whirlpools or my undertows. There is no explanation (don't even bother looking for one) for the free swell of life, what can we do about it, we can't control it. You say to me that passion has taken away your freedom; that's because you haven't experienced passion through freedom itself. I imagine you a tiny figure huddled amongst stainless steel spider webs and wearing a little blue perspex jacket."

My father is in Santiago studying law, my father is in Madrid, my father is in America, in the state of Illinois, I can see it from the envelopes, some of which have been preserved; otherwise he's at the Quinta Blanca, but what does that matter, what does it matter now, when all that counts is the murmur of the somnambular tide on which the lost text of these letters reaches my cave, now that the Eugenio to whom they were addressed and who kept them for years is condemned never to be able to read them again, his name cast to the winds, reduced for ever to a generic initial: E for enamoured. While the S of the secret, on the other hand, has risen up and flowered.

"Sila, Sila," I whisper, "draw the noose of the negative more tightly about my neck, you won't hurt me, tell me more, Sila, talk to me, talk nonsense to me across the void, tell me who taught you to write like that, ah, how long you've taken to arrive, Sila. We were born to meet."

And I tremble when I say her name. Knowing her name has upset all my tentative literary plans, dissipating any doubts I had about where in this narrative I should place the scraps of another narrative – which I perceived as distant and unfocused – about which tense I should use when setting down on paper the fragmentary tale told in these letters. At last, I know the name of the person who wrote them – a name concealed from me until now – briny and immediate as a huge wave that brings with it only the present, the present continuous of stories that suddenly converge on our lives and subsequently form part of their waters for ever. There it is. The matter is resolved. I was travelling blind, but from the moment I emerged from the dark tunnel of that S into the light of that unequivocal name, which can now stand in line with those of Gerda and Kay, Sila says all she has to say in the present tense, that is the only rule; her time overflows and mingles with mine, because she's saying it all to me. Go on, Sila, I'm listening. You are talking to me, aren't you? Of course, she says, who else?

What's even odder is that her letters reveal other affinities, literary ones too. As children, we both liked "books that give you vertigo", as she puts it (and I smile when I read that), the shyness of the romantic hero who, on the one hand, is infected by the vastness of the night, the sea or the storm, but, on the other, is quite incapable of apprehending those phenomena.

". . . it's the same with love, why do you find it so strange? You just have to receive it, like an electric shock; you can only enjoy what is transient at the very moment it explodes, but, at the same time, you have to look at it as though it were fixed in a painting, because you can't take the sea home with you, not even if your home happens to be as big as the Quinta Blanca. How on earth do you think you'd find room for it?"

You're right, I say to her, that's what art is for. Friedrich, for example, knew how to embody in his paintings the longings for the infinite which unbridled nature arouses in the seemingly fearful figures contemplating and enduring the scene, always with their backs to us. I remember that when I was in Berlin, I sent my father several post-cards of Friedrich's work – perhaps I'll find them here mixed up with your letters and with those from my grandmother – postcards which I signed "the outsider", what else could I put, although I was almost sure that he too would find them exciting and that they would remind him of the turbulent love affairs he later sought in novels. What I mean is that when I discovered Friedrich, I was thinking as much or perhaps more about you, Sila, than about my father, even though I had never met you. That was four years ago I think, when I still used to write to him. It had been a dazzling discovery and, while it lasted, I plunged into what I was seeing as if I were actually hearing the sound of the wind and the waves. It was very early in the morning; there were no other visitors. But when I left the museum, there was nothing: just the people in the street, in the cafés, getting on a bus, as if all the rest had been a lie, and there I was with my dilemmas about belonging or not belonging, which seemed as tedious and impersonal now as the boarding houses I was staying in and where I would lie waiting for sleep to come and trying to banish my childhood memories, alone in the bed or by the side of some transient lover – foreign bodies. Everything seemed strange to me, nothing touched me, or, rather, I made every effort to make things turn out that way, so it's absurd to imagine that the outsider fleeing from himself could have addressed his father in a language even remotely like the one I'm using now, which was unleashed the moment I saw your leap into the void, Sila. And I was right, because I think now that he never understood your meaning either, which is as mad as your leap, cancelling out time, verging on the ineffable. Or perhaps I'm being unfair, why shouldn't he understand you? Let's be quite honest about this, what I'm feeling is jealousy.

". . . I know that after we've kissed, we are both full of desires that separate us. Don't assume that you're more intelligent than I am just because you notice that feeling of 'not being there' which happens to everyone once the warmth of a kiss has cooled. I'm more aware of it than you are, but it doesn't make me angry; I find it natural. It's like having a nap when you're tired. You say to me: 'You're evaporating' and it sounds like a reproach. I call it simply entering a new scene. I told you so yesterday, and I can't see what's so terrible about that. I'm glad I said it because that's exactly what happens to me at such moments. For example, when I don't pay you any attention and I sit there looking out to sea, there's no point you asking me angrily: 'What are you thinking about?', forcing me to look at you and take my eyes off the sea. Don't pester me, leave me alone, I can't explain what I'm thinking, only that when I look at the sea, it's like eternity. That's all I know. I can see yesterday and tomorrow and what will happen after I die, though it's all very vague. And I enjoy that feeling of vertigo."

God, that's lovely, Sila! But he used to kiss you. I understand you better because I haven't kissed you. I used to feel something similar sometimes, when I would escape to the cliffs, and the waves would be breaking down below against the island of seagulls: a confused but certain sense of eternity – something which, later on, Friedrich's painting gave me back second-hand – as if my mind were thirsty for space and wanted to break the bars of the body in order to merge with nature, because just looking at it isn't enough, as if my mind grew agitated trying to imitate storms and clouds and tides, only to realize that it can't – do you see what I'm saying – because the body is the mind's cage.

And she says yes, of course, how could she not understand when all I'm doing is putting into other words what appears in those books "that give you vertigo", the struggle between our own smallness and all the things we would like to embrace, "flying dreams" she calls them in another note, but the word "vertigo" is the one that best sums up the implicit fear in those dreams, which is neither more nor less than the fear of madness, albeit concealed, a fear that one hides because one doesn't want to frighten other people, that's what happens to her and has ever since she was a child. And it happened to Ellida too. In Old Norse Ellida means "he who comes with the storm" and she identifies herself with that character, a man's name borne by a woman, a name you sometimes hear bandied about between my father and Sila, like a clash of swords. The name rings a bell at first, but it takes me a while to locate it.

". . . Don't tell me you're going to start feeling jealous of Ellida too? You say that your mother should never have lent Don Antonio that book and that he should never have let me read it. Don't be so stupid. I've been like this ever since I was three years old, long before I read Ibsen. If you don't believe me, ask my grandfather, although, since what's happened between us, I know you don't like talking to him; by the way, he's noticed; he says to me: 'What's got into Doña Ines' boy?' Anyway, it's up to you. If you carry on like this, he'll come to suspect what he'll never find out from me. For him, you're still the older friend who looks after me a bit and laughs at me, as you did when I was a child. But coming back to Ellida, the apparent root of all evils, surely you're not going to say that I also copied being born in a lighthouse from Ibsen – though you're quite capable of it."

Too many facts at one time, too many spectres slipping into this amalgam of life and literature which is growing denser as I read. Let's begin with Ibsen, who knew more about ghosts than anyone. I hadn't thought about Ellida for a long, long time. *The Lady from the Sea* lay submerged and now reappears with the solemn, enigmatic gesture with which she continues to throw her ring into the sea, in the present tense, like the voice that comes to refresh a story which, years ago, I found so moving. And another subterranean channel opens, because I suddenly remember (it hadn't occurred to me until now) that Hans Christian Andersen was born on an island near Odense, some years – not many perhaps, I'll have to check – before Ibsen was born in southern Norway; those two cold, foggy places can't be many miles apart on the map either, and Henrik must have heard of Hans Christian, he might even have met him, I don't know. But at any rate, in this notebook their texts have become interwoven in such a chance, mysterious way, just as my vision of the rocks complements the vision that Sila brings as she leaps down from them – vertigo on vertigo – what a gallop we're going at, we'll crash. "No, hold on tight, we're riding together now," she says.

Ellida, the daughter of a lighthouse keeper, marries Wangel, a respectable Finnish widower, but she remains faithful to the memory of a mysterious sailor, a symbol of the sea, who appears not to exist, but to whom one day she swore eternal love. Wangel asks her about him, asks her to tell him what they talked about. And all at once, I remember her reply:

"We almost always talked about the sea, and about storms and calms, but mostly about the seals sunning themselves on the rocks, about the gulls and other seabirds. It seemed to me that all those beings were somehow his brothers."

It was a book bound in red, I can still see it, published by Sucesores de Hernando, Arenal 11 in 1914. My grandmother had the works of Lope, Moreto and Calderón in that edition, and it was in that same volume that Sila read the story that I read later on. Perhaps some of the underlinings in pencil were hers. It's so exciting to be remembering it at the same time, because now we're heading downhill together. I hold on tight behind her and close my eyes, as I did when I used to ride on the sledge with Gerda and Kay. I feel dizzy, Sila, we're going to crash.

". . . 'I've decided to go off in search of treasure,'" says Sila. "'I'm telling you in advance, granddad, so that it won't come as a shock later on. I want to cut my ties with this corner of the world, because I was born to leave, or just because, just to know that I can.' He asked me if this was the shock I was warning him about, and I said it was, and we both laughed. And then he wanted to know if going in search of treasure meant that I still dream of one day finding my father, and I looked at him very seriously and I said: 'Yes, granddad, he calls me like the sea, you've always known that. And I'm going to meet him. I'm sure of it.' And then neither of us laughed. In the evening, my grandfather told Don Antonio that he was afraid, because he sees in me signs of my mother's mental unbalance mingled with 'that man's' boldness – that's where I get my independent spirit from. And now it worries him that he's always encouraged me to be so independent. They were talking quietly, but I heard them. I tiptoed down the spiral staircase and went outside and sat on the rocks. It was very windy. What I most enjoy at times like that is breathing in the air until it almost hurts. I looked at my hands and my feet and I realized that they can take me anywhere I want to go. I don't feel weak or wretched, I'm nowhere and yet I'm everywhere too; the same thing happened to Ellida."

Some of the pieces of paper are pages torn from a notebook, possibly, judging by the tone, extracts from a diary. And I suppose they must have been sent to my father some time after they were written, stuffed into envelopes that flew over great swathes of sea, the vast expanse of sea that sometimes separated them.

There comes a point when I can bear it no longer, when I need a breathing space, the breathing space afforded by dates. Let me get a breath of air, because it's terribly stuffy in here. Now, Sila is the granddaughter of the last lighthouse keeper; he died before I was born and Rosa Figueroa – my grandmother's former servant – occasionally referred to him: country tales that left a trail of curiosity and mystery behind them until they, too, came to seem oppressive to me, until they lost their aura of surprise, and then I hated them with the same intensity with which once I had loved them. The last lighthouse keeper lay buried with them. However strange it may seem, we know that he was Sila's grandfather, but when I suddenly learn that she did eventually run away, as planned, following the faint tracks left by an English sailor she had never even met, I realize that I need more information, that I need to step into a different scene, just as she used to do.

The vertigo I'm experiencing reaches such a pitch that I jump off while the sledge is still moving. It's too much. I will not drain this particular draught to the dregs just now. Cut off from the daily course of events, immersed in a period of time which I have entered as a stowaway, lost in the suffocating garden of the imagination, elementary common sense advises me to open the window and let in other voices, other witnesses.

I pick up the papers signed with an S and put them slowly back into the green file. I'll continue another day, but now I know that they are mine. And I know too that my father and I have finally made our peace, that he not only likes what I'm doing, but he also likes the way I delicately pick up what until only a short time ago was still his. The transfer of powers has taken place with his blessing. He leaves the floor open to me.

And I turn to my grandmother, just to see what happens. My grandmother is another absence, but her handwriting, even though it merely poses more riddles, is as dependable as the voice setting those riddles, something familiar that protects and consoles. The slightest change in her calligraphy, however insignificant, tells me what mood she's in. And thus I leave one scene and enter another.

* * *

Six years before I was born, my father had finished his law degree and was in Chicago. I don't know what my grandmother felt about the fact that he had gone there, whether she was pleased or not. That is what I want to uncover, but, in that respect, the clues left in the letters that she writes to him from the Quinta Blanca are contradictory. It seems to have been a sudden decision, as if he were running away from something.

"You think I don't know what's happening to you," she says to him in a letter, "but the more you talk to me about money, business and the important people you're meeting, the more clearly I see what it is you're hiding."

And in another:

"I've always liked the fact that you know what you want – of course, why wouldn't I? – but it's dangerous to bury what is not entirely dead, so be quite sure of what you're doing."

Occasionally, she seems to show pangs of conscience.

"It may be that I am to blame for exactly what I complain of in you," she says, "you're right there. I complain that your letters sound as if I were writing them for you, and you complain that I'm always looking for what's hidden behind the mask, even though I have no proof that there is anything. It's true. But I wouldn't want you to lie to yourself either. I'm confused. I know I spent many years encouraging your ambition and urging you to leave this backward country full of legends in which I am so firmly anchored, to escape my influence and other worse influences. But tell me truly, are you really having such a good time there, have you become so very cosmopolitan? All I can say is that it seems very odd to me."

On the other hand, the information about the motive and arrangements for the trip, which takes up most of the text, essentially agrees with the information I had as a small boy, and I skip that because it bores me. My grandmother's handwriting in those sections is impeccable, without a tremor, like the voices of leaders when they make a speech. And not one sentence questions, even obliquely, her only son's solvency, or his will of iron. He's gone to Chicago in order to sort out some family business, related to the iron industry in fact, and to settle accounts with an associate of his grandfather's, a slippery, untrustworthy person who needs to be taken in hand. My father's legal baggage and his gifts for diplomacy will lay the foundations for his future fortune. It isn't clear if this individual deceived grandfather Leonardo or if they were collaborators in some bungled bit of trickery which it was up to his orphan son to untangle. It doesn't matter. I don't know, either, how long my father had been an orphan before he left for the States, but it seems unlikely that he inherited his stubbornness from his father, for his father, it would appear, was blessed with only sufficient strength of will to escape the clutches of those trying to impose their wills on him. Anyway, it's an old story that I knew about before I started rummaging around in the safe. Whenever she referred to her husband, which was not very often, my grandmother used to raise her eyes to heaven and say: "The poor, unfortunate man, may he rest in peace," an expression in which any warmth was cancelled out by her tone of voice, so remote and opaque that it failed to ignite in me even the tiniest spark of curiosity about the person who once bore my name and surname. I started to believe that they had invented him, that he had never existed.

I only remember having seen my other grandfather once when I was little, when he visited us in our house in Madrid, which he had bought for his daughter as a wedding present. He didn't sleep here, though; he stayed at the Ritz. He wasn't in the least affectionate towards me. He was tall, had very pale eyes, and was very elegantly dressed. In the study, there's a framed photo of him and his daughter, probably in the era when my father first met them. They're standing at the foot of a staircase in a luxurious, colonial-style house, and in front of them sits an Alsatian dog.

My grandmother, who was by nature suspicious, found it odd that my father should have gained the confidence of those people so quickly, "because the businessmen there must have their own ways of doing things, especially in this day and age". She also advises him to behave always as what he is, a gentleman, and not to beg any favours from anyone. And if he's going to fish in other people's waters, then he should at least make sure that he catches a good-sized trout.

My father's letters are missing, so it's like trying to make out the design on a piece of embroidery from the wrong side only. With a dash of imagination and some help from the *Encyclopaedia Britannica*, I did manage to get an idea of what the atmosphere in that great city must have been like shortly after the end of the Second World War, when people's eagerness to forget about conflicts and to enlist in the modern age was growing as ambitiously as the buildings, and which was, at the same time, both the driving force and the mainstay of a new religion ruled by money. The name of one of its chief officiants, Walter Scribner, involved in the projected O'Hare Airport, must have appeared in my father's letters very early on, although my grandmother, not knowing that he was to be her son's father-in-law, referred to him only as "that rich gentleman who's always inviting you to his house"; the alarm bells only begin to ring when she realizes that there's a daughter involved too. At first, she assumes that the daughter will be as ugly as sin, not because my father deserves no better, but because the family is loaded; then, he must have sent her some photos and she begins to suspect that perhaps the girl is pregnant, but no, Gertrud is very much a feminist and is far from sure that she wants to go through the hell of childbirth.

"It isn't like that, Eugenio, it's natural for women to give birth. But what really worries me is that I can't tell if you're in love or not, that's the worst thing. I still say I'm not convinced. She looks very pretty in the photos, but a bit stiff."

From then on, it's as if she just shrugged her shoulders and awaited news of that strange wedding. Anything she couldn't control, she simply ignored. The haughty tone initially evident in her comments is gradually replaced by a sort of fatalism.

But it's absurd to talk in terms of "from then on", "initially" or "gradually". That succession of events is just an invention of mine really. When you sort through old papers, the hardest thing is piecing together all the details of the story they tell. Words do away with chronology and remake a new meaning with a new order.

I was warned about this once by an archivist friend of mine at the University of Verona, someone with whom I almost had a romance. Our relationship never came to anything, although the quiet conversations that we had during our evening walks always had certain Shakespearean overtones for me. It was as if the text of *Romeo and Juliet* hovered above the roof tops, urging me to perform similarly ardent feats of verbal prowess, forcing her to believe what I said and provoking some response from her. Her name was Clara. She was like an ingénue in the silent movies, tiny, with shadowy eyes, and she had never had a boyfriend. I haven't thought about her in ages, and certainly not with that sudden feeling of tenderness and nostalgia – a cool breeze riffling through my grandmother's letters and muddling them up with Sila's, some of which have somehow found their way into this pile too – what a mess! One in particular attracts my attention, a letter sent to Chicago from London, in which Sila is presumably referring to my father's engagement to Scribner's daughter.

"What is most noticeable in your letter," she says, "is the display you put on of perfect equilibrium. That's what worries me. The 'you' you have drowned will surface one day like a living corpse. I only hope I won't be the one who has to deal with it then."

I wonder if it's just chance that the doubts expressed by Sila and my grandmother about my parents' marriage should have ended up together. It is, at the very least, a shocking piece of information, and not entirely innocuous either it seems to me.

It was the order or, rather, the disorder of old documents that Clara was telling me about. She was doing research into Alfieri and she said that the worst thing was that there were just too many documents all jumbled up together.

Now I know exactly what she meant! I stopped going out with her after one particular spring evening that we spent sitting outside the church of San Zeno. I was only half-listening to what she was saying and, for the first time, she placed her hand on the sleeve of my jacket and looked longingly into my eyes; usually she did exactly the opposite – she was always the one who lowered her eyes and I was always the one trying to catch her gaze. "Senti, Leonardo, dimmi." She wanted to know if I understood, if I realized the chasm that lay between life and mere documents. I trembled. I've always been afraid of romantic love and that relationship could clearly not be viewed from any other angle: I had seen the eyes of Juliet, that same mixture of boldness and candour. A few days later, I got myself involved with another girl, more banal, more brazen.

I'm not dragging all this up deliberately; it just resurfaced of its own accord. What Clara said – she was doubtless infected by the poetry of the evening – is true: the words in old letters do rebel, like soldiers breaking rank, and they don't only go back over what happened earlier – which, chronologically speaking, may be later – sometimes, without meaning to, they get snagged on lost scraps of our own memory. The swifts were chasing each other, screaming, across the bruised sky. Two lions, static and eternal, guard the entrance to the church of San Zeno. What will have become of Clara?

"Capisci, Leonardo?" she asked, blushing, her eyes shining. "Capisci? Dimmi."

And I said: yes, I did understand. But that wasn't true. All I understood was that she was falling in love with me. Until today, I had never understood what she meant about papers and the effects of disorder, until now, when my research into how my parents met was suddenly interrupted by the look in those blue, forgotten eyes. They look at me, trying to hold my gaze. I'm not making this up, it didn't happen to someone else, nor is it some story out of Ibsen or Shakespeare. She looked at me one evening in Verona – do you understand? Tell me, do you understand? – such a deep, urgent look that I feel obliged to abandon other arguments and confront that lost scrap of my own memory to give a proper reply to a question still awaiting an answer after all these years, when there is no longer any trace of the person who asked it.

Yes, Clara, I do understand. I would so like to resume that dialogue with you, a dialogue muddied and cut short because of me, because of my neurotic fear of those transparent eyes seeking shelter and acquiescence in mine, not in the eyes of someone whom I supplant. Yes, Clara, I do understand, because now I find myself in a very similar situation; I can get under your skin, which is, after all, the only possible way of understanding things, by breaking one's own boundaries. A dead letter comes to life again with the heat generated by the person struggling to piece together past episodes whilst he or she is living in a present whose accretions, however, no one can simply dismiss, because the task itself sometimes evokes apparently irrelevant stories.

That's exactly it, that's why you have burst in and suddenly risen up like a great rainbow stretching between my handwriting and the writing on these family papers that I am currently cannibalizing and trying to put into some order, just as you were trying to do with Alfieri's papers: an ephemeral, fecund rainbow. Please, don't fade just yet; let the buildings on the shore of Lake Michigan fuse with those of the little squares and streets of Verona and the Blackstone Hotel where my father was staying, let the fourteenth storey sprout a pink balcony where Juliet is just about to appear. I look up and I see that the taut curve of those seven colours has slackened and is now rippling in the wind like a streamer.

And from the resulting S I see again the black-and-white figure of an adolescent stepping out into the void, and the scene is no longer the façade of the Blackstone Hotel or the Capulets' balcony, but the rocks beneath the lighthouse – mind-blowing! It must be the effects of the hash.

You've made me quite breathless, Clara; it's a long time since my blood beat in my veins like this. I'd like to go back to that evening outside the church of San Zeno and force it to another conclusion.

It's burning out now, the joint that I lit before lying down on the sofa in order to imagine that change of course from the moment when you placed your hand on my forearm until the first stars began to come out, and the stone lions closed their eyes. If I had your address, which, thank heavens, I haven't, I would stop everything so that I could write you an endless love letter in the style of those letters signed with an S that my father received at different stages of his life, rambling letters in which the addressee sometimes seems to be a mere pretext. My whole body lights up with desire to imagine how that untimely declaration would arrive and impale itself, like a dart in the back, in your life now, in your papers, Clara, sweet ghost, a fleeting, already fading mirage.

But there's still my grandmother, she of the riddles that could never be solved, she who never tired of telling me to be patient, that I shouldn't try and understand things without first taking into account their natural complexities. "If you see everything all neatly lined up, this first, then that, all the mystery's gone," she used to say, "and without mystery what a foolish affair life would be."

Well, she must be very happy; she's got a disciple like the ones you get in stories, a child lost amongst papers that may or may not contain an explanation for the inexplicable, in search of a path which he can't be sure he'll recognize amongst all the other paths he comes across in the wood, paths he sometimes has to walk along backwards, his only guide a few vague clues: you'll see an oak tree with golden acorns, you'll have to dig a hole, but make sure it's at that exact point; if you're frightened by the fire-breathing dragon, then everything is lost; go straight on, don't let anyone steal the talisman from you.

They were conflicts common to every adolescent faced by the need to grow up and sharpen his wits, advancing in all weathers through grave dangers, skirting precipices that threaten his memory and sap his determination.

I get up from the sofa again. I wonder if you're happy, grandma.

VII

Down to the dining room

If I want to maintain the necessary degree of concentration to continue writing, I've realized that I need, above all, to bring some order to my new life.

The first thing I've done is consult the small ads and hire a woman to come every day to tidy up the house a bit and cook for me. I've told her more or less where to find everything she might need; I've given her the keys to various cupboards, taking them from the bundle of labelled keys that Don Ernesto left me; and I've asked her to bother me as little as possible because I have a lot of work to do. She seems efficient and she's a good cook too.

Yesterday, I also made a long-distance call to Chicago and spoke to Aunt Ingrid. I feel no affection for her whatsoever; I've only met her twice in my life, but it seemed to me logical and proper to talk to her. We spoke in English. The line wasn't particularly good, but good enough for me to notice that she was trying very hard to sound caring. It seems that my mother had been undergoing treatment and that they had been thinking of admitting her to a convalescent home. I asked if my mother had been driving the car at the time of the accident. My aunt said that she had and that she couldn't understand how my father could have let her. There was a note of reproach in her voice. They have been cremated. Then, out of pure politeness, she asked me various questions about my life and my plans for the future, to all of which I responded vaguely. She wanted to know if I was married, and when I said that I wasn't, she suggested that, if I was lonely, I could go and spend some time over there. I told her that I needed to be alone and that, besides, I can't travel abroad at the moment because my papers aren't in order; this was followed by an embarrassed silence. I explained that I'd had problems with the police, and she said: "Really? Are you kidding?" in a strange, metallic voice. She didn't ask me to explain what kind of problems. It was clear that we had both abandoned any attempt to get closer.

As soon as I hung up, I went over to the piece of paper I had pinned on the study wall. It was a list of matters pending, and, feeling a genuine sense of relief, I drew a red line through the words "Aunt Ingrid". Once you've solved one awkward matter, any remaining problems always seem so much easier to resolve.

Underneath "Aunt Ingrid", I had written "Notary". I'd spoken to him twice on the phone, but I was going to have to go and see him.

I went down to ask Pilar, the cleaning lady, to press my grey flannel suit; it's the only decent one I have, although now it's a bit big on me. She was in the dining room, polishing the large mahogany table in the centre of the room, and she seemed glad to be asked to perform such an urgent task related to my personal cleanliness, because she probably considers my appearance to be entirely out of keeping with this luxurious house.

She took the clothes and went into the pantry, pushing open the swing doors with one foot. When she had gone, one of the leaves continued swaying backwards and forwards, creaking gently, until it stopped altogether.

This was the first time I'd been down to the dining room. Everything there was clean and tidy, just as it had been the last time I saw it, and the atmosphere in the room provoked in me the same sense of pointlessness, the sense that it was just an inert, luxurious façade. I stood there leaning on the mahogany table, staring at the white swing doors, as I used to during the tense, silent meals I sat through before I left for good, by which time the lines joining together our particular triangle had become high voltage cables. Then came the main course, then the sweet. The only relief from that unbearable ceremony was the occasional opening and closing of the swing doors. My eyes found a refuge there, awaiting the appearance of an impassive figure which was topped by vague, ever-changing faces. I can scarcely remember the names of any of those maids and servants, who were continually being replaced and who, when they entered, were always staring straight ahead, concentrating on balancing the tray, bearing the new dishes sent to fill up the silence.

I ran the tips of my fingers over the polished surface of the table and, looking up, I saw myself reflected in the oval mirror, like an incongruous ghost flanked by two naked women each holding a bronze candelabra. I had never noticed before that the one on the right is smiling and the other is not. I looked from one to the other, just to make sure that it wasn't my imagination, and the more I looked at them, the more challenging the smiling statue seemed to become, whilst the other seemed to grow more taciturn. I stood there paralysed, as if my image were imprisoned inside one of those strange photos that you find years later in the bottom of a drawer. ("The first time that I came back and my parents weren't here, when I realized suddenly that all this was mine and that I would have to do something with it, and I noticed that the woman with the candelabra on the right was looking straight at me and smiling, whilst the other was looking down.") Someone might be behind me preparing to capture that scene on his Kodak, because it certainly was a memorable occasion. My father always had an instinct for choosing moments he considered significant and a remarkable capacity for dissimulation when it came to capturing them. The photo of Sila flying is one of the finest examples of those gifts. You didn't even realize he was taking a photo until you heard the click. I had, unwittingly, stayed quite still, waiting for that figure to appear behind me, in the stagnant waters of the mirror, his face hidden behind the black box. Click. "Got you. The return of the outsider."

I acquired the name "the outsider" on the day that my father compared me to the protagonist in Camus' novel, which I had lent him. I already identified with the character myself, but my father was the one who gave me definite confirmation of that identification when he returned the book and said that he wasn't in the least surprised that I liked the book so much, because the hero was just like me. And he gave me a very penetrating look, as if he had no option but to accept the incomprehensible nature revealed to him by that work of literature.

We lent each other books tentatively and even slightly fearfully, but it was never a matter of indifference. A strange complicity grew up, the kind you associate with shared vices, and as long as we were living in the same house, we had to keep up that exchange of books and the subsequent, more or less trivial commentary, a ceremony from which, of course, she was excluded. It was a way of sizing each other up, of sending up observation balloons so that we could each explore the other's territory. Indeed, as I grew older and began to stay out until all hours, he was as troubled and intrigued by my adventures as I was by his, however hard we both tried to hide that fact. And through our freely expressed literary and cinematographic preferences, it was fairly easy to imagine the models we clung to for our respective modes of behaviour. We had no other sources of information.

He loved the nineteenth-century novels of adultery, especially Eça de Queiroz's *Cousin Basílio* and Clarín's *La Regenta*. For example, he would rave about Clarín's description in the latter of Ana Ozores walking through the streets of Vetusta dressed as a penitent and Álvaro Mesía watching her passionately from the balcony of his club with the keenness of the hunter when he first sights the prey he has yet to catch, his soul transfixed by the sight of her bare foot rhythmically appearing and disappearing from beneath the hem of her purple robe.

"That white foot," he would say, "embodies all the eroticism in the world. But what would you know about that? What would those girls you take on the back of your motorbike, the girls you pick up at discotheques know about eroticism? It's all so easy, you don't even have to talk, one girl is much the same as the other."

"Come on, Dad, don't get into things you know nothing about. I never say anything about the girlfriends you might have had."

But that "what would you know" aroused feelings of envy in me, imagining that in his youth he must have experienced some romantic love affair of the kind that simply doesn't happen any more. And I was quite certain that Gertrud Scribner – the daughter of a Chicago financier who made his fortune in the years of the Great Crash – had never been the love of his life.

He, in turn, was always trying to read in my eyes the novel he knew nothing of, with its disconcerting plot cloaked in shadows. My father was a keen cinema-goer, perhaps eager to pick up ideas for a tentative scenario for that stark novel of mine – some smoky, low-ceilinged, strobe-lit dive. If I half-close my eyes, I feel as if I had almost inherited the pictures that doubtless filled his imaginings. There is mist, a lot of mist. I'm not entirely sure where I am either, and, however hard I try to step back in time through the dining-room mirror, all I can remember of those years is the sound of a record player being played at full blast in a room I visited one night because a friend knew someone who lived there. The question always remains as to which of the friends of your friend is the owner of the apartment you've ended up in; it's generally not very welcoming, although you can fit plenty of people in, not because it's spacious, but because you don't seem to need much space between bodies. And it takes you a long time to find out, if you ever do, who is with whom or how many beds the house has or who's going to sleep in them or if the fact, which is taken for granted, of ending the night lying next to someone else will be arranged before-hand or will be a chance combination, depending on how the evening develops – something on which our arrival may even have had some influence, although no one seems in the least surprised to see us and no one has asked us our name, and, at most, they've given us a wave of the hand; and the presumed owners of the house and their presumed visitors are sprawled in shabby armchairs or lying on the floor, just as they have been since God knows when, all wearing the same transfixed, sleepy expression which fails to arouse the curiosity of the new arrival, heads and feet moving to the strident rhythm of the music, hands reaching out for a bottle or crumpling up an empty cigarette packet – "Got any fags?" – eyes staring up at the damp patches on the ceiling or at a giant poster of Marilyn Monroe, eyes that slide from her mouth to her divine calf to her provocative foot which no purple robe of peni-tence threatens to conceal. And nothing leads one to believe that the night could yet take a passionate turn, even though, after a while, one of the girls, who has got up to turn over the record or to go down a corridor that probably leads to the kitchen or the bathroom, looks at us rather more insistently when she returns or even changes her seat and we find ourselves stroking her bare arm, and no one is surprised, not

even the person who might have been her partner on previous nights;
the girl may be sad or have problems, but she usually tells you about
it in a boring, incoherent, lacklustre way. It's a story like many others
we have heard before, and which we never connect with the face that
told us the story, should we ever see that face again: she's left home,
she hasn't got a job, she hasn't got any money or she's pregnant, she's
thought of a terrific plot for a novel, she wants to go off to Ibiza, she
knows some people there who can put her up. A lot of girls have told
us similar stories in similar places, places where fellow drifters meet up,
united by their shared status as shipwreck victims, but who never listen
to each other, who imagine sadly that they are telling you some sensa-
tional, shocking story. My father, however, would doubtless have given
his eyeteeth to be able to listen at the door of one of those unimagin-
ably squalid flats, to be able to enter with no need for a talisman or an
open sesame, with no one demanding a password which, backwards,
spells Sil, with no one asking him what he does for a living or if he's
married; they would make room for him on the imitation leather sofa
facing an unknown, but strangely unmysterious corridor, because it
never leads to the forbidden room, to the forbidden door that troubled
my dreams; but it would perhaps excite him to imagine what might be
happening in one of those rooms along the corridor into which a couple
disappeared some while ago: do they take their clothes off as soon
as they go in? do they leave the light on? do they talk to each other
or do they say nothing? He would give anything not to feel tense in
such a situation, to be able to sit there without looking at the clock or
expecting something extraordinary to happen, aware only of the
rhythms of his own body, all immediate plans for the future cancelled,
all his speeches and value judgements melted away in the warm and
unusual feeling of beatitude that makes him drop all his defences to
allow himself to be invaded little by little by the smell of the girl who
has made room for him next to her, but has not as yet opened her
mouth, the girl who is not wearing Diorissimo perfume, but who keeps
looking at him, idealizing him because he's going grey at the temples
and has the antiquated air of a mature gallant. A frank, unequivocal
look. He must often have dreamed (as often as I have imagined an

encounter with some enigmatic lady) that someone would look at him like that, close to, one of those girls who used to phone me up or ride pillion on my motorbike – barely glimpsed female presences who provoked his fear and his anger, whom he must have experienced as a wall against which all his dreams of becoming an ageing Lothario would inevitably crash, a Lothario with an inscrutable son who never tells him anything – you never even know whether he's gone out or is closeted in his room – a son whom it is sometimes best just to forget about: "I didn't know you were in. A girl phoned," "I didn't know you were in either." We lived beneath the same roof but thought such divergent thoughts that we were always startled when we met. The notion of his existence was far more doubtful then than it is now. It was so odd to see him suddenly appear, to bump into him at night, when I least expected it – "Sorry, Dad, you gave me a fright; I thought you'd be in bed" – and sometimes it was clear that we were both equally startled because we were both so immersed in our own affairs. You could tell by that few seconds of nervous blinking as we struggled to clamber out of our personal submarines and erase from our face that look of distance and indifference. On many other occasions, though, it was clear that the encounter was not in the least fortuitous, but the result of a conscious lying-in-wait on his part or on mine, and the one who had been prowling around in order to surprise the other was always the first to look away – "I didn't know you were in here" "Well, here I am, do you want something?", "No, nothing" – a shadow spying on another shadow, over time, along corridors, in corners, through windows and cracks in the doors, those doors that hide secret opinions and lock in the smell of an evanescent presence.

But the collision between those two shadows had never been so real as it was now – when all contact was impossible – in the sepia waters of the mirror, flanked by two naked women, one of whom has just revealed the snare of her terrible smile, hidden for all these years. Although I had not heard him come in, I could sense him approaching, his face hidden behind the black box of his Kodak. "Don't bother," I say, "the photo won't come out, there's not enough light." "And what if I turn on the lights in my candelabra?" asks the woman on the right with her breasts bared and her eyes staring straight ahead. "The occasion certainly merits it, don't you think, Eugenio? The Prodigal Son has finally returned, your very own dear outsider."

Those were the words with which, years later, he would always open the letters he wrote to me after I flew the nest, until he finally lost track of me because I lost track of myself, along with my memory, my peace of mind, my equilibrium. He always sheltered behind that distancing formula ("Dear Outsider") in order to approach me in the only way I would allow him to, adorning the barrier growing between us with literary references and a few touches of humour, as if he wanted to exorcise any bitterness resulting from my abrupt decision to leave them, or, rather, her, although he never said if it was for better or worse. It didn't matter; that complete, irrevocable split had been with her, and we both knew that, although her name was never mentioned between us – cowardice on his part, disdain on mine. It was a clandestine game played behind her back, and I helped keep it going, I gave him the opportunity to continue weaving between us that strange refuge with the only thread that still bound me to an identity that was becoming ever more doubtful and remote.

Staring at my reflection in the oval dining-room mirror, I surprised myself by remembering how often I had replied to his letters over the years, signing myself "L'étranger" (I always wrote it in French), from points on the globe as various as my states of mind. I would even be filled by a kind of guilty sorrow if more than a month passed by without my sending him a new address – that of some casual acquaintances, of a hotel or a poste restante. It wasn't just postcards either, but letters too. Perhaps he's still got them in some drawer in his study – there's still so much to look at! I'm sure he wouldn't have torn them up, because he liked them. He said I wrote better all the time, and I would try to describe for him landscapes, people, places, adventures while hitchhiking, the customs and oddities of the different countries I was visiting, as long as it did not commit me to anything or give any clue as to my exact whereabouts: the shapes of windows and roof tops, the colour of buses, the design of boats, a visit to a museum, political news, wisps of transient mist, and only very occasionally some allusion to my attempts to get work as a photographer, a painter, or a journalist, or as a teacher of Spanish in Bergamo and Verona, a tourist guide, a waiter or an occasional actor, because I did all kinds of things. He used to say that it made him really happy just to see my writing. He said it rather coolly, but it sounded sincere, and there was always a touch of resignation and restraint about his deliberately jovial replies. His comments on my letters – which I dashed off and launched immediately on to the blue waters of oblivion – gave me back an image of myself as a mere remnant of a figure in a state of perpetual metamorphosis, and gave him, in passing, the opportunity to think out loud and to exercise his much-regretted, latent literary talents. He never got bogged down in anything personal or bothered me with sermons; it was a tacit understanding – as if he were resigned to the idea that one day I would stop writing to him, and he would never have dared to ask me to go on writing to him for ever. "My mother kept me tied to her apron strings for far too long," he had confessed to me on more than one occasion.

My father was a past master at hiding his feelings, and so I have no idea how he took my abandonment of that epistolary relationship of ours, when it finally ended. Once he said that the strangest thing in the world was not so much habit as the shift from one habit to another. It's true that such a transition doesn't fall from heaven or rise up from hell just like that; whenever some unfamiliar change first shows itself, it has already passed through a stage as a woodworm gnawing silently and tenaciously at the beams of the building.

I only know that, as my replies became more infrequent, the letters and postcards that he continued to send to me – sometimes forwarded from my last address to the next – contained an unexpected novelty. In the upper corner of the letter there would now be a slanting note that always said the same thing: "Love, Mama". A love as sharp and aseptic as her writing, a love that gave no sign even of remorse; it was just a way (possibly suggested by him) of reminding me of her inescapable presence at home, a testimony to a symbiosis maintained at all costs.

Needless to say, such a novelty – regardless of whose idea it was – proved counterproductive. The incursion of her signature not only tempered my father's words and tarred them with the brush of conventionality; it dulled the spontaneity of my response, just as her presence, hovering silently at the apex of the triangle, had always inhibited the relationship between the two lower corners. We would have to talk more quietly because she was asleep or had a headache or was just about to come home; you could never discount the possibility of a sudden phone call or appearance which would immediately put paid to any magnetic charge that might just be beginning to flow between us, an intimacy that the dumb reproach of her mere presence transformed into some culpable deviation.

So, the outsider, confirmed in his role, forswore his roots and gave no further sign of life until chance and fate returned him to these shores in search of tracks he had thought erased.

The presence of the outsider had never been quite so evident as it was in those moments when, at precisely the point when a change in his very nature was about to take place, he was waiting to clothe himself in grey, in the guise of a decent, respectable orphan, in order to visit the notary's house, while, still absorbed in thought, he asked his double in the mirror what was the date on the last letter signed by him to arrive at this luxurious, three-storey house, where he had only rarely felt happy, but which he was now going to be free to sell, renovate or even demolish as soon as he was ready to round off the abstruse clauses of some boring document with his clear, harmonious, responsible signature, this time without the unfortunate accompaniment of fingerprints: L. Villalba Scribner.

I suddenly smiled, dismissed the scrawl of my former image and turned my back on the two bronze watchers, the one who smiled and the taciturn one.

Opposite me, on the other side of the table, were the sliding doors that separated the dining room from the living room, the small panes of glass framed in dark wood. I went over and opened them. They slid smoothly back. Inside, the blinds were down, and in the half-darkness of the room I could make out the white covers that she always put over the sofa and the armchairs whenever they went on a trip. It was an obligatory ceremony; she would rather have missed her train or her plane. Those covers seemed to me now like a shroud on the ashes of her own body, on that vain endeavour that ruled her life – to cancel out the marks of time and all signs of wear and tear. Everything was intact, as if nothing had ever happened nor ever would.

When the cleaning lady came in carrying my pressed suit draped over her arm, she found me ripping the covers off the sofa and the armchairs. She handed me the suit and started picking the covers up and folding them neatly. She said it might be a good idea to have them dry-cleaned.

"No, please! Just throw them in the bin. I never ever want to see them again!"

I went upstairs, whistling, to have a shower. I put on the grey flannel suit along with a shirt and tie belonging to my father and topped it all off with a black raincoat. I look good when I'm dressed up like that. I look the part of the indolent but prudent heir, who has finally taken charge of his affairs.

VIII

My grandmother's funeral

By the time I reached the notary's house and they showed me into the waiting room, the theme of the outsider, which had come to life again between the two candelabra in the dining room, had been mingling with that of the Snow Queen as I strolled down Calle de Serrano, leaving behind me buildings and shops that were all doing their best to distract me with other memories. What prevailed, though, was the combination of those two literary tales, interweaving and amplifying each other like an invasive melody around which everything else was organized.

I think I read Camus' book in the same autumn that my grandmother died so suddenly, and it was at about the same time that I ceased to feel any obligation to go and sit with my parents at the mahogany table in the dining room. I'm not sure, though, because the death of my grandmother left a very strange scar. The time before that has become confused with the detritus left by the time that followed, the way two converging currents crash against the sides of a breakwater, unable to contain the fury of the wild, intermingling waters leaping over it, crowning it with foam and scraps of seaweed, and finally drowning it beneath the eddying waves.

Of course, when the tide goes out, no amount of make-up can conceal the ragged edges of the scar. For a long time afterwards, I would wake from a dream in which she appeared and it would take me several minutes before I remembered that I couldn't phone the Quinta Blanca to tell her about the dream, that I would never be able to do so again, and then it was as if I had just been told the news of her death for the first time, or as if I had simply guessed what had happened, as in fact I did.

It happened one afternoon. I had just come in and, for some reason, I wandered into the dining room – why I don't know, since it wasn't time to eat and I hadn't gone in there to look for anything, and since it was, moreover, a symbol of everything I most hated. I stopped at the foot of the stairs, my hand resting on the caramel-coloured ball that adorns the end of the bannisters. It was some banal matter to do with parking my motorbike that made me pause for a moment, but these thoughts vanished beneath the tide of whispers filtering out through the half-open door. I tightened my grip and the caramel-coloured ball exploded before my eyes like a soap bubble, filling the air with rainbow reflections as it dissolved. They were in there talking in low voices, and my feet carried me purposefully, unhesitatingly in that direction. I pushed open the door and went in, despite my dislike of interrupting other people's conversations or of butting in. I was breathing hard, in the grip of a terrible presentiment. They were standing by the mahogany table and when they saw me, they stopped talking. My father was holding a telegram in his hand. They were both looking down.

"My grandmother's dead," I said and I myself was surprised by the utter calmness with which I spoke those words.

It seems even odder to me now when I remember it, because I hadn't heard them mention her name and she hadn't been ill. The strangest thing of all, however, is that I could accept so easily what I had always held to be entirely unacceptable, that I was capable of saying in a clear, firm voice: "My grandmother's dead", without all the clocks stopping, without the image of her motionless body blocking out everything else that was going on around me. There are certain terrifying sentences that secrete a strange anaesthetic when you say them, as if they distanced from our living flesh the very events that they describe, an event which, had we imagined it only a few hours before, would have made our hair stand on end and which becomes frankly unbearable as, with the passing days, we begin to take it in.

My mother didn't go to the funeral. My father and I travelled in the red Mercedes with Luis, the chauffeur, since we both assumed, without even discussing it, that neither of us was in any fit state to drive. We barely exchanged a word during the whole trip, and so the possible memories or anxieties tormenting my father are just one of many unknowns that I have yet to resolve. I was thinking about Kay when he was kidnapped by the Snow Queen and how the giant snowflakes, beating against his face, made it impossible for him to recognize the landscape he was passing through. I tried, in vain, to remember our last conversation. She had phoned me one afternoon when I was in a hurry because I was meeting someone in a bar in Argüelles, a guy called Enrique Williams, who wrote poetry and had a really good record collection. I said: "Bye then, Grandma. Shall I get Dad for you?" And she said no, that wasn't necessary.

It was late by the time we arrived and it was raining. Earlier, we had stopped briefly at a roadside restaurant and I had taken two sleeping tablets with a cup of herb tea. I had felt feverish for several days, but I hadn't been to the doctor.

"You're going straight to bed the moment we get there," my father said. "You look terrible. I'll look after everything, my dear, and tomorrow, well, tomorrow is another day."

I looked at him, smiling, feeling forlorn and grateful.

"All right, Dad, but I want to sleep in her room."

I did, in fact, sleep in the room from which her body had just been removed, and I remember that, to reach it, I had to swim against a strong current, through a tide of confused, weeping figures whose dark clothes exuded a smell of burnt wood, eucalyptus and sour milk. From amongst that magma of childhood aromas, a few arms reached out from the wall towards me, as if to imprison me. I concentrated all my efforts on resisting both their cries and the intense nausea I felt at having to walk straight ahead like that, looking neither to right nor left, intent only on not foundering in the midst of that choppy sea. However, I could not help but notice the blaze of torches to the left, in the large piano room, where they had arranged the funeral chapel. At that point, the moans and the grasping swell of hands trying to seize my body and turn it from its path reached a crescendo.

"Let him through," my father was saying behind me. "He's absolutely exhausted. He doesn't need anything, he just needs to sleep. Really, Rosa, just leave him for the time being."

At last, a door closed behind me.

I lay down fully clothed on the sheets that she had only just left. I did not even want to turn on the light. Just as I did a few nights ago, I lay huddled and shivering in the dark on the big bed with the mattress that dips in the middle, imagining where the furniture and all the other different objects were, imagining the dimensions and corners of that room which was so familiar and in which, suddenly, I felt lost and utterly alone. For example, her sewing basket must be somewhere, and not being able to pinpoint its exact location provoked in me a feeling of disquiet bordering on delirium. My grandmother's long, gnarled fingers, hovering over the diverse geography of threads, reels, ribbons, fringes, bits of wool, remnants, safety pins and buttons, began to glow phosphorescent as if they were in their last throes: flashes of light left behind by hands that only yesterday had fluttered over that tangled nest of tasks, premonitions and memories, whose silken threads can still be followed, whose knots can still be undone. However tightly I closed my eyes, the tremulous, brilliant whiteness of those hands, like wings battling against the scissors of death, reached me from every corner, through the barrier of my closed lids, like a shattered symphony. It frightened me to think that I might one day cease to be in the world and that familiar objects would no longer bear my mark, and I knew that the notion of death is both lateral and oblique, it slips inside us from out there, from the stillness of all those orphaned objects which endure, parasitical, useless.

I soon fell asleep and I heard my father sobbing nearby, but it wasn't me he was calling for. I knew it was him, although it didn't sound much like his voice and I couldn't see his face. It doesn't matter. That happens in dreams. On the other hand, I clearly heard the content of that incoherent conversation, because it wasn't a monologue; he was phoning someone whom he missed terribly. "I need you so much. What I'd give just to have you here; seeing you here, now, would be like being able to breathe again; I'd sell my soul to the Devil – not all of it, of course, just the bit you've left me – in exchange for seeing you for just ten minutes, even if you didn't speak to me, just to see you and look at you now." It was a howl of weakness and passion.

The following morning, when we were sitting opposite each other in the kitchen having breakfast, I suddenly looked at him, stunned, as if I didn't recognize him. The telephone was in the corridor, next to my grandmother's bedroom. I wasn't entirely sure that I had dreamed the conversation. What I did know, however, was that, hallucination or not, my mother was not the recipient of that clamorous plea, never in a million years, not even if you could turn back the wheel of time. No, the pieces did not fit.

They put my grandmother in a cedar coffin which, as I heard someone remark, she herself had commissioned a long time before from an old cabinet-maker in the village; it had a little glass window in the lid so that we could see her smiling until the very last moment when four of her fellow villagers came to bear her away on their shoulders.

No one thought my mother's absence odd; at least, no one asked after her. My father and I walked behind the funeral procession, closer than we had ever been, two men in black, of about equal height, our heads bowed, and behind us came the whole village. It was a grey morning of chilly, purple clouds. It was only a short distance to the little garden surrounding the church, short but infinite, like that vertiginous downhill ride on the back of the sledge that took Gerda and Kay to the square.

After Don Anselmo, the village priest, had said two prayers for the dead in Latin, and when they were already putting the ropes around the coffin to lower it into the ground, it began to drizzle, and you could hear the soft drumming of rain on wood. Then I knelt down on the ground and, for the last time, lifted the little shutter with which they had covered the window. During that long, eternal moment, my grandmother continued and continues to smile enigmatically, her eyes closed.

"You're taking everything with you," I shouted, weeping, "everything!"

And I beat on the cedar wood with my fists. They had to drag me away, like a child, although I hadn't been a child for quite some time. That was the last time I cried.

It was also my last visit to the Quinta Blanca.

When I returned from the cemetery, I did not even want to go back into the house. I wandered about the garden while my father talked to various people, embracing some, giving orders to others, sorting things out or making the occasional phone call, whether real or imaginary I couldn't say.

Quite some time must have passed, because I got very wet, although the rain was fine and warm, almost like dew. There was one very intense period of time – how long I don't know – which I spent sitting on the last bench next to the big statue of Minerva, staring at the back of the house. That was when the scar began to form. I had the feeling that I was witnessing something that had already happened, something remote, which, once the cycle was complete, before it broke away from me entirely, left something like the aura of a mirage. Above all, I felt afraid of the future, because at that moment, if I closed my eyes, I could still imagine, with absolute clarity, my grandmother's voice calling to me from the kitchen window. ("Leo, are you mad? Come on, come inside, you're getting soaked. I've just lit the fire.") I could really hear her voice, I could spontaneously reproduce its exact cadence, with no need for adjectives, as now, when I say that it was grave, mysterious, authoritarian, melancholy, or whatever. I could simply hear that voice, I could still hear it. It occurred to me, in a sudden flash of insight, that the day would come when I would forget it, when I would no longer be able to wrap her voice about me, and that seemed to me the most terrible thing in the world.

Afterwards, we went back to Madrid and I spent several months ill with hepatitis; I had been sickening for it for some time it seems. I lost all desire to eat or speak, but I read a lot, for hours on end. I wrote down some of my ravings which were almost always about rooms full of forbidden doors. I had nearly finished my course in philosophy and literature but I missed that entire year.

My parents treated me with more delicacy than usual then, as if they were slightly afraid. When I got better, I took advantage of their new respect for me by declaring that eating with them put me off my food and that I had no intention of joining them in the dining room ever again. I said it coldly, like someone throwing down a challenge, and since they agreed to my demand, or at least did not dare to argue with me, there began, with the tawdry feeling of victory that their weakness allowed me, the silent period of sadistic acts and blackmail that culminated in my final departure.

Around that time – whether before or after the scar began to form, I cannot tell – I discovered Baudelaire, Poe, Camus and Bataille; I was excited by their ideas of destruction and sin and I identified with those heroes of evil, and, in the grip of the cruel, Olympian naivety of early youth, I believed myself capable of peering, unmoved, into every abyss. I plunged with secret pleasure into that dialectic, at once murky and dangerous, the same dialectic that had already been apparent on the threshold of my childish consciousness and which had led me to reject the second part of the Hans Christian Andersen story.

One day, my grandmother had said to me: "I know what it is, you're jealous of Kay." I got angry with her, because it was true. For from the moment, early one morning, that Gerda put on her little red shoes and, refusing to accept the evidence of Kay's disappearance, ran away from home with no idea where she was going, determined to find her friend, Gerda moved further and further from me. She crossed the narrow streets and went out through the gates of the city towards the river.

"Tell me," she asked the river as she sat on the bank, "have you taken Kay away? Where is he?" I would go down to the cliffs and sit there watching the tide come in, and I would feel Gerda near me, because, although I never knew the name of the river in the story, I knew that all the rivers in the world flow into the sea and bear away with them the tears of those who weep on their banks. The worst thing was when she got into a boat and set off on the long and dangerous adventure that took her still further from my enclosed paradise. She had left me completely alone and refused to cry on my shoulder. Deep down, I envied her because she was free and had had the courage to set off into the open country. I decided to wash my hands of her, but I couldn't forget her, because I couldn't follow her.

Then I would go and sulk in my room and paint pictures of a very ugly, hunchbacked little girl with her dress all torn into grey shreds. "I'm turning bad like Kay," I thought, and sometimes I would feel regret and, at others, a confused, secret joy, because I was tempted by the suspicion that perhaps you had to be bad in order to be loved. Besides, in order to be very good – which was still my preferred option – there had to be some evil against which to struggle, some curse to break, something that would urge me on towards some adventurous goal. I wanted to be either extremely bad or extremely good, but there were no dangers in my life; I felt safe and I could only strike out blindly against grey shadows that came to nothing. How different from Gerda!

Half the book was taken up with her many valiant adventures (down the river, through woods and across plains, encounters with witches, princesses and talking animals) until she managed to find the Snow Queen's ice palace, rescue her friend with a kiss and thus secure a happy ending.

Despite the icy winds, she arrived mounted on a reindeer, and her encounter with Kay really was exciting, however unlikely it was that she could have managed to slip through the cracks of that frozen, inaccessible building in which his white jailer had locked him away. She found him kneeling in an immense, glacial hall, bare of all ornament, trying to do a jigsaw puzzle made out of fragments of ice. He was trying to piece together the word "eternity". He was wholly concentrated on that game, whose name still makes me tremble: the Game of Cold Reason. When Gerda saw him, she ran towards him and threw her arms around his neck. "Kay, my dear Kay! At last I've found you! The journey has been so long, so full of dangers!" But Kay did not move. He sat there rigid and indifferent, looking at his friend without seeing her. Then she started weeping disconsolately and her hot tears, flowing down the boy's chest, opened up a path into his stone heart. That is what struck me as most absurd, that a piece of ice, buried inside someone for so long that it had formed a crust over it, would melt just like that in the warmth of someone else's infectious tears. But that was what Hans Christian Andersen said: the moment Kay's eyes welled with tears, they carried away with them the splinter of diabolical mirror, and his cheeks, until then blue with cold, immediately blushed rose-pink. At the same moment, he recognized Gerda, called her by her name, embraced her and asked her what was going on, what was he doing in that huge, unfamiliar room. All in the winking of an eye.

"I don't know why you find it so odd," my grandmother would protest when I voiced my suspicions. "Snow White was brought back to life by a loving kiss."

To me it seemed that such a terrible change could not be erased with a mere kiss. If the first part was true, then the second part must be false.

On some afternoons, when it was bad weather, I would disobey my grandmother's prohibitions and escape to the lighthouse and stay there shivering, staring out at the terrible, dangerous waves, feeling myself buffeted between those two contradictory poles of good and evil, prosperity and calamity, that trouble the waters of all children's stories, each sending their lights out into battle, until one of them is extinguished. But why was it always the evil light that went out, that was finally rendered harmless, as if it had never existed? I would return home with my clothes drenched and triumphantly face my grandmother's scoldings. From the cliff near the lighthouse, where I could hear the screaming of seagulls above my head, I would dream of the Snow Queen's ice palace and of the boy who had lost his memory, who knelt on the tiles of that vast hall, his cheeks blue with cold, struggling all alone to decipher an incomprehensible jigsaw puzzle.

"Gerda is stupid," I would say to my grandmother. "I don't know why she has to interfere. Kay is just thinking his own thoughts, he wants to solve that puzzle on his own. You're always saying that you have to find the solution to hieroglyphs on your own. Perhaps he doesn't want anyone to find him. Besides, if he is bad, let him be bad. They should just leave him in peace."

"He isn't bad. In the end he becomes good again," my grandmother would remind me.

But her voice had the prim tone she used when she recited the mysteries of the rosary.

"It's a lie, the ending is a lie. You don't believe it either, you never sound enthusiastic when you tell it."

"You're the one who's not enthusiastic, but if you like," she would add, sighing, "if you like, I will try to tell it better."

"No, I don't want you to. I've told you, I don't want to hear it."

"As you wish. Honestly, you are a ridiculous child! Anyway, don't go down to the cliffs by the lighthouse; one day you'll hurt yourself."

Once she was dead, the only thing that seemed worth doing was to continue on down the cliff of the literature of evil that promises us a glimpse into every abyss. The odd thing is that my desire for transgression, fed freely now by my readings of adult literature, was turned more and more against my father. My decision, from then on, to create a character diametrically opposed to his, was a tribute to him. It was as if I suspected that behind his apparently measured and patient appearance lurked a rebel angel (albeit bound and gagged) very similar to me.

During the period immediately following my grandmother's death, his relationship with my mother was, as I recall, at its most strained. However, what remains in my memory are not gestures or attitudes, but the complete absence of them, as if they were two maladroit actors disconcerted by the lights, complete strangers to each other, incapable of continuing to perform a role that was entirely beyond them. Then, more than at any other time, I had become convinced that it was my existence that contributed to making the whole tedious, thankless rehearsal so insuperable a task. Around the same time – whether before or after the scar began to form, I don't know – I began to become obsessed with the idea that he might have a lover. He was often away, for days or even weeks, and he would return looking absorbed, attractive, mysterious.

One morning, during one of those absences, when I was convalescing from my illness, I woke up and I saw that it was snowing. There is always something miraculous about snow, something that abolishes routine and relegates us to the sidelines, as if any movement we might make while it is snowing becomes questionable, unreal. I had got up some time before and was sitting at the window watching the snowflakes falling on to the garden when there was a knock at the door, and my mother came in. Her sudden appearance made me jump, because she didn't usually come up to see me. She was wearing a white velvet dressing gown. She asked me how I felt, asked if I was studying – all useless circumlocutions, because I realized at once that she had come to tell me something. At last, she sat down and took a very thick letter out of her pocket. Even before she held it out to me, I recognized the handwriting on the envelope that read "For Leonardo", and I snatched it from her hands, feeling the blood rush to my head. My grandmother had been dead for months. Why had they not given me the letter before?

"You weren't well. The doctor said you shouldn't get over-excited."

While I listened to her words which struggled to convey concern and affection, I clutched the envelope in my hands as if it were a talisman and thought that the doctor had nothing to do with it, that neither they nor the doctor had understood anything if they had failed to realize that the cure for all my ills lay precisely there, in that hoped-for confession from my grandmother. For I was sure that there, inside that envelope, would be the story I had so longed to hear, set down in clear detail, with no riddles interposed to throw me off the track; it was the one drink that could infallibly quench my thirst, bring my fever down. "Fever, fever, go away, don't come in my bed today." The light of that promised tomorrow had arrived.

When, after what seemed an eternity, my mother gave me a peck on the cheek and finally left my bedroom, I ripped open the envelope and read the first few lines; I suspected then that the splinter of glass was entering my eye. I went on skimming the words, as fast as possible, looking. There was nothing. In that letter, dated two years before, my grandmother simply stated that she had realized that no one, not even she, could be immortal, and that she knew she was in the final straight and was beginning to die. Behind that preamble, adorned with proverbs that oozed an ambiguous humour, she merely gave me a series of practical and moral pieces of advice about life and cleared up various points that might remain obscure in her will. As soon as I came of age, I would receive my inheritance which would include, of course, the Quinta Blanca, with all that it contained. "I am not the kind of person," she said, "to impose my will on you, still less when what little that remains of me will already have been food for the worms, but I would ask you never to sell the Quinta Blanca. I know it needs a lot of work doing to it, especially upstairs, which is falling to pieces, and I know too how lazy you are, but don't be in too much of a hurry to get rid of it, because one day you won't be so lazy and then you will be sorry that it was left to others to carry out the work." This was followed by a long inventory of all the things that were wrong with the house, but which she no longer had the strength to do anything about, mixed in with more or less jocular comments, a description of the furniture, a meticulous drawing of vaults and corridors, whose rather wobbly outline was interrupted here and there by little red crosses that pinpointed the places where the rain came in or where the beams creaked most ominously, along with a list of errands to be run, references to complicated legal fees and detailed accounts.

While the snow thickened outside, I glumly devoured each paragraph of that interminable lecture, hoping against hope that, crouched amongst them, there might yet appear the longed-for confession, the story I had asked for so many times, or, at the very least, a clue. I didn't find it, because it wasn't there. I looked again and again, picking up the sheets of paper that had fallen on the floor, going slowly through each word from start to finish. The lines intertwined, forming an incongruous arabesque. They danced before my eyes, and not because my eyes were clouded with tears. No. My eyes were dry as dry, they burned as if someone had lit a fire inside them. I had lost the ability to cry. The moment I opened the envelope and read the letter which closed the door on all my questions, there leapt into my eyes a splinter of glass from the shattered mirror of the gods of evil in those irrecoverable days of "once upon a time", and that piece of glass was slipping down into my heart, sliding vertiginously down to freeze my tears, my nostalgia, my memory. I was condemned to play the Game of Cold Reason for all eternity, fitting little pieces of ice together on an infinite, unfamiliar, white surface. And no Gerda was coming to rescue me.

The following week, when my father arrived, I told him that I wanted to sell the Quinta Blanca, as soon as possible, at whatever price. I didn't want to know any details. I wanted him to take care of everything.

Since then, I have had plenty of time to play the Game of Cold Reason, to rewind that afternoon and watch it again and again in slow motion, dry-eyed. But until yesterday, when I was reconstructing it as I sat in the notary's waiting room, as a way of rounding off my stroll through the streets, I had been incapable of deciphering it. There in that anonymous room where I was waiting in my grey suit for someone to appear and say: "Come in", with my eyes fixed on a door that concealed no mysteries and from behind which there emerged only the click-clack of typewriters, a ray of light suddenly burst through.

You're right, grandma, it does take a long time to decipher things, it is all a question of patience. The solution to the mystery can be set within the same mysterious text that camouflages it, as happened with your riddles. Now I know why it wasn't your son who brought me the letter, or why I didn't find it on the table or why the notary didn't send it to me by registered post. She came in dressed in white, carrying the letter in her hand, and shortly before that it had started to snow. Fate chooses its messengers carefully, that much I have understood. I have understood the essential truth, the one you never wanted to tell me, perhaps so that my heart would not freeze over completely. When the messenger who brought that letter – a messenger whom I had always kissed and, rather apprehensively, called "Mother" – drew it out from amongst the folds of her white cloak and held it out to me, she was giving me a clue to her own identity: a clue deciphered too late, when both she and you, grandma, are just a pile of dust, a handful of immemorial time. But I want you to know, wherever you are, that I have finally understood it for myself, without anyone's help. Your posthumous letter was brought to me by the Snow Queen herself.

IX

The strange tenant

"Honestly, Leonardo, I just don't understand you. It's as if you'd lost your memory."

"Well, as I said before, I have partly. It's only now, thanks to the writing I've been doing, that I'm beginning to recover it, little by little. It's the aftermath of being in prison. But anyway, even if what you say is true, I mean, that I was the one who wanted to sell the Quinta Blanca . . ."

"Of course it's true! It wasn't a case of just wanting to, you couldn't wait to get rid of it. Your father was terribly upset. Do you really not remember coming here, to this very office, in order to give him power of attorney and put him in charge of everything? Have you forgotten the hurry you were in? You acted as if it was a matter of life and death. You were going abroad, to Morocco I think, don't you remember?"

Don Octavio has a very persuasive voice. For a while now his voice has sounded more like that of a psychiatrist than a notary. He's a lot greyer, but his face is still familiar to me. He was a good friend of the family, and his kindly expression and calm voice have always filled me with confidence. I sit looking at a bronze bookend resting on the great dark wood table separating us. It shows Don Quixote standing, lance at the ready, looking up at the skies, about to launch into some impassioned speech. Yes, of course I remember, I'd been very aware of Don Quixote on that other afternoon too, making him a witness to a crazy decision which, at the time, I thought heroic, irrevocable: to rid myself of my grandmother's legacy once and for all and as quickly as possible, so that I would never ever have to look back again.

"Why was my father so upset?" I asked. "I never got that impression."

A melancholy smile appears on Don Octavio's face, as if he had just remembered something else.

"Well," he says, "he had a difficult relationship with you, things weren't exactly easy between you. That happens sometimes with children. Have you got any yourself?"

"No, not that I know of."

"Well, when you do, you'll come to realize that you just can't get it right; you can forgive your children anything, but you never understand them. Maybe our children understand us better, but they don't let us get away with a thing."

We fell silent. It was beginning to get dark. Not a sound came from the office. Earlier, he had told me that there was no one else in the waiting room, that he had deliberately left me till last so that we could talk without feeling pressured.

"Anyway, I don't know whose fault it was, but I could see there was a certain tension between you. I don't think I'm telling you anything you don't already know. Eugenio was sad that the Quinta had to be sold, of course, but it was more than that, I think; it was that he didn't understand the reasons for such a sudden decision; he didn't think it was anything to do with money, at least not fundamentally. I don't know, perhaps you should have given him the chance to ask you your reasons and to discuss them."

"Maybe. It never occurred to me."

"Did you give him a chance? I mean, did you at any point consult him about the Quinta Blanca? Did you ask him his opinion?"

"I can't remember. Probably not. Do you think he expected me to?"

"Leonardo, your father always expected you to make the first move, something he was incapable of doing; rather the way one hopes for a miracle. He didn't want to bother you or influence you in any way. At least that's what he told me. After all, it was your inheritance, and you were legally of age."

"Of course. What did he care if I sold the Quinta Blanca? In my grandmother's last years there it brought him nothing but problems and expense. I imagined it would be a relief to him."

"Hardly. Eugenio's whole childhood was there, as much or more so than your own."

"Yes, but even so. And as for my mother, she never set foot there."

Suddenly, albeit vaguely, the memory of an ancient argument surfaced. I must have been quite small. It had to do with a village woman who came to do the housework, Rosa Figueroa, the same one who used to tell me stories about the late lighthouse keeper. I took her part in the quarrel. What was it they were quarrelling about? My grandmother looked very serious and my mother had a fit of rage. I don't think she ever went back to the Quinta Blanca after that.

"But your mother has nothing to do with it," said Don Octavio. "I was asking about you; what were you thinking about, how could you consider letting go of that house, whose existence has once again become an obsession? We weren't talking about your mother; please, don't confuse things."

I think to myself that talking to another person, heading off along the roads that he or she marks out for you, just confuses things and adds to the complexities of those other topics that simply happen to crop up. But I say nothing, I simply make a note. I realize that remembering with Don Octavio sitting on the other side of the table is harder work than trying to tie up loose ends on my own. It's not that I find his presence objectionable; I even think it might be worthwhile making the effort, for it could be like broadening out a panorama by giving it another dimension. For example, he sounded quite agitated when he mentioned my mother, he probably knows things about her that I don't. The fact is, however, that such a dialogue requires a gymnastic ability which, being somewhat out of practice, I lack. I have spent many days of solitary work remembering things like someone doing a crossword in his own language, only to find that all the down clues are in Latin.

"As I said, your father was sure it wasn't fundamentally a question of money," Don Octavio goes on. "He said it would be hard to find a more disinterested person than you, and you're more than demonstrating that to me yourself now. Learning that you've just inherited a vast fortune seems to leave you completely cold; all you're interested in is recovering what you yourself once despised and sold off cheaply."

We look at each other and I feel like asking him for help, I feel like confessing that I find it hard to follow his arguments because my thoughts are starting to drift off along other paths. I don't know quite where this speech of his is leading; it's already spent a long time meandering through a strange landscape of deeds, documents and figures, and yet it always stagnates as it approaches the Quinta Blanca, changing it, the moment it heaves into view, into a mirage, a kind of Utopian goal. I have only to reach out my hand and it crumbles before my very eyes, dissolves. I will never be able to recover it because it may never even have existed. I draw a hand across my forehead and breathe deeply, as if I needed air.

"What's wrong, Leonardo? Aren't you feeling well? I haven't said anything to hurt you, have I?"

"No, no. I was just remembering something, only I can't quite remember what. I'm very slow, as you know, and sometimes I just go blank. It would be best if I came back another day. We've talked about too many things today as it is."

"As you wish. You'll have to come back anyway, because the execution of the will is going to be a long-drawn-out affair; there are still an awful lot of loose ends to tie up and I need your help. There's plenty of time. The main thing is that you're back; you can't imagine what a weight that is off my mind. Your father named me his executor – you know how fond I was of him – and I hope that you will look upon me as a friend and come to me with any problems you may have, any problems at all, I mean it. Will you do that for me?"

"Of course," I say. "Who else would I go to? I trust you and everything you do. But you'll have to be patient with me. I'm a bit of a disaster area at the moment."

My own voice sounds so strangely faint to me that I hardly recognize it. Not since Maurício left have I felt that sense of unease, of impotence, at the idea of being alone. I sit paralysed in the armchair, staring down at my folded hands, as afraid of moving as I am of restart-ing a conversation that arouses such feelings of anxiety in me, conscious that, if I don't leave now, I'll be forced to say more, or to burst out crying. What was it like to cry? I remember that the last time

I burst into tears was at my grandmother's funeral, but, even more clearly, I remember my stillness afterwards, in the rain, sitting in the garden on the bench farthest from the house, with my eyes – dry for ever of tears – fixed on the rear of the house, where I could still imagine with utter clarity the sound of the voice that used to tell me riddles and call me in to tea.

Don Octavio gets up and comes and sits in the chair next to mine. The table of the Law no longer separates us. Earlier he was telling me that he has a twenty-year-old daughter, Fanny, who has gone off with a rock singer and that they haven't heard from her in months. She was studying medicine and had been getting on really well.

"Tell me what's wrong, Leonardo, please. What are you thinking about now, or, rather, what is it that you've been thinking about for a while now?"

"I was wondering what they will have done to the Quinta Blanca," I reply without hesitation. "About the work they might have done on it."

A deep sigh of relief helps me raise my head, as if I had risen to the surface after being on the point of drowning in a whirlpool of abstractions and lies.

"Because they're bound to have done some work on the place," I go on, looking at him as if at an oracle, wanting him to refute my suspicions. "They won't have left it exactly the same, they could easily have torn down walls, completely redesigned the garden. Of course, they'd be perfectly within their rights, I know that," I add, when he remains silent. "But I can't bear the idea. As soon as I buy the Quinta Blanca back, I mean to restore it to the way it was before, whatever the cost, you can be sure of that. Otherwise, what's the point of being rich?"

Don Octavio is smiling.

"Well, it won't be that easy. You can't solve everything just by getting out your cheque book."

I notice a troubling tone in his voice which I can't quite decipher.

"Why do you say that? Do you think they've got very fond of the place? I was thinking of offering them double the asking price. What sort of people are they? Do you know them, the buyers I mean?"

"There's only one buyer, she's a woman, and of course I know her. She came here with your father to sign the deeds."

"And how come a buyer turned up so quickly, because she did, if I remember rightly. And it can't have been that easy to sell the Quinta Blanca, with the furniture included, in that remote part of the world. Only an eccentric would buy it. What are you laughing at?"

"When you came to hand over the power of attorney to your father, on that afternoon which you seem to have forgotten, you said exactly the opposite. You said that the world was full of eccentrics, that it wouldn't be hard to sell at all, if it was put on the market at a reasonable price."

"I'm always saying different things, don't remind me, I'm contradiction personified. But what's she like? Rich, I imagine, but what else? I suppose she must have bought it on a whim and only later seen all the snags – that's what usually happens. I wonder if she even goes there, she probably has the house shut up most of the year, and leaves it in the hands of caretakers."

"You're wrong there. Apparently she loves the place and has settled there for good. I don't know anything about any changes she might have made to the house or garden, but she must have had them done while she was living there, because I think she moved in straight away. She comes to Madrid only very rarely. She's a writer."

"A writer? And how come my father knew her?"

"I couldn't say. I only know that she came from Brazil and that she had only recently been widowed when she signed the deed. Perhaps your father was a friend of her husband, that seems most likely. Anyway, Leonardo, why don't you write to her yourself and resolve your doubts that way?"

"That's what I'm thinking of doing."

"Her name is Casilda Iriarte. But now I think of it, I even sent you a copy of the deed; you were absolutely delighted. I've got the letter stating your agreement; Eugenio brought it here so that I could file it with the other papers. do you want to see it?"

"No, no. All I want is to reach an agreement with this lady, to convince her to sell the Quinta Blanca back to me. I'll write to her tomorrow. Has she got any children?"

"I don't think so. But I warn you now, she is by no means a malleable person and she won't be easy to convince. I don't know, though, I've only met her twice."

"Is she an unpleasant person?"

Don Octavio sits staring into space before replying, as if he were trying to evoke a fleeting impression, difficult to put into words.

"No, not unpleasant, but different, very well-educated, very elegant. She certainly didn't give me the impression that she was unsure about what she was doing; on the contrary, she seemed enthusiastic about buying the house. Not that she said as much, but you could tell. Some people are like that, as soon as you look at them, you know that they don't do things without thinking about them first, at least, they don't see it like that. I've spent so much time battling with clients, I know them well. She signed the deed without even discussing the price, she paid in cash and, as you know, the whole sum was paid into an account in your name, from which Eugenio used to draw out money for you, and by the way . . ."

"Yes, I know, tell me about it later," I said, interrupting him, afraid we might lose the thread of what interested me now. "So how long has she been living at the Quinta Blanca? Let's see, five years?"

"At least. We can look if you like, the exact date must be here somewhere," he says, again pointing at the desk.

I feel suddenly depressed. Five years is a long time. I wonder vaguely what my life would have been like had I been capable of spending that much time in one place. What city was I in when I wrote that letter of agreement? What hotel, what bar, what afternoon now erased for ever? Everything is spinning about me, but my reflexes are still fast enough to make a gesture to stop Don Octavio getting up and fishing out yet another file and yet more documents. He's already shown me piles of them and it seems that still there are more. Those documents, thick with misplaced dates, figures, abstract words and references to plots of land scattered across some vague map, form a growing battalion around the Quinta Blanca, concealing it from view. I refuse to look at any more papers.

"Please, don't bother, it doesn't matter how many years it's been. It was a stupid question. If she's quite happy living there, it must mean that she's not bored. That's the unfortunate thing. It's infuriating, of course, but I have to recognize that she has good taste."

"Yes, it seems it was love at first sight; she said it was exactly the place she had always dreamed of retiring to in order to write."

I pull a disdainful face.

"I dread to think the kind of thing she writes."

And the moment those words are out, I hate the childish tone of voice in which I said them. It's just that I don't like losing. Don Octavio shrugs and gives a half-smile which is more paternal than sarcastic.

"Well, look," he says, "I don't know how good she is in her field, because outside of civil law I'm pretty much of a blockhead, but she's just published a book, a collection of essays, which has been a great success. My daughter-in-law was telling me about it the other day at supper; she's a new author, she said, although not particularly young, and her name rang a bell. It took me a while to remember where I knew it from. I kept going over and over it in my mind – I'm a real obsessive about these things – until the penny finally dropped. Of course, Casilda Iriarte, the woman who bought the Quinta Blanca. That conversation could only have been about a month ago, and we talked about your parents too. It's odd how things work out. Who would have believed that they had so little time left to live? Anyway, according to my daughter-in-law, the book is very good. She reads a lot and writes a bit herself too; she's married to Miguel, my eldest son. You remember Miguel, don't you?"

I get the feeling that he has started talking about his family in order to make me forget the tragedy of my own. I nod without much conviction, as I try to hide my lack of interest. Miguel Andrade. I think we went to the same school. My imagination drifts off as I try to reproduce that recent conversation about my parents when they were still not yet dead, trying to imagine what they would have said about me. What I'm finding most tiring is trying to disguise how lost and sad I've been feeling for quite some time now, to disguise the tedium I feel at the thought of having to go home and shut myself up in the house again.

"Miguel is a lecturer in political science at the Complutense University," his father goes on. "At least one of my children turned out sensible, touch wood. Although, as St Teresa used to say: God works in mysterious ways. That's what I'm always telling my wife, especially since this business with Fanny, which has really taken its toll on her. You never know where your destiny may lie; it's like tossing a coin, don't you think?"

"Yes, you're right."

"You see, when Fanny dropped her studies, she said that she had never been half as happy studying the workings of the human body as feeling her own body vibrate to the beat of rock and roll. And if she says that, it must be true."

"Of course, why shouldn't it be?"

"Now, I understand, she sings too, or writes songs, I'm not sure which. Her boyfriend plays the drums. The group's called Cold Comfort, do you know it?"

I say no, I don't, but that it seems like an excellent name. I get up to go. I feel that we're beginning to grow tired of each other or, at least, to travel off along divergent paths.

He accompanies me to the door and says once more that we must see each other again, that we've still got many things to talk about and that I can count on him for absolutely anything. He seems to have noticed my sadness.

"You have to be brave, Leonardo," he said. "You're still very young and that's a great privilege, to have so much life ahead of you. It can all be put right. You're through the worst of it now."

And he embraces me, having urged on me two or three pieces of advice which, judging by the tone of his voice, must have been very important, but which, once inside the lift, are wiped completely from my mind – because they had nothing to do with Casilda Iriarte.

It's already dark when I go out into the street, and it's quite cold. I pause for a few moments on the pavement, not knowing which direction to take. I only know that I don't feel like going home.

X

Puerta de Alcalá

It's raining as if in a dream. Amongst the shifting silhouettes of the other passers-by, a shop window reflects the back of someone in a dark raincoat standing on the edge of the pavement, slowly turning up his coat collar and staring abstractedly at the red light. He is the protagonist of the film, the one in charge of his own thoughts.

"What are you thinking?" my cell mate used to ask me sometimes. He was older than me and eager to hear stories in order to forget his own, some sordid affair involving embezzlement or something, a nice chap, I've forgotten his name. "What are you thinking about? Tell me."

He always asked me so earnestly; it worried him "to see me thinking" as he put it. He couldn't rest easy until he'd got a reply, even though my words subsequently went off on some tangent of their own. I would just shrug my shoulders. I used to say that I needed to wash myself clean in the rain, that I was a rainy person, and that I would like to die on a showery day in Paris. I used to quote Verlaine to him too:

> Pour un coeur qui s'ennuie,
> O le chant de la pluie!

Sometimes I would imagine myself sauntering off, with no particular direction, lost amongst the anonymous people crowding the rain-wet streets of some strange city, out of which would gradually emerge familiar street corners, statues and balconies, squares that took on colour as I remembered them. At other times, though, I would imagine myself sitting at a large desk, which was overflowing with papers, and writing furiously in the greenish light of a table lamp while the rain beat against the windows of the large, soundproof room.

They were my two favourite daydreams when I was in prison, so closely bound up with the absurd that, for a while, my fervent efforts to escape reality managed to annul time and space. Both daydreams were a distillation of my urgent need to use the gifts of solitude that I practised and refined there, to make the most of them in some less hostile setting.

The lights change to green. It's raining more heavily now. I still don't move.

The fact is that, up until now, all I have done is give in to the option of cushioned seclusion, to the distant rain, to the water that doesn't make you wet. On the other hand, the sharp, voracious, pointed words have become a persistent downpour and are – I thought – becoming rather like tyrannical lodgers in my room, thinning the air that I breathe there.

I thought all this while I was still standing on the pavement, and the word "there" liberated my body from being condemned to stay within the four walls of an inherited study in which my recent memory sits cloistered. It is a setting that has suddenly gone into reverse, trans-forming itself into something else. The word "there" sent spinning off into space, into the redoubt of dreams, that house and garden situated in a select, salubrious area, the house bought by Walter Scribner in 1951 for what now seems a ridiculously low price – a wedding present for his daughter Gertrud. I've just found out all the details, and that six-figure number, along with words like dowry, put option, taxable income or joint property, was still whirling about and forming clots that inter-rupted the flow of my thoughts, delaying any decision to actually decide anything.

I let the lights change three times before crossing to the other side. Sometimes I get ideas when I'm walking, sometimes when I'm stand-ing still, and all the ingredients that will, later, proliferate, come together in that momentary pause before I move off again, as if their expansive nature determined my need to start walking. Amongst these ingredients, one stood out, like a centrifugal force drawing all the other ingredients round it: the notion – plain, crude and healthy – that I should not be indoors, but outside, feeling the touch of real rain, and open to the potential allure of the street.

The temptation to go down into the churning river of the street to see if I could catch a bit of the shifting present – a kind of reconnaissance trip to find out what is going on outside while still remaining safely immersed in the water – had been at the back of my mind for some days now, like an anonymous gift rejected out of hand, unceremoniously strangled. My reasons for consistently opting for seclusion are not only my obsession with my personal researches and my renewed pleasure in writing – I said to myself as I crossed to the other side and started walking away from Don Octavio's house – but deep down, there are still traces of fear and incredulity, a logical consequence of the dubious mental wheeler-dealing in which I found myself obliged to engage whilst in prison, in order to block out the siren songs of illusory freedom that dazzled and tormented the other prisoners. I had specialized in the demythologizing of those songs, warning the others that they were harmful and fallacious, arguing that they poisoned the present and made it even more putrid than it already was. In support of that dialectic, I resorted to all kinds of metaphors, and I not only managed, to a notable degree, to convince myself, but I even recruited the occasional disciple, although most of the people there laughed at me and thought I was mad. The world is a labyrinth of corners, it buffets you and bewilders you with treacherous questions and proposals, and it corrals and pressures you. Moving from one place to another is merely an illusory notion which does not, in itself, necessarily go hand-in-hand with the kind of inner freedom that means you are the one deciding to make that move; going out or staying in are equally transient and accidental acts, it depends how you look at it, it depends on a focus that is ultimately determined by the mind. That's one thing you must never allow to break down; the only really serious mutilation is the mutilation of one's thoughts. It all came down to a tenacious cultivation of those sophisms, to building them up as a doctrine of faith, knowing full well that any faith can all too easily become indispensable and hard to eradicate: the only residue it leaves behind is fear. I was less afraid of the actual weight of circumstances than of realizing that, beneath that weight, my imaginative abilities were gradually losing their power to take flight and rise above sordid reality, and that the partition wall that separates that reality from the rooms of dreams is nothing but a torn, fragile curtain about to be taken down at any moment. All kinds of creatures and premonitory birds entered through that crack.

And as I let myself be caressed by the drenching rain, on the threshold of a night in late autumn, I had the feeling that I was gradually sloughing off all those survival mechanisms, an orthopaedic solution that had shored up my real life, but had also set it in plaster. I was breathing deeply, letting myself be filled by the cold, free air, by the drops of water washing clean my face and eyes and allowing themselves to be drunk in by a thirsty, greedy tongue. It was like an unstiffening of benumbed limbs, the feeling of "where am I?" that must afflict Sleeping Beauty before her gradual integration into the new reality, the pleasure of footsteps synchronized to the rhythm of a body left to its own devices, whose arms sometimes rise like wings from the flanks of its black raincoat, eyes sliding furtively over the polished surface of the shop windows as I walked down Calle de Serrano. And I was walking carefully, as if afraid of losing that rare balance, that incipient certainty, wary of possible cruel blows from reality, but ready too for surprises, for the intrusion of as yet unexplored moods rich with the promise of pleasurable feelings of vertigo.

When I reached the Plaza de la Independencia, my perception of the rain had gone beyond that point where it still bothers you, when you're thinking: "I'll have to take shelter in a doorway, get the metro or duck into a café." The rain was, I felt, an atmospheric element quite independent of myself, although capable of provoking unexpected emotions and intentions. Naturally, I kept a sharp eye open in order to spot them, but the fact that I was drenched to the skin didn't matter to me in the least.

* * *

As if throwing down a gauntlet to danger and nimbly dodging the cars that were obliged to brake or swerve to avoid me, I ran across to the centre of the roundabout and took shelter underneath the central arch of the Puerta de Alcalá that is crowned by four seated angels standing guard over the memory of Carlos III, whose praises are sung in a Latin inscription. The angel nearest Calle de Serrano is looking at himself in a mirror, or perhaps enjoying being able to see reflected in its oval surface the few traces of goodness still floating about in the world; for – or so I thought – it cannot only be devils who have the privilege of drawing evil into their dark mirrors, as Andersen imagined. And, with the wind beating round me beneath that vaulted stone ceiling, I thought too that if the furious air were to snatch the mirror from the hands of the white angel perched rather precariously above me, and if that mirror were to shatter at my feet, a tiny splinter of goodness might enter my eye and slide down to do battle with its enemy, the splinter of glass-turned-to-ice which, one far-off day, froze my heart and left it impervious to feeling; it might perhaps dislodge it, unclench my heart and open up a channel for all those pent-up tears. Alleluia, at last, Hosanna in the highest. Blessed are they that mourn: for they shall be comforted. Suddenly, with the ingenuousness of the boy who had once drawn pictures of Gerda and Kay surrounded by mauve flowers, I saw that struggle between good and evil as images in a comic strip, the different scenes from which were all taking place inside me. It was a very odd sensation, but stimulating too, a blend of black humour, tenderness and hope, although the tears apparently rolling down my cheeks were apocryphal, a mere consequence of my recent drenching, as I realized, after a momentary shock, when exactly the opposite impression had risen up before me like a mirage. Those tears did not spring from my soul, they were dripping down from my drenched hair. I took a handkerchief out of my raincoat pocket and dried my face, feeling suddenly amused. It was just a story that had somehow slipped into the sombre garden of my digressions – the open air was beginning to make its magical effects felt – a meandering tale that deactivated my tendency to black thoughts simply by landing on them, weightless and silent, like a butterfly on the bristling back of a dragon – just as light conquers darkness – a gentle story, unexpected and slight, that I was pleased to give refuge to and which, of course, I offered up to my grandmother, acutely aware that I was not the one inventing it. I smiled to remember how much she enjoyed novels with happy endings, and from that moment on, I started to feel more at ease in the night and even more disposed to enjoy the gift of being alive and being able to walk freely down the street. On the other hand, the conquest of that strategic position – which, having taking it by main force, I considered to be mine – only added to the feeling of triumph.

"This is great!" I exclaimed, raising my arms as if stretching after a long sleep. "I'm safe, and yet I can see everything; no one is going to oust me from here. I will leave when I choose to and only then."

While I was studying the buildings surrounding that urban island – the dark leaves of the Parque del Retiro and the speeding cars, in which I would occasionally catch someone's darting glance as they noticed my figure there like some crazy apparition – I was recalling too, with the same calm clarity, an old engraving in the Quinta Blanca, where this very scene is presented as a solemn landmark signalling the boundary with some suburbs that no longer even exist, from the time when Madrid was a one-horse town with no electricity and no sewers.

My father was very interested in the eighteenth century and would speak glowingly of the enlightened ministers appointed by Carlos III, during whose reign so many of Madrid's architectural reforms were begun. When I was a little boy, he would sometimes attempt to explain and to convey to me the importance of those early advances, timid attempts to forget about wars and improve life in our own country, to brighten it up a little and provide it with a few amenities. At that time, which few people ever mention now, they erected this arch beneath which no one walks, which cannot even serve as a temporary shelter for some drenched citizen without his becoming the object of scandalized looks. Puerta de Alcalá, a space wide open to the void, a harmonious reminder in stone which, one day, with no need for locks or bolts, marked the boundary between inner and outer – a metaphor, a riddle, a nonsense, a door with no key that is never closed; this, grandma, is my momentary refuge, my island concealed from the eyes of those gesturing equivocally at me, a temporary hiding place from the talons of time. Because now – with the minor difference that I included myself as a tiny figure in that empty landscape – the Puerta de Alcalá was once again the arch in the engraving that my father used to show me as a child: through here you leave a city crisscrossed by carriages. A carriage brushes past me and I have to step back against the stone wall; and the wheels and the horses' hooves echo on the uneven paving stones, heading for Alcalá de Henares.

"Over there, it's over there!" I cried excitedly, pointing with my right hand at the statue of Espartero, who was not, of course, alive then, nor were any of those other nineteenth-century soldiers who were the cause of one fracas after another and whose surnames invade the streetnames of Madrid. I had the powers of past and present by the reins, I could keep them in step at will.

And I imagined the present approach roads to Barajas Airport, to the American outpost of Torrejón de Ardoz, to the hilltops and picnic areas near the River Jarama, leading all the way to a city of pillars and ornate Plateresque façades, to the oldest university in Spain, the cradle of Cervantes – don't die, master, vanquished by the weapons of mere melancholy. Do anything but die.

And suddenly I began to let out the string on the kite of fantasy. Who was there to stop me travelling, dreaming, setting off in search of adventures, weaving the night out of my own footsteps, sailing it, possessing it? There were no bars now between me and the possibility of setting whatever course I chose. And I remembered that song by Moustaki that I used to sing in prison to console myself:

> Sans projets
> et sans habitude
> nous pourrons rêver
> notre vie.
> Viens, je suis là
> je n'attends que toi,
> tout est possible,
> tout est permis . . .

Everything is possible, everything is allowed. To dream, like Moustaki, of a life with no routines or plans. To see visions like Don Quixote. The city and the night lay open before me. Perhaps someone was waiting for me, and, even if they weren't, adventures are things to be dreamed.

After a while, when the rain had eased off and the wind had dropped, I abandoned my temporary island, ready to catch the first bus that passed.

XI

Breakdowns of the soul

I couldn't help but notice that my euphoric mood had sprung a leak somewhere, and I suspected that she was beginning to notice too. The second factor worried me rather more than the first, not only because it forced me to put on an act, but also because it proved an obstacle to my investigating the reasons for the breakdown in my mood. An alien presence always gets in the way of such investigations, especially when that presence does not inspire confidence, when the unknown person has not yet revealed herself to us, adorned with the attributes of the magical companion – nor gives the least sign of doing so – the companion who providentially appears and whose sole mission is to set the hero, who is about to get lost, back on the right track, to warn him of dangers, give him advice or listen to his innermost thoughts. Almost the moment such a character first appears in a story, he is recognized for what he is – at least by the reader whose attention is unclouded and who can view the plot from outside. In my case, of course, for a long time, for far too long, I have been the sole reader of all the catastrophic situations I have found myself in, and, however practised I may think I am in splitting off from myself, I often get confused and start seeing things.

"What I need is another reader, someone who could read me," I thought, in a moment of insight. And the thought struck me as so important that I furtively scribbled it down on a paper napkin. I told her that it was an urgent reminder to myself for the following day and that it was lucky I had remembered to write it down, because otherwise I would have forgotten it.

"If you just screw it up and put it in your pocket, you're bound to forget it, because the night's still young, you know," she said. "I've lost track of the number of bits of paper that I only ever find when they're no longer any use, tons of them, especially telephone numbers, and when you do find them, you can't remember whose they were because you haven't written down the person's name. Of course, the answer to that is a diary. I never bothered with all those diaries I used to be given, not until Mónica convinced me how useful they were. The trouble is that now I just fill them up for the sake of it. If I don't write something down, I feel as if I've wasted the whole day, but that's me – I never do things by halves. As my mother would say: I'm either bald or wearing three wigs. Haven't *you* got a diary?"

"No."

"Well, you can kiss goodbye to that paper napkin, then. It's like pouring water through a sieve, sweetheart."

I shrugged. My inability to shut out that close, troubling female presence was beginning to irritate me. And my desire to flee collided with something which, at first, I refused to acknowledge as a need to go to bed with the first woman who came along. The idealized image of the wild, desperate ex-prisoner reminded me of certain jokes and conversations – just the thought of them made me feel like throwing up. My queasiness was the result of sudden contact with an area utterly resistant to analysis. On the other hand, the combination of gin and hash was increasing both my sense of fatigue and my inability even to attempt to stand up, let alone interpret highly complex symptoms. In these circumstances, I was incapable of being a reader of myself. I got into a terrible mental tangle, because I started to try and force the metaphor of the reader, and it simply burst its banks. I saw my life as a book out of which sprouted a leafy tree and that I was hanging from the branches by my feet, struggling to decipher the words on the pages from an upside-down position.

The girl was looking at me hard, as if she were waiting for something. There were other people with us, especially to our right: a sinuous line of shifting profiles, superimposed figures that occasionally drifted apart, lazy, inexpressive faces, heads resting against a rather hard, communal pillow fixed to the wall by small rings and that served as the back of the sofa, also communal, on which we were all sitting in various states ranging from catatonia to total collapse. It was a kind of continuous sofa, dirty white in colour, that bordered the far end of the dimly lit club which consisted of a long, slightly damp room, rather like a hangar. The girl was wearing striped tights and had drawn her legs up on to the sofa so that she could sit cross-legged, with her mouth close to my ear. She must have found that the most comfortable position from which to observe the expression on my face, because it seemed that I was beginning to intrigue her. Sitting across the sofa, like a sort of barrier, she had turned her back on the group to which she had originally belonged – and which had apparently lost all interest anyway and was ignoring her – as if her turning away had divided the sofa into two zones, and as if the right angle that her body formed with mine was an indication that she was transferring her interests elsewhere – a declaration of an exclusive intimacy which I had perhaps unwittingly encouraged.

One of the members of the zone which her body now concealed from me was a guy called Clemente, who was sitting immediately behind her. Before that transfer of interests, we had been talking for a while, I think, and she had mentioned his name, a name that the others present kept repeating in compliant tones, a name that reached my ears with the crunch of an icebreaker, as the one unequivocal fact about the other zone – Clemente – a fragile guarantee of reality amongst the discordant, fragmentary tide of unfamiliar voices. They invoked his name the way people might light a swaying lantern in the darkness, and there he was, that sharp-tongued, disdainful young man who always had to contradict everyone else, who never lost his cool and whose silences were as significant as what he said. I didn't need to see his face, I could tell by the tone of voice in which they asked him for a light or for a cigarette paper. People who know that they are the centre of a group are always the same – unmistakeable amongst the confusion that they themselves have often generated, its magnetic pole. I've known plenty of them: some were genuine, but most were phonies. The latter are characterized by the immediate urge they have to lock horns with anyone they suspect of being an aspirant to the same rank. I know the kind of person I'm dealing with because – sometimes deliberately, sometimes not – I too have been the kingpin of such groups or have allowed people to treat me with the mixture of respect and unease that the slightest whiff of eccentricity provokes in others – a dupe who passively allows it to happen and then, later, encourages it, until such time as he begins to weary of it.

There were a lot of people standing up, moving aimlessly back and forth, although the bar and a platform in the corner at the opposite end stood out as the centres of greatest activity. Three extremely thin young men had just climbed onto the platform, each bearing an electric guitar, and the audience, who received them with enthusiastic whistles, gathered round to sit on the steps or on the floor. The microphone was not properly adjusted – it whined slightly – and the artists hadn't quite got the hang of it. They were folk-rockers. They sang in passable English and writhed about.

The bar was packed too, but with a constantly changing personnel. People would stay there for a while, forming random groups; they would pause to say hello to someone, then, sooner or later, glass in hand, they would move off and wander slowly back across the arena spread out before me, as if listlessly seeking some ideal corner in which to find refuge. They never did. It was a place that could have been defined precisely by its lack of cosy corners. There were no windows and the air was thick.

"We build an imaginary room about our body. For the great dreamers of corners, nooks and crannies, nothing is ever empty," I said, as if mumbling a prayer.

She noticed my lips moving.

"Speak up," she said. "I can't hear you."

"Do you know *The Poetics of Space*?" I asked.

"Is Sean Connery in it?"

"No, it's a book, an essay."

"Oh, I hate anything like that. My flatmate, Mónica, is a great one for essays though. And she remembers everything she reads. You'd love her. I'm really going to miss her. She's going to live in Melbourne, for good; real burning-your-bridges stuff. She's fallen in love with a guy over there; he's as mad about books as she is. From the photo I've seen of him, he looks a bit of a cold fish to me, but there you are, she likes him. He sends her poetry and that. Sorry . . . What was that book you mentioned about?"

I made a dismissive gesture with my hand and plunged into an even more hermetic silence. The mere idea of trying to summarize Bachelard's theories in that particular place and for the benefit of that particular person reinforced both my desire to be alone and my sense of having my train of thought interrupted; it also increased my nostalgia for a world filled with corners, caves and hiding places. Amid the cigarette smoke rising from the plain, I watched the blurred, abstract figures changing as capriciously as the spirals of colour in a kaleidoscope, as if they were no more than smoke themselves, the smoke from half-burnt-out lives. I felt sorry for them. I felt too as if they were actors in a play whose plot I found all too familiar. They're like me, I thought, they are my generation. It was like discovering the Mediterranean, except that it produced in me a mixture of panic and surprise.

The girl reached out her arm to pick up her half-empty glass of whisky and, after brushing back a lock of hair, she slipped her other arm in the space between the back of my neck and the back of the sofa. It was a furtive but deliberate move, as I soon realized. First, she took a long sip of her drink and then replaced her glass on the table. The pressure of her fingers on my shoulder increased.

"What's up?" she asked. "You've gone all silent. Was it so important, that note to yourself about this thing you've got to remember tomorrow?"

She had leaned forward to speak into my ear in a voice as rich with implied meanings as her smell and the way she pressed her body to mine. In the grip of that physical closeness which dimmed all judgement, the words I had written on the napkin dissolved in my consciousness. I tried, rather half-heartedly, to return to the meditation to which they alluded, whilst my hand in my jacket pocket crumpled up the piece of tissue paper and mechanically rolled it into a ball between thumb and middle finger. It had been something about a reader, but it hadn't sounded, as it did at that moment, like an advert for a university post. What was it I was trying to put myself on guard against? Who knows? A message written in smoke, escaping through a hole in my pocket to join the smoke in the club.

"Sorry, I can't honestly say." I said, not daring to look at her. "It's nothing to do with that. It's more general."

"Right," she went on in a still more insinuating tone, "that's what I'm complaining about. You leave a person wanting more. You're an odd one you are, I can't quite categorize you."

"I'm not some sort of beetle, you know."

"I can see that."

"What do you mean then?"

"I don't know; first, you were zooming along so fast I couldn't keep up with you and then, for no apparent reason – because you really were bucketing along – you suddenly slammed on the brakes. Does that often happen? I mean, don't answer if you don't want to."

"Bucketing along?"

What really bothered me was having to give some account of my ghostly behaviour, having to try and retrace the route taken by my words before the silence began to fill up with the gas leaking out of my soul, and all the while her caresses, focused now on the back of my neck, were growing more insistent. She burst out laughing.

"Yes, bucketing along, but don't look so worried. All I'm saying is that I like the way you talk."

"And how do I talk?"

I may have asked the question rather abruptly, but I needed to know, to find out to what extent I had provoked those caresses which, first, grew more tenuous and then stopped. I looked at her. She seemed embarrassed, and, from the expression on her face, I doubted that she would be capable of keeping to the subject.

"I'm not very good at summing things up," she said, "and it's even worse if what I've seen or heard is something really nice. I can't retain anything; it was the same at school. You talk really well, but you do sort of leap from subject to subject. And so, of course, when a deathly silence falls, apart from the fact that I forget what you've just said,

I think: he must have realized that I'm not up to it, he'll have said to himself 'no point casting pearls before swine'. Normally, in places like this, with all this noise, there's not much point remembering what people say to you and so you just switch off, but it's different with you. I'd like to remember everything you've said to me from the moment you arrived, so that I could tell Mónica about it later. I expect that sounds silly to you."

"What do you mean? Does she interrogate you afterwards?"

"No, it's just that blokes always say really cool things to her, it's always her they give those great long speeches to. I'm jealous really."

"She probably makes it all up, there are plenty of mythomaniacs about," I said sympathetically, now partially resigned to abandoning my initial investigations.

"You may be right. For example, it does seem extraordinary that after one of her long telephone calls with her current boyfriend, when they can't even see each other's faces, she can still remember everything they said. And they speak in English too, don't forget, because all he can say in Spanish is 'tortilla de patatas' and 'olé caramba'. But then, if Mónica does invent those fascinating conversations – because sometimes I do wonder if she isn't just making it all up – well, all I can say is that I envy her even more. With people I know really well, I know where they're coming from and I don't really have to listen, because I don't expect any surprises, and with new people, especially if they're a bit odd, I don't know, I just get lost, because, on the one hand, it's nice to hear new things, however difficult they are to follow, but, on the other, you start thinking, well, I do anyway, what is he on about?, which is what happened with you, it's a bad habit I know, but my concentration just goes. According to Mónica it's all a question of concentration, because if you don't concentrate you don't learn anything and you miss the best part of life. You see, she listens; she can listen to several things at the same time. I just can't."

The boys with the electric guitars had changed their style. After stepping back a little, one of them announced a female name that provoked loud applause, and he handed over the microphone to a girl with straight blonde hair who launched into a fairly convincing rendition of a Patsy Cline song from the sixties: "I fall to pieces". Now, I didn't find it such hard work listening to my companion's stream of consciousness, abandoning myself to the tide of its comings and goings.

"I'm really going to miss her," she went on. "Don't think I don't care about her, just because I said I was jealous of her. It's more that I admire her, that I'd like to be like her. I mess everything up because I talk too much, and talk a lot of nonsense too. The thing is you have to be bright to talk a lot. You've either got it or you haven't. Am I boring you?"

"Not especially."

"Tell me what you're thinking."

"I'm thinking that each of us has to make the most of what we are. There's no point worrying about it. And I was thinking too how nice this song is. Forget about Mónica for a moment and listen to the words. 'I fall to pieces each time someone speaks your name.'"

She shrugged. She seemed depressed, incapable of exorcising the ghost of her friend, or so I thought.

"I don't know any English," she confessed. "Why don't you translate it for me?"

"Let's see. Give me that diary you always have with you."

She opened her handbag, which was scrunched up against the wall, and delightedly handed me the diary. It was bound in grey leather. She took out a pen too.

"Shall I write here? This is December."

"No, wait. Write on the lined pages at the end."

> I fall to pieces
> each time someone speaks your name,
> I can't bear you to think of me as just
> another friend.

"Haven't you got nice writing. And you write so quickly too."

"Be quiet, please, you're confusing me!"

You want me to behave
as if we'd never kissed.
You want me to pretend
that we've never met,
and I've tried and I've tried,
but I just can't do it.
You walk by and I fall to pieces.

"Well, that's more or less what she's saying," I said, returning the diary to her, when the applause had died down and the blonde girl had launched into another Patsy Cline number, "Always".

We used to listen to it round at Enrique Williams' flat. He was a friend of mine at the time when I was just beginning to take on the role of "the outsider" and Patsy Cline had died in a plane crash a few years before, definitively "fallen to pieces". Enrique told me the singer's story; his father, a soldier on the American base in Torrejón, was a great admirer of hers. Enrique had a very good record player. He was tall, with blue eyes. He introduced me to Patsy (I now realize) on the very evening when I heard my grandmother's voice, for the last time, on the telephone. It's odd how clearly and unexpectedly whole lost sections of memory surface: objects, gestures, lights, as well as connections that you might think utterly banal. At that time, I was still capable of feeling moved if I saw a girl looking sad or if I listened to some heart-rending song. The splinter of glass had not yet entered my eye. I wonder if I was happy then.

"That's lovely!" the girl in the striped tights exclaimed admiringly. "Thank you. You're a real love. And, in future, I will try and accept myself more."

She put the diary away in her handbag, finished what remained of her whisky and once more slid her arm between the back of the sofa and the back of my neck.

I remained silent, immersed in the images revived by Patsy Cline's music. As I consciously tried to put myself on guard against mere desire for someone who inspired in me neither curiosity nor interest, I was wondering how many women I had hurt without realizing it.

However needy my body was, I could not desire something unless it offered some contrast, or helped raise me up above the thorny problems of past and present reality, and dispelled my fears or slaked a different kind of thirst. And with the same clarity with which I could see the tables, the stage on which the blonde singer was standing and the figures moving about in that cornerless place, I saw and almost felt the awful void that would succeed any future coupling with the girl sitting next to me – the cracks in the ceiling of some unfamiliar room, the two of us lying on our backs, still and naked, and she perhaps asking me: "What are you thinking? Did you enjoy it?"

"I don't mind if you don't say anything," she said suddenly. "I like you when you're quiet too. You've got lovely hair. I can take almost anything, but I can't stand dandruff or crinkly hair or baldness, to mention only three. Mónica says I could write an MA on the subject. Her boyfriend in Melbourne hasn't got much hair, he looks a bit like a monk. It's not often you meet someone whose hair turns you on, and, believe me, I've had a lot of experience. You've got fantastic hair, but I expect people are always telling you that."

I changed my position slightly. I felt a kind of emptiness in my stomach.

"I don't know. I don't remember. Can I ask you a favour?"

"Yes, of course, what?"

"If you want to put me at my ease, will you try and get back to what I asked you before, would you mind? I'm losing the thread. What was I talking to you about? Don't think about what you're going to tell Mónica or anything, just try and remember. What was I talking to you about? One example will do, just the most important themes, you must remember something."

She looked at me bemused.

"When though?"

"I don't know, before, when I first sat down here. When you first met me, whenever. I can't have been sitting here that long. Otherwise, just make it up, improvise. It's really important."

"You do ask some strange things!"

But she was smiling, looking pleased. Then she tried to concentrate, staring across at the bar. She was biting her thumbnail.

"Well, for example, you started by saying that it was pouring with rain outside, and you did actually look as if you'd just been helicoptered in from Bombay, and you were saying how everything looks different, the street, the people, the storm, everything. The sort of thing that makes you think 'Where's this guy coming from?' I was listening to you and it was like I was hallucinating. It was probably the hash that did it."

With my left hand I felt something wet on the sofa: the black raincoat that I'd taken off when I arrived. And before that, of course, there had been my visit to the notary, Puerta de Alcalá, and an abstract but intense desire to sail the city in search of some valuable fossil hidden in the crevices of its sewers. And I saw myself soaked to the skin, standing under the dirty glass canopy, shaking off the water like a poodle, while the curtain of slanting rain took on an intermittent, red glow. You had to go down a winding staircase – the steps were lit up – and it was a long way down, and as soon as you started going down, what came up to meet you was the smell, the smoke, the gurgling of some subterranean, forgotten place where you might well have lost something. It wasn't the first time I'd been here, I didn't just stumble upon it. It was near the Telefónica in the Gran Vía. My footsteps, divorced from any fantasies about finding adventures, had obeyed the rule of the devil you know. And the place was still there with its red neon sign: GO LIKE THE CLAPPERS. I needed some hash, that was what I was looking for.

"You're not gay, are you?" the girl asked suddenly. "Just so as I know."

She had leaned away from me slightly to get a better look at me, and that allowed me to move and feel less boxed in. For the first time, I noticed the emptiness and candour of that abstracted gaze, circling round the momentary light she may have imagined she had found in mine, and I was afraid of the compassionate lie with which one consoles one's fellow shipwreck victim. I stroked her hair briefly and seized the opportunity to get up.

"My grandmother used to say that riddles are something you have to work out on your own. She was a very wise woman. I'm going to get another drink. Do you want anything?"

"Yes, a whisky. But come back, won't you?"

"Don't worry. I'll leave you my raincoat as surety, all right?"

XII

Old acquaintances

It was a great relief to get up and stretch my legs. Moreover, as I made my way over to the bar, I realized that the feeling of surprise with which I had viewed it from afar was disappearing. I relived in vivid detail the moment of my arrival at the club and my conversation with a waiter with curly hair, who had shown every sign of recognizing me the moment I came in, a scene that was added to other previous performances, as if the curtain had been raised on a revival of a familiar spectacle. The waiter had greeted me with a broad grin:

"You're looking very smart! It's good to see you. What's with the Humphrey Bogart raincoat?"

"It needs drip-drying, as you see," I said, taking it off. "Give me a gin and tonic, will you? I don't suppose you've got a hairdryer on you, by any chance?"

He laughed and asked how I was doing, and said what an age it was since I'd last dropped by there. I grabbed a stool and said I was fine, that I was living somewhere else now. He could see that, he said. I'd obviously gone up in the world. Nothing like a bit of success. He kept calling me Leopoldo.

"Anyway, it's good to see you, Leopoldo. As you probably remember, the clientele here changes every two or three months. They're opening up so many new places around here, there's a real glut. The other bloke I haven't seen around here for a while is Javier, you know, Tiny. He got into a bit of bother, didn't he?"

I shrugged.

"I thought you lived at his place," he went on, "or perhaps I'm mistaken?"

"We all make mistakes. Your mistake was believing that it was his place and mine was paying the first instalment – money down the drain. Well, I was wrong about other things too. Not that it matters. I don't want anything more to do with them."

"Did they do the dirty on you then?"

"Yes, I think they did, but then, I probably treated them equally badly. I wasn't keeping score. Come on, give me that drink."

I stayed there a while longer, until I'd finished the gin and tonic and the next one, because, normally, I enjoy sitting at the bar. But I felt uncomfortable, trying to exorcise troublesome ghosts from the past – heavy clouds possibly laden with hailstones – and, from my vantage point there, I kept a sharp eye on the constantly changing groups of people, in case I spotted something in their behaviour that indicated some secret conclave or deal that would prove fruitful to me in my search. On the other hand, I felt that I too was being observed; I felt more exposed than out in the street. The false sense of security that the vision of the night had injected me with as I left Don Octavio's door, and the impulse I felt then to step out and explore the rainy city, incognito, was gradually crumbling and giving way to the paranoia of the ex-jailbird who sees prying eyes everywhere. And yet I couldn't leave either. There came a point when I only felt safe and secure when the curly-haired waiter came by and smiled at me. I had established that his name was Fabi, that he enjoyed a laugh and was rather more popular than his colleagues. He was terribly busy, though, because he was in demand from all sides.

When I ordered my third drink, he again stayed with me for a while. He obviously wanted to continue our conversation about my former friends.

"I imagine you know about the girl with the red hair," he said suddenly.

"No, what happened to her?"

"She gave birth prematurely, and the child was born dead. She nearly didn't make it. Esteban, the tall one with the curly hair, was telling me about it last Sunday. It happened recently; she's still in hospital."

"I didn't know anything about it."

"Well, you wouldn't if you don't see them any more. She's a nice girl, Ángela. She's put up with Javier for a long time, you know, but she's ten times brighter than him. God knows where it will all end. She's had a lot on her plate."

"Maybe, but it's all ancient history to me."

"Don't be too sure, Leopoldo," said Fabi. "There's always some old mammoth lurking, waiting to leap out and attack us when we least expect it."

"What a nice image!" I said, laughing.

He was right, though, because the withdrawal symptoms I had been suffering from suddenly got worse. Finding myself suddenly free of that child of smoke that might possibly have been mine aroused in me feelings that were a mixture of liberation, emptiness and uneasy conscience. I remembered, despite myself, the anxious, pleading eyes of the girl who used to come and visit me occasionally in prison and who never knew what to say to me, perhaps because she too had an uneasy conscience. She brought me clothes or food, as if she were my girl-friend, a sort of clandestine, unreal girlfriend, with dark rings under her eyes, who was always on the point of bursting into tears. I would sit there, still and silent, just looking at her, as if none of it had anything to do with me. An endless sequence of silent close-ups, slow and painstaking, through the pierced plastic screen in the visiting room. What script did those shots belong to? I didn't want to question the motives behind anything. But there was the mammoth, I could sense his black bulk behind me, like an immense, threatening shadow. I urgently needed to smoke some hash.

I saw vaguely familiar faces around me, but I trusted none of them, and I trusted my memory still less, which is the only compass that can prevent you making a false move or getting into awkward situations. So, before he went off again, I decided to consult Fabi about the matter that had brought me there. He looked around as if scanning the horizon; a rapid, expert glance. Then he leaned towards me.

"The people on the sofa at the back," he said in a low voice, with a lift of his chin. "I don't know if they'll have much left to sell, but they have some really good stuff. Do you know Clemente?"

"I don't remember."

"I'm sure you do, but it doesn't matter. Just ask for him, he's the second on the right. Tell him Fabi sent you, that'll do it. He's a great guy."

And that was how I had arrived, with a fresh gin-and-tonic in my hand, at the sofa at the back of the club. And after smoking a couple of joints, I had, it seems, managed to dazzle the girl in the striped tights, the girl from whom I was now escaping.

"You've got a very odd way of escaping," I thought to myself, after a visit to the gents in order to undrink everything I had drunk, to splash my face with cold water and stare at myself for a moment in an anonymous mirror, like someone touching base. "It's always been the same. To stay or to flee, that is the question."

It was like a set phrase, catchy, like the chorus of an old song that was struggling hesitantly to open up a path towards a healthier, more workable analysis of the situation.

Entrenched now at the far end of the bar, where even Fabi would have found it difficult to spot me, I remained firmly out of the limelight, and gradually withdrew still further until I was leaning in a corner, not far from the illuminated staircase, which continued to vomit forth customers; I stood very still, dizzy with the music and the smoke, having completely forgotten my intention of buying another drink. Besides, the Patsy Cline songs had finished, and the roar of mediocre rock music was growing in intensity. Why didn't I leave? What the hell was I doing there, cornered, skulking in the very place where the giant shadow of some black mammoth might suddenly leap out at me? And I'd been warned now.

I thought vaguely of all the men and women who, at that hour, would, like me, be hiding from something amongst the swarming, anonymous masses in subterranean places in countless cities, gripped by the fear of returning, reluctantly, blindly, to the surface to confront the glum night that had lost the transient iridescent gleam that had embellished its wings when it first took flight; they would be in retreat now, alone, carried along on the whim of some zigzag path. They all hide their intentions behind an inscrutable mask, although few – still less at this hour – can actually remember what their intentions were, if they had any, or how those intentions gradually changed, how they have been reduced to nothing but fear. People don't like to be reminded of their fear, for that is where the mammoths lie in wait. They are all running away from the same thing – we all are – running from what we thought we had left safely buried behind us, as we plunge down roads that lead nowhere.

And why don't you just go home, if this is all so old hat, if you really have run out of steam? Take a good look at the night, this squeezed lemon that you're still sucking, and just throw it in the bin once and for all, because there's no more juice in it, and you know it.

Despite all my muddled philosophizings, I had to admit that what kept me there was the call of the grubby sofa that I had just left and which was slyly urging me to change my position so as to find a strategic viewpoint from which I could observe the sofa from afar. Within that spatial reference, the girl in the striped tights was taking on an unusually important role. Her figure – the main target of my vigilance – appeared and disappeared, occasionally obscured by the different strata of heads that interposed themselves between us, just as the swaying branches of trees hide the tiny, hopeful, but possibly dangerous light in the strange house which the lost child in fairy tales, stopped in the middle of the woods, believes he has seen.

When I left her, intending to escape, I had wanted to erase myself at a stroke from her slender, uncertain memory, to possess the gift of invisibility, which everyone longs for when they find themselves in a jam, so that she would not even have seen me get up or heard me say goodbye, and only when she tried to speak to me again and failed to find me by her side would she have begun to question my existence as a real, known entity, as well as her feeling of perplexity at my absence – the aftermath of that suddenly vanished mirage. Now, though, watching her without being seen (because that was precisely what I was doing from my precarious watchtower), I looked in vain for some sign of perturbation, for she gave no indication of it at all. She didn't once look over at the bar, but she didn't seem particularly pensive or absorbed either, as you would expect in someone who believes themselves the victim of an hallucination and wants to reconstruct behind closed eyes an image seen in dreams, to go over the astonishing words she had heard, in order to tell her best friend later on and to feel herself the object of envy: "He was different, the sort of bloke *you*'d go for. He appeared out of nowhere and then he was gone. Do you know what he said to me?"

No, I don't know, what did he say?, because if you don't remember and don't even want to remember, I cease to exist. I need you to look over here, to give me a reason to tell you about my experience of transience, about my old dilemma about whether to run away or to stay; I need to hear myself say these things out loud so that someone else will remember, even though, afterwards, I have no idea what I said and even though, having said it, it weighs on my soul and leaves me feeling empty; I need you, forgetful girl in the striped tights; I have spent too much time on my own; tonight you are my counterweight, my geometry, please pick up the thread I throw out at random and which is as likely to become horribly snarled up as it is to become lost in a tangle of smoke signals, just blink a little, let me sense something of my presence in your interest for my whereabouts and in how I came to be cast up on these shores: who is he? which door did he leave by? what's become of him now? why can't I see him? Give me a moment's respite so that I can recompose myself, so that I can draw breath; I could tell you some marvellous lies, just you wait, because you don't know me, I'm an outsider and my mammoths will never be the same as your mammoths. The riddle begins with an L, like the *lis* in *flor de lis*; look this way, seek me out, O fickle young woman. The outsider with the nice, soft hair wants to play with you.

But she wasn't looking for me, she wasn't taking out her diary, she wasn't dreamily stroking the black raincoat that I had left with her as surety. She was no longer sitting crosslegged and, having rejoined her own group, she was now in a close embrace with the companion on her right, Clemente, the one who had sold me the hash.

From that distance, I couldn't tell whether she was accepting his embrace enthusiastically or as a matter of routine. She did allow it, though, just as she allowed his increasingly passionate caresses. And that evidence brought me to an enlightening conclusion which was confirmed when I looked away and studied other areas of the club, where, with utter spontaneity, similar scenes were taking place. For good or ill, I had spent more time without sex than the girl in the striped tights had and doubtless than any of the other young women there whom I could easily have tried to pick up. It didn't imply any inferiority, it was just something to bear in mind, and it would mark any amorous adventure, should I choose to embark on one, with an unfamiliar undertone, a mixture of hunger and caution. I evoked previous periods of my life when I had blithely let myself be swept up by the instantaneous intoxication of being liked by a woman, when love presented itself as an implacable state of violence and ecstasy, an unpostponable, unapologetic fire, when the gap between wanting and achieving one's desire was minimal.

However, the evocation of those scenes provoked no nostalgia in me, as one might have expected, only curiosity and a thirst for analysis which spurred me on. There doubtless exists some process of disenchantment, of maturity too, by which any astonishment at each new amorous experience would have gone spinning on until it burst forth simultaneously with an awareness of its own transience, along with the realization that the people who live alongside you are always emissaries of something else. I wondered when and how that ambition would be born in me, the ambition to distance myself from some object of desire and change it into something more controllable, into an object of meditation, a sliver of ice seeking its place in the jigsaw puzzle of Cold Reason, the game that froze the memories and emotions of Kay during his captivity in the Snow Queen's palace.

I remembered a lost beach in Tangiers, when I was just beginning to get into drugs. We had been barbecuing fish. There were a lot of people there, amongst them Javier and Ángela. We had taken blankets and had slept on the beach, all bundled up. I woke with the first rays of sun and I saw her, with her back to me, bathing naked. I started walking swiftly across the sand, in the opposite direction.

"If you start trying to trace the origins of your alienation from reality, you won't come across just one mammoth, you'll come across several," I said to myself, trying to make light of it.

Yes, it must have started earlier than that, before I was arrested, but prison, of course, had provided me with an ideal place in which to sublimate enforced abstinence into fantasies about infinity: breaking down the frontiers between the real world and the dream world, transforming, for example, a cell into the open sea. I had become a real expert in such exercises of sleight of hand, difficult to define and, to be frank, a complete waste of time.

"Pure fantasy, love, I could write a thesis on it, just as you could on the subject of men's hair," I thought as I directed one last look at the grubby sofa where my ideal interlocutor was now almost buried beneath Clemente – I don't know what rating she would have given his thick, black, curly hair. "Goodbye. The tendency for people to part is like a sort of natural cancer. A nice phrase for your friend Mónica, if you remember it. But remembering things isn't your strong point. Goodbye and thanks anyway. Have fun."

I didn't feel like becoming a second-rate voyeur, nor letting my breathing quicken; that's what porn movies are for. So, as nonchalantly as I could, I relinquished the wall I was leaning against and headed slowly for the staircase, although I was still not quite sure what my intentions were. My head felt clear, though, the way it does after a cold shower. It was comforting to have set a different course and to feel eager for alternative paths along which to explore that new thinking alone.

By the steps that led down to the toilets, the stairwell broadened out to house the cloakroom. It had a small imitation roof to it and the girl in charge, behind the counter, also sold cigarettes and tapes. She was talking to a grey-haired man, who was presumably a friend of hers, because they were laughing a lot. I went over and leaned one elbow on the far end of the counter. It was like a toy shop. The poetics of space had at last provided me with an example that night of a corner where I could seek refuge. I had read a lot of Bachelard while I was in prison, so much so that I had learned whole paragraphs by heart. It served me as a guide in my mental acrobatics.

"Any corner in a room, any small space where we feel tempted to curl up inside ourselves, provides a moment of solitude for the imagination, that is, it contains the seeds of a house. Ensconced in his corner, the dreamer remembers all the objects that accompanied him in his solitude, objects that are a souvenir of solitude. He sees again an older house, a house in another country. The corner becomes a store cupboard of memories."

That had happened to me in prison, in that cell where I would crouch to read words that formed a rope ladder, out through the bars, or a child's swing beneath the moon. And the dreamer would once more see an old house, always the same one; his prison cell was filled with the smell of the sea, of home cooking, of old books, and, from a picture that hung above a certain piano, a lady in a wide-brimmed hat would step out and stroll defiantly through my dreams; she would sit on my bed, a far more real and palpable presence than the red-haired girl who sometimes gazed at me through the pierced plastic screen in the visiting room, as if she herself were not entirely convinced of her own existence.

I wonder what happened to that engraving that always hung above the piano in the Quinta Blanca? The question came to me suddenly, the first sharp stab since I left the notary's house. I hadn't asked him what had happened to the furniture, whether or not the new owner had got rid of it. Of course, he would have shrugged his shoulders and, quite rightly, reminded me yet again that I was the one who had insisted on selling everything, and that the only thing I had wanted to keep had been my grandmother's bed. I clearly still had a lot of things to discuss with him, a lot; I needed to sit down and make a proper list of them. I had wasted quite enough time already.

"Can I help you?" the cloakroom girl asked. She was quite short and had her hair dyed a kind of mahogany red; she wore it in a spiky style that made her look rather like a porcupine. She must have been looking at me for some time without my realizing it, immersed as I was in my obsessions. Her friend had left.

"You wouldn't happen to have a pen, would you?"

"Nothing easier. Anyone would think you were asking for a Molotov cocktail."

"I mean, can you sell me a pen? I need one desperately."

"Here you are. I'll hire it out to you for free," she said, holding out a yellow biro.

"Thanks. And have you got something to write on too?"

"What do you mean something to write on? Whatever next. Will this card do?"

"It's a bit small. How about selling me that little notebook you've got there?"

"Of course, why didn't I think of it! Because I need it to keep my accounts in, that's why, but I'll tear you out a couple of pages. Will that be enough? Or are you planning to write a novel?"

"That's exactly what I am planning to do actually. But those two pages will do for now, thanks."

She watched as I leaned on the far end of the counter, noting down urgent messages for Don Octavio and for Casilda Iriarte whose name I had only just learned, but which was etched into my memory like a tattoo.

Suddenly, the idea of going home seemed like a liberation. I put the sheets of paper in my jacket pocket, returned the girl's biro and, when I went to thank her, I caught a knowing look in her smiling eyes. With her friendly, eccentric appearance, she reminded me of a mocking fairy sheltering in a hollow tree-trunk.

"Thank you, Puck. That's who you look like, Puck," I said. "Although you've got prettier ears. You know who Puck was, don't you?"

"Of course I do. I suppose now you're going to ask me if I've got the complete works of Shakespeare on me."

I burst out laughing.

"No, for now, I'll make do with a packet of cigarettes."

I waved to her from the foot of the stairs. We were friends.

When I reached street level, I stood for a few moments sheltering under the canopy that let in the reddish, intermittent glow of the neon sign. I took a deep breath. My mind was going like the clappers with all those fragments of stories flooding in. I was dreaming of an as yet blank notebook beneath the soft light of the green reading lamp. There were puddles in the street, although it wasn't raining now, and, at once, the memory of my raincoat – abandoned in the depths of the grotto – stood like an unexpected obstacle in the path of my escape – so nearly achieved – an obstacle that halted all further action. How often that happens in myths and legends, in fairy tales! Looking back or seeking wild, new paths, noticing landmarks along the road, deciding which way to go at a crossroads. The hero in the story always has to take the initiative in resolving his own dilemmas, no one can do it for him. And he has to act with both boldness and prudence.

And I thought of Gerda as if I were thinking of a friend who had become lost because of me, of that part of the story in which I sat behind her with my arms about her as the sledge carrying Kay to his perdition sped down the steep street. It was a scene as real as the barbecue on the beach in Tangiers, as real as my efforts to hold a conversation in the prison visiting room, or as the meetings in Enrique's house to listen to Patsy Cline records. Gerda had been very close to me during that journey, just before the arrival of the Snow Queen, so much so that I could feel her shoulders trembling. When we reached the square, though, I abandoned her in order to plunge into my own conjectures, and when I remembered her, it was already dark and she had left; all I embraced was a handful of snowflakes unravelling against a black backdrop – the archway through which Kay's sledge had disappeared yoked to that of the driver dressed all in white. And that was when I realized that distance can unite two unfortunate beings even more indissolubly than physical proximity. We were united – and are still united – by the desperation of our respective but utterly different searches, she in search of Kay, and I, without knowing it, in search of someone as brave as she was. Our voices touch but do not meet. My grandmother was right. The real adventure, the raison d'être of the story, lies in Gerda's tenacious search, which I found so hard to accept, in her refusal to listen to the siren songs that try to dissuade her and turn her from her path – the story is a true lesson in refusing to accept one's fate. And I smiled to remember that rich, unmistakeable voice: "It's very long, this part of the story, and you're determined to be bored because of your wretched impatience, but, believe you me, if you read it carefully, there's a lot of substance in it. In fact, what you need is another Gerda." I wonder what happened to that grey book? I've lost so many things in the crevices of the Quinta Blanca. I don't know if it can ever all be sorted out.

"Do you need a taxi?" asked the doorman who had obviously been watching me for a while, intrigued. "You'd be best off trying in the Gran Vía."

I was about to tell him that what I really needed was to make an inventory of lost objects and to reclaim them as soon as possible from a woman I had never even seen.

"Thanks, but I've got to go back in. I left my raincoat in there."

As I was going down the first illuminated steps, I heard him say:

"Well, it's no night to be out without a raincoat. Winter's on its way."

My step was now rhythmic and determined. My entrance into the club was not only different this time, the whole place was different, easier to cut a path through, more innocuous. The musicians were taking a break. I noticed that the blonde Patsy Cline impersonator was sitting on the bottom step of the stage, responding with evident ardour to the caresses of a dark, young man with thick, curly hair. It was Clemente. I walked past them and, as I approached the sofa, I saw that they were being watched intently, grim-faced, by the girl in the striped tights, who was so engrossed that she didn't even notice me there. While I silently recovered my black raincoat, she remained utterly still, despite the fact that I had to tug a little at the coat, because the belt had got trapped beneath her. I wasn't sure whether to say anything to her or not. She resolved my doubts for me.

"Are you leaving already?" she asked suddenly, without looking up at me.

"Yes. What's wrong?"

Close to, I saw that her eyes were full of tears.

"Oh, nothing," she said. "I'm better off keeping my mouth shut; the moment I open it, I put my foot right in it. What a bloody awful life this is! It's hard to know what to do for the best. My mother says that, in her day, people just accepted what they had and that, nowadays, because we want everything, we don't know what it is that we do want any more. Anyway," she concluded, getting up, "I'm leaving too. Do you mind if we leave together?"

"No, of course not, why should I?"

She paired up with me and as we passed the place where Clemente was still busy kissing the blonde girl, she looked away and took my arm. It seemed to me that he noticed the manoeuvre, but he didn't react.

Out in the street, she buttoned up her jacket. A low, damp mist now filled the air.

"It's been very nice meeting you," she said. "Can I drop you anywhere? Or, perhaps you'd like to come back to my place for a nightcap. I've got my moped with me. Over there."

She spoke in a dull, sad voice, as if nothing really mattered to her. I surprised myself by accepting her invitation with alacrity.

"Sure. Do you live very far?"

"No, not very."

"Let's go then. And cheer up."

Then, driving down the Gran Vía, my arms about her waist, my face wet with misty tears, I remembered Gerda again and I shivered. We were both very silent.

She stopped abruptly at a set of traffic lights, and turned her head a little.

"Are you OK?"

"Yes, fine, I love riding on mopeds."

"I'm glad. If you like, we can go for a spin."

"It's a bit cold, isn't it? But if you want to . . ."

"I don't know what I want, I'm very bad at making decisions."

"That makes two of us."

In the rearview mirror I saw that she was smiling at me.

"By the way, what's your name?"

"Leonardo."

"Mine's Almu, short for Almudena. Pleased to meet you. Hold tight, we're off."

The wind tangled our hair. I savoured once more the pleasure of being out of prison, the intense taste of freedom. At the Pompeya they were showing a Woody Allen film, *Manhattan*.

XIII

Mónica's luggage

It was a fourth-floor flat with no lift; the worn wooden staircase was cramped and steep. The door opened onto a rather narrow red-tiled corridor with rooms at either end. The rooms to the right were in darkness, the others were lit. I watched a suddenly angry Almu walk briskly towards that source of light – the source too of occasional bursts of music – not even bothering to see if I was following her or not, almost as if she had forgotten I was there. I closed the front door and waited, leaning against the wall. The music was Albinoni's "Adagio". All along the corridor there were bundles, books and untidy piles of clothes. A small white dog with black patches came to greet Almu and tried to leap up at her, wagging its tail excitedly. That seemed to make her disproportionately angry.

"Get down, Rosco!" she shouted. "And what, may I ask, is this animal doing here? I thought you said you were going to take it to your cousin's."

She had reached the room on the left and hesitated for a moment before going in. It was a double door with frosted glass. She pushed open the door that was standing ajar. The ochre-coloured paint was peeling off the wood, and it was edged with a fine golden strip of metal. The bolt with a rounded knob at one end was positioned exactly halfway down the door and was identical to one in the living room in the Quinta Blanca. This was the first time I had ever seen another one like it. Through the frosted glass I could see a woman's silhouette moving about, then she walked past the gap in the door, looked fleetingly at Almu and disappeared again. She was a dark young woman with long straight hair and very graceful movements. My recognition of the bolt and my tendency to fall in love with things glimpsed through unfamiliar doors cast me in one of my favourite roles, that of passionate detective. I spotted a black canvas folding chair leaning against the wall amongst the packages. I carefully opened it and sat down on it without making a sound. I was half-concealed by an elongated hat stand. With luck, they would forget about me.

Almu still had her back to me, peering in at that scene which was as yet unknown to me. The music had been turned down to a mere murmur. The dog rushed into the room again, brushing past the legs of the new arrival, who was becoming increasingly aggressive.

"Well, he's not staying with me a single day, do you hear! I've been telling you that for ages now and you take no notice. If your cousin doesn't come for him, I'll put him out in the street and he can fend for himself. You don't believe me? You don't know me then. What right have you got to come into my room like this, Mónica? Haven't you got a room of your own? You really are the limit."

"I'm sorry, but you told me you were going to sleep at Clemente's house," I heard the other woman say in a calm, modulated voice. "I was going to leave everything exactly as it was as soon as I'd finished, honestly. Anyway, why are you getting so worked up? I did ask you."

"You did?"

"Yes, when you were coming out of the shower, and you said that would be fine, you said what you always say: no problem; but then, of course, since you never remember anything . . ."

"I know, that's the problem," said Almu, her voice suddenly tired. "And I don't listen, I don't pay attention, that's why I'm in the state I'm in, I know."

"Oh, don't start whingeing, please, I've had a really tough day. I had a bit of a cry earlier on."

Almu's voice softened.

"Poor thing, I'm sorry. Is it because of your mother? Haven't you made it up yet?"

"No," came the brief reply, "but let's not talk about that now. The time's flown by and I'm in an almighty mess sorting out what I need from what I don't, that's the worst thing, and I've been on full alert since yesterday. See what you think. I'm leaving the books

I'm not taking with me in my room, as well as any clothes that you might be able to use. There's heaps of them, or rather two heaps. One for winter things and the other for summer things. We'll look at them later. For example, the famous green three-quarter-length coat is there."

"The green coat? Oh, you are sweet. Is that for me?"

Almu had gone into the room now, but you could still hear their voices clearly, Mónica's being the lower one.

"Yes, of course, and lots of other things too. Shoes as well. And handbags. Honestly, the things you accumulate. Come on, help me choose, or are you very tired? Tomorrow, I'll be leaving you in peace once and for all."

"You're going tomorrow? God, that's right. Oh, what a drag! I'm going to miss you so much."

"Well, I'd never have guessed."

"Fancy going all that way away."

"And don't worry about Rosco. Gerardo is taking me to the airport tomorrow in his car and he'll take Rosco with him then, that's what we've arranged. Come on, give me a hand getting this suitcase off the bed, it weighs a ton."

The phone rang in the room. Mónica again walked past the doors and turned the music off.

"It must be Clemente," she said. "He phoned earlier. Shall I get it?"

"He phoned? When? When? Tell me!"

"About five minutes ago. God, you're jumpy."

"And why didn't you tell me? Leave me on my own now, go on."

"I was going to tell you when you gave me a chance. Calm down, I'm leaving. It's not exactly fun listening to you two quarrelling. Come on, Rosco, out!"

The telephone stopped ringing and I heard a voice, half-sensual, half-mournful, saying "Hello?" Then I heard nothing more, because Mónica came out into the corridor, preceded by the dog, and closed the door. In her arms, she was carrying a sports bag overflowing with books. She started when she saw me sitting there behind the hat stand, and some of the books cascaded on to the floor, mainly those perched most precariously on the top. I found myself kneeling down and picking them up.

"God, you gave me a fright! Who are you? Did you by any chance come in with Almu?"

"Yes, purely by chance. But don't bend down, or all the others will fall off too. I'll get them for you, don't worry. Well, *The Fear of Freedom*, who'd have thought it!"

"Do you want it? It's one of the ones I'm leaving behind. I'm going away for a long time, did you know that?"

"Well, yes and no," I replied.

I'd stood up again with the books in my arms, and we were looking at each other. She had hazel eyes and was studying me with frank curiosity.

"What do you mean 'yes and no'? That sounds like a riddle."

"Well, it's one of those riddles that starts at the end. Yes, to the last question, I did know you were going away, and no to the first, because I've read Fromm's book before, many times. Thanks, though."

She smiled and started walking off to the right, signalling to me to follow. I obeyed. The dog went ahead of us.

"Me too," she said. "Too many times and now I think I'm about to lose a little of my freedom. That's why I'm leaving the book behind. I'm leaving a lot of other things that might interest you too. Come on, I'm having a bit of a clearance sale in here. Can you switch on that light, please?"

She pointed to a switch by a double door identical to the one opposite. I flicked it on and we went in.

The room, which was quite spacious, had two balconies that opened on to the street and, to the right of the door, there was a bedroom separated off by a half-drawn curtain. Mónica dumped the bag on the floor against the wall, then she went into the bedroom and continued talking to me from there, while she moved around in the somnambular light of a low-voltage bulb. The dog gambolled about her feet.

"Sit down, if you can find a place," she said, "I'll be right out. And take your time."

The room was sparsely furnished, nothing matched, and the whole place was in a state of turmoil. I put the books I'd picked up on a table, along with a lot of other things, and I sat down in an old office chair, one of those chairs that spin round and can be adjusted to different heights, doubtless a flea-market acquisition. I felt comfortable there. Sometimes, I would glance out into the street at the ghostly glow of the street lamps surrounded by mist and, at others, over at the half-concealed area where the young woman was struggling to bring order to a chaos I could not even begin to understand.

"I say take your time," she went on, "because when Almu starts talking on the phone to Clemente, well, you know what she's like."

I looked at her. Mónica had her back to me, bending over the bed folding up a few items of clothing. She had very nice legs.

"No," I said, "I hardly know her at all."

She turned round.

"That's typical of her, she's always bringing home people she hardly knows. Anyway, it's horrible. I've never known a couple like them; they only have anything to say to each other when they talk on the phone. If you see them together, it's like a film by Antonioni, all close-ups, silences and each of them looking the other way. The phone bills, though, are astronomical. I've no idea what they say to each other but, generally speaking, they seem to cultivate the gentle art of the insult."

She had returned to her task and there was a brief silence.

"Excuse me," I asked, "do you mind if I put this light on?"

"Of course not. For the moment, the room is still mine."

I turned it on and then I started rummaging about in the books scattered over the large table. Perhaps they belonged to the batch to be given away. There were books in English and French and a lot of literary criticism. There was a lot of philosophy too. Since it didn't look as if anyone was in much of a hurry, I drew the chair over to the table and passed the time leafing through some of the books. It was a very agreeable occupation, like being in a secondhand bookshop in a foreign country, with the owner sitting dozing and indifferent. As if she had exhausted all her information about Almu's possible delay, Mónica fell silent again, a silence interrupted only by Rosco scurrying around or by the noise of some object being moved to one side – a few dull, pleasant sounds that evoked a forgotten familiarity.

Quite a long time passed and I was enjoying the pleasure of reading in the presence of someone who doesn't bother you. It was a quiet, shared peace, as if we had known each other all our lives.

It was rather like dancing with someone to whom you've just been introduced and noticing that you immediately fit smoothly together, something that usually only happens after long hours of rehearsal.

Mónica was in the habit of carefully underlining certain paragraphs in pencil and noting down her own thoughts in the margin. I soon came to recognize her small, neat writing, because the same writing was repeated over and over. And I contrasted that penchant of hers for taking notes about what she read with the generosity shown in her readiness to give her books away. I noticed a quote written across the upper corner of a chapter: "Memories are sacred time. Pilgrimages through places that evoke memories (especially if undertaken alone) have a purifying, renewing effect on the soul."

There were blank sheets of paper amongst the sea of books on the table, and there was a pen too. I copied out that quote and then a few others that she had underlined in the text. The book was *The Sacred and the Profane* by Mircea Eliade. Clara, the girl in Verona, the one who found disorderly dates so bothersome, had given it to me in an Italian translation. It's odd how things tie up sometimes! And, as she used to say, it's always a thread of words that binds them together. When all else is lost, there is no other thread. I lost that book. In my neurotic desire to travel light, my belongings have been left scattered the length and breadth of a variety of countries, but, as I discover every day with growing unease, those attempts at a diaspora have their price. Inevitably – interrupting my feeling of well-being – the memory of all those orphaned objects resurfaced, all those objects in the Quinta Blanca, abandoned without a thought. I reimmersed myself in Mircea Eliade's words.

"Settling in a particular territory is tantamount to making it sacred – placing yourself."

I was just writing that down, when I suddenly felt Mónica behind me, but I went on writing, feeling no embarrassment whatsoever, as if I were alone.

"You've got lovely handwriting," she remarked.

"So have you. I assume it was you who wrote the notes."

"Yes, but don't bother writing anything down. The books in that pile are for whoever wants them, as well as the ones in the bag I was carrying, now where did I leave that? Ah yes, there it is, look, against the wall. Just take whatever you want. *Ad libitum.*"

"I really like the fact that you're so unpossessive. It's quite rare. Are you like that in love too?"

"Well, in love, it depends," she smiled. "But books are to be read, not to be treasured and then left to gather dust. The people who are keenest on keeping them and counting them are the ones who are least bothered about what they say, wouldn't you agree?"

"Absolutely. You have to make what they say your own and weave it into your own life, when what they say is worth it, of course. You start to create a symbiosis between what you've read and what you live and think; it can be quite frightening sometimes. A book then is like the grave of someone you've loved. You can go and put flowers there, but it's no use. The person's soul isn't there, it hovers over the places where it left its seed – inside ourselves."

I was staring out at the balcony. The mist had grown thicker. How many hours had passed since I started remembering my grandmother's funeral while I was in the notary's waiting room? It seemed incalculable to me. What a long, complicated journey! At last, though, I had found a welcoming inn.

Mónica placed her hands on my shoulders.

"I'd really like to write down what you've just said too. It's a shame I'm so tired. Where did you meet Almu, if you don't mind my asking?"

"In the Gran Vía. In a club called 'Go like the clappers'. Sorry, the name's not my idea."

She burst out laughing.

"I shouldn't think it was. You're unlikely to find much sacred territory, the sort that Eliade talks about, in a place with a name like that."

"Probably not, but you know, if you want to, you can learn from almost anything. In the end, I took shelter beneath a kind of little roof, next to a girl selling matches who had read Shakespeare, and my mind just took off. Unfortunately, I didn't have a notebook with me, which reminds me . . . ," I added, patting my pockets. "Of course, I didn't have my raincoat on then! Do you mind if I take it off."

"Not at all. What are you looking for?"

"Nothing, a few bits of paper. I've got them here in my jacket. The things you've just written down always seem terribly important, don't you find?"

"Sometimes," said Mónica.

And she yawned. I saw her cast a weary, distracted eye over the disorder on the large table.

"Do you know what time it is?" she asked.

"Yes, it's a quarter past one."

"Well, I'm shattered. I'm going to lie down for half an hour. I just can't stay on my feet a moment longer. Don't leave, though, not if you don't want to. It's nice to have company."

I thought it odd that she should refer to my future presence in that house without even mentioning Almu's name, as if that particular reference point had vanished, and I had become her guest instead.

"Are you sure I'm not in your way?"

"On the contrary, you're making it much easier to say goodbye. I've been very much on my own all day. Before you set off on a long journey, you always feel full of fears, doubts and thoughts that sour your decision. Well, I won't tell you about the minor battle I've been fighting, but it's rather like dying a little, do you know what I mean? Anyway, I feel better with you here. I may not even sleep, we'll see. And I'm delighted to have you rummaging around amongst my books. You could try talking to me now and then if you like. Aren't you sleepy?

"No, but I'd be happy to watch over you while you sleep."

She still hadn't removed her hands from my shoulders, and I was becoming used to having her close, to her smell. Every now and then I looked up at her, not daring to ask her to move, and not daring to move myself, afraid that something, what I didn't know, might break.

There was a silence and she bent towards my ear.

"It's almost as if heaven had sent you," she murmured.

Then she moved away from me, tore a leaf out of a small pink notebook and started drawing. I got up from the revolving chair and gave her my place, which she accepted with a smile. I stood close by, watching her, my hands resting on the table, leaning over her slightly. She had slender white fingers with short nails and she wielded the pencil with skill and confidence. Gradually, the silhouette of an angel reading a book appeared. She took special care over the veins in the wings and the little lines that represented the words in the book. Underneath, she wrote in English: "The farewell angel". She sat looking at it for a moment and then held it out to me.

"Here you are. Keep it along with your other bits of paper," she said. "I assume you know English."

At that moment, the door flew open and Almu appeared.

She clearly was not heaven-sent. On the contrary, her contorted face revealed the unmistakeable signs of her own private hell. Almost without looking at us, her voice quavery with tears, she announced from the door:

"I'm going to Clemente's house. I've got no option."

Mónica got up, went over to her and put an arm around her shoulders.

"But, what's wrong?" she asked affectionately. "What do you mean you've got no option, why not? It's always the same old story. Have you two had another row?"

Almu nodded, staring at the floor, looking downcast.

"Then why go?" Mónica insisted. "Honestly, you drive me to despair. It's as if you enjoyed suffering. Tell him to go to hell."

"Don't get angry with me. He hung up on me and I can't bear him having the last word. That's why I'm going. To tell him to leave me alone, that he's a complete bastard."

"Yes, and then you'll end up spending the night there. We've been through all this before."

Almu, who had calmed down a bit, looked at her watch.

"Well, we'll see. It depends how late it gets. When are you leaving?"

"Not again! You know very well that I'm leaving tomorrow at midday."

"Don't worry, I'll definitely be back before then. I couldn't not be."

"That isn't what worries me. All I mean is, instead of always saying to each other 'leave me alone', why don't you just do exactly that: leave each other alone. You need to take drastic action, there's no other way. Anyway, if he hung up on you, it must be because he doesn't want to see you. He might be in a really foul mood when you get there."

"No, he won't be. I know him, and I know he's expecting me. Things aren't that simple, Mónica, I was really horrible to him too. I need to see him. Talking helps."

"But you never talk! Oh well, it's up to you. I haven't got the energy to nag you just now. I haven't got room for any more of your stories, Almu. I'm up to here with it all. I just feel very, very fragile."

"You're right, poor thing. Your life will be so peaceful without me. I'm always getting you involved in my problems, and then, when it comes to it, I'm never there for you when you need help."

Mónica rubbed her eyes and yawned again.

"OK, Almu, no speeches, please. If you've got to go, go, but at least say goodbye to your friend."

For the first time, Almu glanced at the table I was leaning on, as if putting two and two together. Then she looked back at Mónica. She seemed disconcerted.

"Hey," she said, "do you two already know each other?"

"Yes, Mircea Eliade introduced us."

"Who?"

"You wouldn't know him. He's a Rumanian professor."

Almu's voice grew suddenly warmer.

"Isn't that a coincidence, and I was just saying to him, wasn't I, that I've got a friend he'd get on really well with. Didn't I say that?" she added, looking at me.

"Yes, you did, and you were right too."

She gave a theatrical sigh of satisfaction.

"That's a bit of luck, then, because I never really get on with anyone. You don't mind if I leave you here with her, do you? If not, I can drop you off somewhere on my bike."

"Don't worry, really. I'm fine here."

She came over to the table and kissed me on the cheek.

"See you soon then. And sorry."

"Don't worry. I hope you have better luck and that things turn out all right for you."

"Yeah, yeah. For that to happen, I'd need to begin my whole life over again and even then . . ."

"Come on, don't start," said Mónica, pushing her towards the corridor.

They went out together and stood for a while outside, whispering to each other, while I studied the angel that Mónica had drawn on the pink sheet of paper. Underneath it I wrote the date. I don't know why. Perhaps as a homage to my friend Clara, to all those other things that have been lost and forgotten, to everything that is jumbled, broken, incomprehensible, to the Madrid night, to hieroglyphs in general.

When I heard the front door close, I got up and went to find Mónica. She was leaning against the wall in the corridor with her eyes closed, as if her head were spinning. I went over to her and I saw that she was crying.

"Do you feel faint?"

She pushed her hair back and stood away from the wall, roughly wiping away her tears with her hand.

"A bit. Poor Almu. She's so crazy. Well, generally speaking," she sighed, "we're all so crazy. It's as if we were tied to a water wheel that kept going faster and faster. It's frightening. It gives you vertigo, yes, vertigo. One day, we're all going to crash."

I took her hand and we went back into the room. She let me lead her as if she really were at the very limit of her strength.

"It's best not to think about that now. Go on, lie down for a while; you're worn out. Can I help in any way?"

"I don't know. I just feel terribly deflated all of a sudden. And I'm so cold!"

We had stopped by the curtain half-concealing the bedroom. Now

I could see more clearly the chaos that reigned in there. I looked at Mónica and understood the reason for her depression.

"It's awful," she said. "You get invaded by things. The more you get rid of, the more there is, and they're all demanding their rights, demanding attention. I feel like setting fire to the whole lot. Honestly, I don't know where to start."

"Shall we start by clearing the bed? That seems to me the number one priority if you want to lie down for a bit."

"Yes, but the problem is, where are you going to put the stuff. You can see what a mess it is. And Almu's room is just the same. Packed to the ceiling."

"Come on, don't panic, we can just put anything that's in the way on the floor. It won't go anywhere."

I went into the room with her and helped her to clear the bed of clothes and packages. She flopped down on the rumpled bedspread, gave a deep sigh and covered her face with one arm. She didn't move or say anything. I took off her shoes and then covered her with a check blanket that I'd seen draped over an armchair. It was almost impossible to move without bumping into something. Rosco jumped up and lay at her feet.

"Shall I turn out the light?" I asked after a brief pause.

When she didn't answer, I went slowly over to her, although it seemed odd to me that she should have gone to sleep immediately. A kind of rainless storm was shaking her, sending brief spasms through her body, as if the storm had not quite broken. I sat down by her side, and she immediately put her hand on mine. I squeezed it.

"I'm afraid," she said in a faltering voice.

"Of leaving?"

"Yes, and of staying too. I feel both those fears pulling me in different directions. It's hard to explain."

"You don't need to. It happens to me every time I leave a place. It has ever since I was a child. But then, when you grow up, it gets worse, precisely because you try to explain it to yourself, and you go over and over it, instead of just letting it pass of its own accord, by allowing yourself to sleep or cry. If you can, of course."

She sighed, then yawned, and the trembling in her body stopped. There was a long silence. We sat there holding hands. I noticed a poster on the opposite wall. It showed two women's heads, both wearing a bathing cap. They were in profile and were, in fact, the same woman looking at herself. Their mouths were joined by a giant bubble of pink gum.

"The thing is, I'm going a long, long way away and for a very long time," said Mónica. "My mother is angry with me; she says I'll regret it. Earlier on, I phoned her to say goodbye and she hung up on me."

"She'll be the one to regret that. What matters is that you want to go. You do, don't you?"

"I don't know. Do you know that book *Peter Schlemihl*, about the man who lost his shadow?"

"Yes, I do."

"Well, that's what I'm like, like that character in Chamisso's novel. My shadow is lost somewhere in my childhood, in some trees that swayed while my mother sang to me. It's a story that has no solution, however hard you look for one. Living without a shadow gives you vertigo."

She had curled up beneath the blanket and was talking in a very low voice, as if to herself.

"But the feeling of vertigo only lasts a short while," I said. "The cure is to sleep. Don't think about anything, don't worry about anything any more. Do you want me to recite you a poem?"

She nodded with her eyes closed. Her breathing was more regular now and rhythmic, like that of a child about to fall asleep.

I concentrated, trying to remember. Clara had recited it to me on the evening when we sat outside the church of San Zeno. It appeared in a book I bought later on, when I began to miss her; another book that got lost. It was a poem by Cavafy. I began reciting it very slowly, in that chaotic, ill-lit room, as if it were a lullaby for the memory. I didn't know to whom I was dedicating it, probably, as usual, to myself. I split into two profiles facing each other, trying to inflate the bubble of the night, to put one more patch on it.

When you start on your journey to Ithaca,
then pray that the road is long.
To arrive there is your ultimate goal,
But do not hurry your journey at all.

I paused, suspecting that I had left some lines out. I couldn't remember any more. Mónica let out a groan of pleasure.

"You don't feel like crying any more, then?"

She shook her head. She was smiling sleepily.

"And what about you?" she asked after a while, still not opening her eyes, in a voice so muffled I could barely understand it.

"Me? No, of course I don't. Farewell angels never cry or sleep. I'll be out here, making a shadow out of your old dreams to go with you on your journey to Ithaca. I'll sew it to your feet; that way the story will have a happy ending. It may only be a temporary repair, because everything in this world is temporary, but you can enjoy what is ephemeral too, don't you think?"

She didn't reply. She had fallen asleep.

I sat looking at the confusion in the room with a marked sense of unreality. Yet I was also absolutely certain that, for the first time in a very long while, I was in the right place and had said the right thing. It doesn't often happen. And I sighed, feeling pleased. It seemed odd even to me that I had been capable of offering sweet consolation to a desperate soul, and even odder that it had come so naturally to me. I stood for a while longer watching her sleep, with the dog at her feet, and I waited quite a while before I dared remove my hand that had remained trapped beneath hers. She stirred slightly and, in her dreams, murmured: "Peter". I switched off the light and tiptoed to the room with the books in it. It was ten past two in the morning.

I lit a cigarette. I was filled with a new energy and I felt much calmer and more lucid than at any other moment of that long, strange night of wanderings. It had been like a long pilgrimage! One by one, I started reliving each episode, each eddy – as if wanting to decipher them – now that they were all threaded harmoniously together in my memory like beads on a necklace.

What I didn't know was that I still lacked the diamond clasp that would fasten the necklace, for shortly afterwards, searching in the bag for some interesting book to take away with me as a souvenir of my time spent with Mónica, one book surfaced encircled by tongues of fire, the mere sight of which made my heart beat so fast it frightened me. I was crouching over the bag at the time and I had to sit down on the floor, take a few deep breaths and lean back against the wall. "It's not possible," I murmured, "it's just not possible." I had closed my eyes, but I was still holding the book in my hand, and when the feeling of dizziness had passed a little, I opened my eyes again to look at it once more. I was afraid I had been the victim of an hallucination, but no.

On the cover was a reproduction of one of my favourite paintings by Friedrich, "Traveller looking over the sea of mist". The book was entitled *Essays on Vertigo* and the author was Casilda Iriarte. It was doubtless something that the night owed to me. I picked it up, wrote Mónica a note of farewell, put my raincoat on and went out into the street.

XIV

Attacks of vertigo

The slide from normality into decline can happen in what seems like the winking of an eye. I learned from certain novels – particularly the novels I most like – the fact that ruin does not give you any advance warning, that you are the one who has to be perpetually on guard, so as not to be too surprised when it happens, that is, when you wake up in the morning and find every corner of the room invaded by rodents and beetles, when words sound like gunshots, when no one can be bothered to open the blinds, do the dishes, pick up the broken glass, give shelter to the pilgrim, call the police or to keep the books, barely glanced at, from piling up on the floor and gradually blocking off all access, until they form a geography as capricious and inaccessible as certain mountain ranges.

But you must realize that this danger also brings with it its exact opposite and all the demands which that implies, because, when you think about it, is it worth it, as an antidote against future ills, to accustom yourself to keeping guard, with the obsessive tenacity of a sentinel, in order to defend your one cubic metre of identity from the onslaught of objects, places and meteorological accidents?

I've made a start by getting rid of Pilar. I did so several days ago and already I've begun to notice that everything is dirtier and colder, that this house is much too big, and that it is into these closed rooms – which, before, I had tacitly left to her care – that anxiety surreptitiously creeps, spreading along unknown pipes, like air that rarefies the air in the other rooms.

My mother would have liked Pilar. Indeed, I think she does like her and considers my sending her away just like that to be a waste, one of my many blunders, because the truth is she gave me no reason to dismiss her.

"She's refined. She's a refined, discreet woman. You should try to get her to stay on permanently, you've been luckier than I ever was. Haven't you noticed how clean she leaves the kitchen? She never gets phone calls and she doesn't eat very much. Plus, she shows initiative. That's the most important thing, that she should show initiative. Just remember how it was when she first came here. You really should buy her a uniform or, rather, two. One for cleaning and another one in black with a satin apron and a lace collar, for when she opens the door, because, one day, you'll have to start inviting people round. Besides, in the trunk in the storeroom there are lots of maids' uniforms. One of them is bound to suit her. You know how many servants we've had through here and I never was one for throwing anything away. The fact of the matter is she looks pretty good, and she's the perfect age, about forty-five I'd say. The way she walks and the way she presents herself remind me of Andrea, the one from Burgos, who started work here as a cook and then became my personal maid, do you remember, Leo?"

My mother usually talks to me about domestic problems just after I've turned out the light and I'm searching for a comfortable position in which to fall asleep. I never answer her. If I did, I would be obliged to remind her that Andrea lasted less than a year in the house and that the main charge against her, as Andrea herself confessed to me, was that she showed too much initiative – "I have too many ideas, she says, as if that were a sin". After I reached a certain age, some servants in my house used to tell me their problems and, behind my mother's back, we would address each other as "tú". And I would also have to remind her – which would be no fun at all – of her failure, generally speaking, in trying to mould the perfect servant, while dismantling along the way the fallacy of her supposed gifts as lady of the house since, according to her code, surrounding oneself with efficient and well-uniformed servants was the main factor in keeping a firm grip on the reins of a household.

I close my eyes and pretend to be asleep until she gives up and I stop hearing her voice. I don't enjoy having to humiliate the dead. Besides, even if I did manage to convince her of something, which seems most unlikely, there's nothing to be done about it now.

But her opinion may have sensitized me to the increasing discomfort that Pilar's silent presence provoked in me, like a pulling of invisible strings, restoring a dull gleam to the house bought by Walter Scribner. Pilar was the servant of Walter Scribner's daughter, whom she consulted and wanted to please, she was the one for whom Pilar did the accounts and took bedspreads and curtains to the drycleaners. The only way I could stop the process was by asking her to leave.

My own domestic incompetence strips the house of any vain pretensions at homeliness and, with that temporary varnish now cracked and peeling, the house sometimes has the feeling of being somewhere simply to hole up in, the very feeling that made me inhabit it in quite a different manner during the now distant scene of my arrival in the garden and my encounter with Maurício Brito. He was a distinctly mysterious person, incidentally, especially since it is hard to imagine how my mother put up with him for three whole years, as I believe he said. Of course, he may have been making it all up. And yet, I'm deeply grateful to him. My vehement desire to write springs from the conversation I had with him that night. He had left saying: "The sun rises on even the darkest night." A good introduction to a fairy tale.

Pilar was a great help, but she was also a protective dyke that would crumble just before I began to think of her as indispensable. It was lucky that I spotted it in time.

I told her that I was going on a journey, that I might call her when I came back. She shrugged.

"A change of air would do you good," she said. "It always does."

It was a remark that revealed neither affection, reproach nor even curiosity. We did not relate to each other as human beings, and it was clear that it would continue to be like that. I paid her off lavishly. We said goodbye with a cold shake of the hands. I'm sure that she would have played to perfection the role of maid to a refined household, the kind my mother so admired in drawing-room comedies. What I'm going to say will sound odd, even to myself, but I'm sure I'm right. Pilar and my mother got on very well, they complemented each other, they were made for each other, precisely because they never had any actual dealings with one another, as when you fall in love with a character in a novel. That's all. I refused to take advantage of a *fait accompli* they were handing to me on a plate.

Do I miss her? I don't think so. And yet, I must admit that she did dispel my fears and soothe my disquiet. Now that she's gone, the conflict between actor and scenery grows more pronounced and I'm left with an overwhelming feeling of wrongness, pointlessness. What has become painfully clear is that this house was never mine nor am I going to make it mine by edict, although, for the moment, I remain holed up in it, imprisoned, as if I were the victim of some gruesome siege.

I haven't slept for several nights and I've started having hallucinations again. I must confess, though, that I am the one who feeds those hallucinations and that I enjoy watching the walls separating fiction and reality come crashing down again. More conscious than ever of its own limitations, thought refuses to accept them; it hurls itself on them and demolishes them, though it knows full well what disasters may be incurred in the attempt. It's like suffering a relapse of some old, devastating illness from which I was recovering really well, and which now, by contagion, grows worse.

This time, moreover, I know perfectly well where the contagion comes from. I also know, at the same time and with equal certainty, that that "where" is neither spatial nor temporal, neither false nor real, but a mixture of all that and more, many more things, of everything contained in a book that I have already read three times, that has become grafted onto my mind and whose subject is vertigo. Because the "where" coincides with the geography of that book and with the unstable cardinal points indicated by its winds and tides. My delirium is rocked by the murmur of what those winds and tides alternately show and conceal. A while ago, I wrote in one of the margins: "At last, a book touched by the sea!"

I spend hours on end during the night drawing fantastic landscapes that have just been shaken by an earthquake. The sea invades the woods, surrounds the buildings, drowns the permanent inhabitants of the area, casts them out. Ancient animals with mermaid tails or walrus tusks appear in cracks and on balconies, warships have run aground on the roof tops alongside flowerpots planted with box trees, and the corridors of skyscrapers have become navigable; they burst and vomit forth cascades of water and mud. The rubble dragged along by each cataract cracks the walls, leaves them peppered with shrapnel. And from a battered balcony on the Chrysler Building someone is distributing pamphlets in praise of vertigo. The figure always has his back to me, and in other versions has disappeared completely, having hurled himself into the void. He is wearing a jacket. I try to imitate (in deliberately distorted form) Friedrich's "Traveller looking over the sea of mist".

It's a long time since I threw myself into drawing in such a convulsive, continuous way. I paint some of the better sketches with watercolours. And above, below or in the centre, there is always a streamer, a flag, a cloud or a piece of foliage, which all contain fragments from Casilda Iriarte's book in tiny, neat writing that contrasts with the reigning chaos. The work absorbs me completely as something necessary and done entirely for myself. Earlier, I spoke of the book being grafted onto my mind. I expressed myself badly I think. It is more as if the book scattered seeds that demanded to be fertilized; it's closer to what I feel when I try to write than when I sit down to read. It isn't just a matter of identifying with someone else's text, as has often happened to me, it's that the text is mine; I feel as if I were giving it form, as if I were writing it even as I read it, and I realize how much I have had to strip away in order for that to happen. It's a provisional text, because it isn't closed, it changes and asks questions and roars like the sea. It has carried on what I began, it replaces me. And on the other hand, it has a tremendous amount to do with what I have become since I was born.

It is, of course, very odd and it does give me vertigo. It's like standing right underneath a very tall building in a crowded street and looking up, with your head right back, your eyes fixed on the distant, travelling clouds up above the pointed summit that is also moving, at the same time feeling the people brushing past behind you, pushing you in different directions. You end up not knowing who is moving and who isn't, where the outside begins and where the inside ends, where anyone is going, far less yourself. It happened to me once in Brasília; I was experimenting, and they had to pick me up off the pavement. Well, I've never actually been to Brasília. It must be something that happened to Casilda Iriarte, but the vertigo is mine.

I let time pass like waves over my motionless, rapt, absorbed body, making no decisions, merely asking myself now and then, as if I were dreaming: when did I write this? how is it that I can't remember having written it? Perhaps that is why I'm so keen to see it written down in my own handwriting, to see if I can remember.

The use of watercolours has added an extra element of confusion and stickiness to the desk in the study, where, alongside my brushes, there are also empty yoghurt pots and fruit peel. Yesterday, I spotted an ant.

When I woke up this morning, it was snowing. I knew it even before I looked out of the window; you can tell by that special silence that the snow leaves behind when it has fallen heavily during the night. Perhaps Gerda, mounted on a reindeer, is about to arrive in order to rescue Kay. Kay is in the hall of the huge castle, trying to fit together symmetrical pieces of flat ice in search of a word he cannot make: the word "eternity". The Snow Queen said to him, before leaving on an inspection of the volcanic lands: "If you ever manage to make that word, you will be master of yourself and I will give you the whole world. I'll also buy you a new pair of skates." And he has been left alone and thoughtful, condemned to play the Game of Cold Reason that one always plays alone, without any visible companion, obsessed by one's own icy calculations. Gerda is about to arrive mounted on a reindeer. But he doesn't know that. How can he know it, if he has lost all memory of his origins? In my drawing, he is kneeling down, one hand on his forehead and the other moving the icy pieces of his jigsaw puzzle. His hair is dishevelled and his eyes wild and cold. Since that is very difficult to show, I draw a black eye-mask on him and fill it in with Indian ink. I colour his cheeks blue.

There is an almost imperceptible murmur, like the rustle of a curtain opening, and I feel someone behind me, just as when I was copying out quotes from the book by Mircea Eliade and Mónica came over to me and we started talking without looking at each other. It *is* Mónica, although, this time, she hasn't placed a hand on my shoulder. I hold my breath. She says that I'm very good at drawing too, as if she wanted to return the compliment after all these days or to discover a further affinity between us. For the moment, I don't make her say anything else, because I can only vaguely remember the sound of her voice and I don't want what emerges from her mouth to sound false. Perhaps she's comparing the masked figure of Kay emerging from my pencil with her drawing of the "farewell angel". I found it in the pocket of the jacket that Pilar pressed for me before I went to Don Octavio's house; the jacket is buried now beneath the pile of clothes, papers and sundry objects that take up the whole of the large armchair. The angel was, by then, in a very wrinkled state, poor thing, next to a half-empty packet of cigarettes, and I very carefully smoothed out the bit of pink paper until the face of the disinterred angel began to blur. Now I have it pinned up prominently on the wall along with three of my drawings of exploded skyscrapers, the ones I think have turned out best. The others I put in a file, on which I've written "Attacks of vertigo"; the failures I immediately screw up into a ball and throw into the wastepaper bin on the other side of the table. Or, rather, they don't go directly into the bin, because the bin is filled to overflowing and they don't always find a place. It would be a good idea to empty it. Sometimes they skim the surface like war planes, dragging down in their fall any protruding bits of paper. As a result, the floor is now scattered with crumpled paper balls. Some open as they fall, like wounded beings convulsed in agony, and from their folds appear the jaws of sea monsters.

"This room is beginning to look like yours," I say to Mónica. "You were quite right, objects do invade one. It's odd how scenes sometimes repeat themselves, isn't it? I don't know how you managed to get here making so little noise. The snow must have a muffling effect."

I speak cautiously, tentatively. I stop. I can't force her to say anything, only the essential. I sense that if I try to call up a response which will lend colour to that lost voice, I must be daring and say something more affectionate to her, as I did when I tried to help her go to sleep, and with notable success. Of course, the main attraction was Mónica's plea for shelter, her physical nearness, her touch. I concentrate on evoking that gesture of her reaching out her hand and me squeezing it, her sobbing like a helpless child, wrapped up in a blanket. "I'm afraid," she said. "I'm cold. I feel as if I had vertigo."

"And you and I," I add, "we grow more and more like each other too. You've no idea how much I miss you. Even I find it strange."

"Yes, it is strange," she says. "And we were together for such a short time. When I woke up, I thought it had all been a dream."

This time she sounds better, more attuned to the tentative desires of my nostalgia. I take special delight in the phrase "we were together", because it's so ambiguous. Perhaps, when she woke up, when I had already gone, Mónica did look for me beside her in the bed, believing that I had lain down with her. What a disturbing thought, if that were true! I don't want to dispel the thought either, because, ever since that night, it has fed many of my most pleasant daydreams.

"It's not so very odd, if you think about it," I say. "I haven't actually seen you since, but I've seen your handwriting, which is familiar to me now; I've read your comments, often so like my own. That brings people together; it means that a friendship remains unbroken, don't you think?"

My voice creates solitary volutes that are lost in the upper air. I am Kay, looking distractedly at the ice pieces that won't fit together, and while I draw his numb hands, I think how much I would like to feel Mónica's hands stroking my neck, covering my eyes, pulling me gently over to the sofa which would first have to be cleared of the clutter of papers and notebooks. And I would just let myself be led.

"You've seen my handwriting?" she asks, bemused. "Where? I don't recall having written to you."

"In the book. It's so full of your notes that sometimes I can't fit mine in, and so yours and mine intertwine. I have to make a space for my writing in spirals that obscure yours. I know it's not the same as feeling someone's arms around you, but it's similar. My writing and yours proliferate, embrace, like infinite branches that invade the whole area and overflow it, because the text is so provocative and so powerful that it does with you what it will, it's like a wellspring of pure water. It was the lack of space that inspired me to do the drawings I've been working on. The scene is nearly always a sea that bursts into and floods enclosed spaces. Well, the room I'm drawing now has nothing to do with that. Today, the snow has made me forget that story and remember another, one of Hans Christian Andersen's stories that my grandmother used to tell me. This boy is Kay. He's turned out quite well. I've given him a mask because he's lost his memory."

"But what book were you talking about before?" asks Mónica. "I'm getting confused. I don't understand."

"It's a book I picked up at your house, in that bag you'd left by the wall. I'll show it to you now."

I start looking for Casilda Iriarte's book amongst the general disorder on the table; I discover something that upsets me and with a clumsy movement of my hand I overturn an open inkpot on to my drawing of Kay. The figure remains entirely submerged beneath a thick, black lake. It was Indian ink. I get up and look for a rag or something and, naturally, Mónica isn't there. But I go on talking out loud, this time to Kay, while I dab at the drawing with some old rags, which immediately become stained with black. The confused outline of the boy can be seen beneath the stain, like a foetus.

"Poor Gerda won't find you, even if she does come. It obviously wasn't her day, or yours, nor mine; still, there's nothing to be done about it."

I make a bundle with the rags and the ruined paper and I throw it all into the wastepaper bin. Inevitably, it falls on to the floor and doubtless it will be staining that too, but I don't care.

Casilda Iriarte's book was hidden underneath a series of letters and papers that I removed from the safe. They contain clues that would make your hair stand on end. I don't want to talk about that now, but my heart turned over when I saw them again; that's why I spilled the ink and got distracted from what I was looking for. What was it? Too many things all at once. Ah yes, my affinities with Mónica. Right on the very page where the book is open, I see her small writing filling one of the margins.

"Now do you remember the book I was telling you about? Let's read what you've written here. You tend to talk a lot about Romanticism. Forgive me if my voice sounds sad. It's because I know that you won't be able to answer me. The note says 'It doesn't matter what I do now, what decisions I take, because although I don't understand where they come from, those decisions come from before, from another life. The infinite sea unfolds and those waters have burst, booming, into other caves. To create a world in which the I, worn out and wounded by its continuous contact with reality, can expand and live a different life: that is the first impulse of the romantic soul.'

You too are moved by the sea. I would love to be looking at it with you right now on one of those wild coasts in the north. And with her too. The three of us together. Although I'm beginning to feel rather afraid of her. Don't ask me why. It's a complicated story; I'm not very clear about it myself. Anyway, let's leave it."

I pick up the book and a notebook and I go over to the sofa. Sighing, I remove the impedimenta filling it and I wrap myself in a blanket, ready to continue taking notes. The disaster with my drawing of Kay makes me decide to do something else.

I write in the notebook: "I have difficulty in continuing to believe that Mónica came and spoke to me. It doesn't work. I abandon the attempt. It keeps getting interrupted by the other papers about vertigo that my father kept and the ones in Sila's handwriting, or, rather, Casilda's handwriting, since they are one and the same. That was the secret. How did I guess? I still can't quite get my head round it, but it is as obvious as it is surprising. The lighthouse keeper's granddaughter leapt into the air and became superimposed on the other one, the one who has usurped the Quinta Blanca and who writes books that I could have written. The two of them have flooded into me simultaneously like an irresistible tide, together, transformed into one. I must develop the theme of metamorphosis. Up until now, the phenomenon of one person becoming transformed into another had only ever happened to me in dreams. It's like a horror movie, like doing battle with a two-headed monster. In literary terms, it could prove very fruitful. I must try to calm down."

I close my eyes and my teeth start to chatter.

"I feel as if I had vertigo; I feel cold," I say. "I don't know what to do with all this anxiety. We're going to crash, that's what you said, Mónica. If I continue at this speed, we're going to crash. I've got such a headache!"

But I realize that I'm saying this to no one. Only the silence of the snow surrounds me. I snuggle down into the blanket and, gradually, sleep overwhelms me.

The book carries an epigraph: "What tempts me and draws me into the unknown is the power of the sea . . . My mind – my thoughts – my dreams and longings – those you cannot imprison. They strain to roam and hunt – out into the unknown – which I was born for . . ." (Henrik Ibsen, *The Lady from the Sea*).

Although it took me a while to link Ibsen and the lighthouse keeper's granddaughter (my head was too full of recent coincidences), I stumbled across that quotation from *The Lady from the Sea* in the taxi that brought me home that night from Mónica's house. It was like the disquieting crack that opens up before the lost child in stories, and which may perhaps lead to the definitive cave of knowledge: "Dare to enter here and you will be master of your fate." It was very dark and I had to wait for the better-lit streets, or when we stopped at traffic lights, for Casilda Iriarte's words – "straining to roam and hunt out into the unknown" like the desires and longings of the lady from the sea – to serve as a lantern to light that first plunge into vertigo, which rounded off a night that had already been quite vertiginous enough. I opened the book as soon as I sat down, and began leafing through it with a growing sense of apprehension and intrigue, as if I were inspecting a dangerous device, an inspection that cut me off from any other memories or plans, so much so that I didn't even notice when we reached the house and had been stopped for some moments.

"It was here you wanted, wasn't it?" asked the taxi driver.

The taxi smelled of one of those violet-scented room fresheners. Everything about me was spinning. "A deceptive feeling of spinning; sometimes the body seems to spin around the objects and, at other times, it is the objects that seem to be turning. In either case, you become completely disoriented." I looked up from the dimly lit page, and I saw in the man's eyes the distrustful, mocking, condescending expression of someone used to carrying late-night passengers rather the worse for wear – damaged goods. I peered out of the window into the thick mist.

"Don't you recognize the house?" he went on. "You can't see the number very well, but you did say it was just after the petrol station."

"Yes, yes, I'm sorry."

I had another quick glance at the book before closing it, and a phrase underlined by Mónica "confusion between what is outside and what is inside" found its perfect illustration on the cover. The traveller looking over the sea of mist had got into the taxi with us. The boundaries between outer and inner had been demolished. I smiled and the taxi driver saw me smile, because he was looking straight at me. I held out the money to him.

"It's just that, every now and then, some very odd things happen," I said.

And I myself wasn't sure whether I was making excuses or looking for an accomplice. He shrugged his shoulders.

"You can say that again, and they get odder every day. You don't have to tell me that. I've been thirty years in this job, and with the way Madrid is now, especially at night . . . now is this the house or isn't it?"

He had turned to look at me again when he asked me that last question in a rather cutting tone. He suddenly looked like a policeman, and that frightened me. Some feelings are never entirely buried. I had to resort to the memory of Don Octavio Andrade to calm myself. There was a few seconds flashback in the film, the mist dissolved and out of that house, which I could barely see now, emerged Leonardo Villalba walking confidently towards his identity as a respectable heir who would never be thrown by some taxi driver's baleful look. I had Don Octavio's card with his phone number on it in my wallet. Although I could hardly justify hauling him out of bed, it was reassuring to know that I could count on him absolutely if things did turn ugly. "Excuse me, Don Octavio, I'm calling you from the street . . .

what street is this, by the way?" The ghost of a local police station, where I might bump into old acquaintances, provoked me into a swift response.

"Of course I recognize it. It is my house, after all!" I proclaimed in a tone that sounded pompous and artificial even to me. "Keep the change."

He didn't even thank me and he didn't drive off until I'd gone up the four steps to the main door and put my key in the lock. I felt his suspicious eyes on me and my hands shook. I've obviously seen too many movies. We always have our own mammoths waiting to spring out from their hiding place when we least expect it – the treacherous scrap metal of one's former life, like old tin cans tied to the tail of a stray dog, clattering loudly down the street.

"But I haven't done anything wrong today," I said to myself. "On the contrary, I have gently rocked a sad girl to sleep. Besides, I'm smartly dressed, as I was when I left the house less than twenty-four hours ago, much less. I may look slightly crumpled, but I don't look like a delinquent. Although the truth is that so many things have happened since my visit to Don Octavio that I probably do look different. They are inner changes, of course, but they will inevitably be apparent on my face, because, in extreme cases, the outside does invade the inside, and vice versa, that's what she says; it's one of the symptoms of vertigo."

Thus I named her for the first time, "she", although for the last few days or so, that has already become habitual, as if we shared a secret. On the one hand, that feminine pronoun reminds me of the first love stories I read when I was a child, the romantic serials that my grandmother adored, in which the protagonists would take ages to get to know each other and even longer to realize that they were in love – pronouncing each other's name in a passionate voice was something that only happened at the very end; and if the lover was gazing into a sunset, he would sigh: "How I wish she were here by my side!", at a party, he would search for her amongst the other female figures, "She's not here, she hasn't come," and he would dream about her. "She" was like the soul, a generic term for absence, a guarantee of clandestine love. In my case, however, I say "she" because I dare not accept that her name is the same as that of the lady I am going to have to tackle about the Quinta Blanca, nor imagine her writing the book that I now devouring, my elbows resting on the desk that belonged to my grandfather, Leonardo, who, they say, hated tackling anyone about anything. So do I. From now on, though, I will doubtless dislike it even more.

I was thinking this as I went into the hall and switched on the light and leaned against the wall, breathing fast, as if I'd just escaped some danger. I realized that the book, which I was clutching to me, was interposing itself like a new obstacle between my interests and those of the new owner, a rather unusual person according to what Don Octavio had said. The back flap of the book wasn't much help either. There was no photo of her and scarcely any biographical data.

"As a young woman, Casilda Iriarte, now aged fifty, lived in London and later moved to Brazil, where she published three books of poetry. *Essays on Vertigo* is her first work in prose. She has also written an unpublished novel, *The Long Journey*, which she is currently reworking. For some years now, she has lived in a remote village in the north of Spain."

I looked at myself in the large mirror on the coat rack and I saw the face of someone in a state of emotional shock. The experiment was only just beginning though. I rushed up the stairs, wide awake now, almost feverish. With a mixture of eagerness and fear, like Dr Jekyll when he shut himself up in his laboratory, I sensed that if it proved necessary to double the dose, I would simply have to face the consequences. For along with her, with that unusual lady, the sea was beginning to flood into the house and there was no point in building cardboard barricades to keep it out.

The connection between the idea of vertigo and the leap into space from the rocks made by an adolescent girl who wrote strange letters to my father and the initial of whose name forms part of the combination to the safe, suddenly exploded, without my even realizing it, like the first wild thud of a wave.

For some time now, how long I don't know, my efforts to strengthen and safeguard my own writing had kept me away from the other love story hinted at in those papers found in the safe. A superficial immersion in them had seemed to me sufficient and I had immediately brought my head up to the surface again in order to breathe. I felt alarmed, because I had detected certain infectious germs. They were murky waters. "I'll explore all that some other time," I decided, picking them up and returning them to their hiding place behind the picture of a lighthouse on a stormy night. I shut myself off from that story because, at the time, I did not feel that I had either the desire or the courage to peer into any more abysses. It was just an attack of fear, that's all.

What I didn't know when I managed to get a grip on my fear, is that there are forces pushing you towards abysses that have little to do with your own capacity to resist. Well, perhaps I did know that, but I forgot. Many days may have passed. The art of seamlessly linking together fragmentary episodes, however harsh, calmed me and gave me a certain, and I assumed, lasting degree of control, which, through writing, restored my own battered sense of identity. At the first serious sign of danger, I heard the alarm call and rushed to inoculate myself against the madness. And I succeeded. My notebooks are the proof of that.

That morning, though, before I had finished my first tumultuous reading of *Essays on Vertigo*, I once again slid aside the picture concealing the safe and emptied its entire contents willy-nilly onto the desk, obeying an unfathomable impulse, external to myself, something that dragged me along with the force of a hurricane. Day was breaking. That was when I locked the study door, conscious that there could be no witness to what was going to happen from then on, that Pilar was in the way. I needed to dig myself in.

The first result of my frenetic researches, comparable to those of a detective confronted by a clue which he suspects might implicate him, was the hunch that Sila might well be a diminutive form of Casilda. This hypothesis was soon confirmed by the progressive linking of one woman with the other, through textual coincidences that betray, without a shadow of a doubt, a single style. As new evidence appeared, I felt a strange excitement. It was like fitting the features of one unknown face to those of another equally unknown face, almost touching them, experiencing a few anxious moments before their imminent appearance: evasive women's faces, crouched behind the branches of the text, mocking those who come near, constantly changing their hiding places. She is one and the same, she doesn't fool me, she speaks with the same voice, she gets angry about the same things, she shrugs her shoulders in the same way. In fact, almost identical metaphors appear in the book and in her letters to my father, similar rhythms, outbursts of rebelliousness or sensuality that share the same perverse eagerness to rebuild their perception of the world on new foundations. And that is precisely what I identify with most, that is the fire that only intensifies my delirium. I long for what she longs for, I write, dream, die and come to life again like her and with her, keeping time. Besides, we share a secret, a terrible secret. I don't care if she hides. She knows that I know.

After feverishly going through Sila's papers, in which there are already signs of vertigo, I suffered a kind of mirage. I saw the C and S meld into one inside a hexagon that contained all the pink and grey juice of all the twilights that have descended on the island of seagulls ever since the world began, the C embracing the S, the eyes of the girl who looks out to sea and dreams of impossible journeys merging with those of the woman returning from those journeys, the same eyes replacing each other and becoming each other, the same way of looking, the same woman, the same lighthouse. The worst thing is that I am part of the metamorphosis I am contemplating. I too have a place inside that prism of changing colours; she makes room for me, she lends me her eyes. Come, see what the view is like from here, merge yourself with us. And everything becomes a rainbow refraction, the total dissolution of any individual plans.

There is further evidence of the symbiosis between Sila and Casilda, irrefutable evidence that goes beyond mere conjecture. Amongst the papers in the safe, there is a typewritten script of fifty sheets stapled together, accompanied by a handwritten letter, which describes how she wrote it. It is the first draft of *The Long Journey*, the novel mentioned in the blurb on *Essays on Vertigo*. I've worked out that she must have been eighteen when she wrote this draft, straight off, as she says in the letter. I too read it straight off, and I can see its appeal. I don't know what changes she will be making now. It tells, in fantastic guise, the adventures of Silveria, an adolescent girl who is believed by some in her village to be gifted with magical powers, and who, one fine day, escapes as a stowaway in a merchant ship in search of her father, an English sea captain whom she has never met, but with whom she has managed to enter into a secret correspondence. The series of prodigies, coincidences, unlikely events, providential meetings and talking animals that punctuate the plot of *The Long Journey* may conceal what is basically an autobiographical story. Although it is told in the first person, not everything that Silveria describes could possibly have happened to Sila, Silveria being more like a character in a novel of byzantine complexity than an alchemist of her own experiences. And yet, that girl who leapt from the rocks did run away to London and she did meet her father. At least that's what she tells my father. She does not say so outright, but she wraps it in the ambiguities and metaphors typical of a style which is now beginning to be familiar to me. It makes me smile, because it doesn't seem so very different from my grandmother's famous riddles. I surrender voluptuously to her tickling.

"You probably don't believe a word I say," she says on the hand-written sheet, "but I've often told you that I would prefer you to only half-believe my stories, because they only half-happened to me and to you too, to everyone in fact. Does anything ever happen to us completely? I'll soon be able to return your loan, by the way, well, half-return it. Meanwhile, I merely ask your honest opinion of *The Long Journey*. The words simply poured out. I wrote it in a week. It's only a draft, but the Captain likes it. Obviously his Spanish is far from perfect, as I could tell from his letters. He says things that really make me laugh, for example, instead of 'tengo hambre' or 'tengo sed', he says 'estoy hambriente' and 'estoy sediente', but he's an educated man, and I'm managing to worm my way into his affections, because I know how to flatter his baser instincts. He's terribly handsome, you know. Some of what Silveria relates of her first meeting with her father in Plymouth is also half-true. Tell me what you think about the quotation from Cervantes."

She puts the quotation right at the beginning, handwritten. It's a fragment from *The Travails of Persiles and Segismunda*, and I'm amazed that an eighteen-year-old village girl could have read such a complex book. However, I really don't know why I should be amazed. With her, you never know what to expect.

"The harder we look for our route to Rome, the longer and more difficult it becomes. My resolve does not waver, but it trembles, and I would not want death to surprise me amongst all these fears and dangers."

Nevertheless, from the point of view of plot – in the romantic novel my father was involved in, I mean – the oddest thing of all is that this literary draft should, as the envelope testifies, have travelled from London to Chicago. This means that, although he may possibly already have met Gertrud Scribner, my father continued to maintain an epistolary relationship with the lighthouse keeper's granddaughter, the daughter, it seems, of an English sea captain. Or perhaps that's just another of Silveria's inventions.

So now Silveria has turned up too. A name that triplicates the mirage and which begins to be refracted inside the prism, along with those already there. We have two S's and one C, as well as my own sharp L which they occasionally allow through the door even though they know it to be a knife that pierces their curves and sends red foam spurting forth. They create a wonderful kaleidoscope of shapes and colours, especially in the evening.

Meanwhile, here I still am, trying to keep a cool head, rearranging the pieces of the jigsaw puzzle to see if I can make the key word. And as the paths branch off, as the faces fade and are superseded by dates, the siege of papers only increases the chaos in my room and my now confirmed addiction to vertigo. I will have to do something.

I move forward through a forest of signs, as if I were always in need of some support, however precarious it might be, so as not to stumble and fall flat on my face. "My resolve does not waver, but it trembles," as no less a person than Cervantes says. He wants a role in this dispute too. And the more I doubt myself and the stories that invade and cloud my reason, the more keenly I sense that I am very close to the cutting edge of truth. "I would not want death to surprise me amongst all these fears and dangers."

No, not yet. I cannot die without first meeting her, without, at least, having heard her voice.

X V

Contact with the Quinta Blanca

Ever since I dismissed Pilar, as well as spending time on my drawings and on reading the various texts written by Sila, Casilda and Silveria, I have made several failed attempts to go over to the phone and dial the number of the Quinta Blanca, which I know by heart and which, as a call to Directory Enquiries confirmed, remains the same, although now it is listed under I for Iriarte, not G for Guitián. I have also begun a great many letters which have gone to swell the trail of crumpled balls of paper scattered about the floor.

Although ultimately unsatisfactory, these epistolary attempts do release me momentarily from the unease provoked by my recent discoveries and clarify the proliferating confusion that surrounds the name of Casilda Iriarte. When I begin my drafts with the words "Dear Madam" or "Dear Señora Iriarte", I try to forget any information other than that given me by Octavio Andrade. Regardless of whether she's a successful author, regardless of whether she was a friend of my father, she is a person to whom I have to write in order to start negotiations about the one thing that really interests me: the recovery of my grandparents' house, or, rather, of my house, since this one is looking more and more like a run-down boarding house. For openers, I'm ready to offer her double what she paid for it, cash on the nail, taking into account the rise in the value of property and land over the past few years, including any expenses she may have had in improving the place, plus any legal fees incurred.

I don't know if she's so rich or so disinterested as to refuse an offer of this type. Perhaps I shouldn't be so direct, perhaps I shouldn't appear too keen – I don't know, I've never been much of a diplomat. The fact that I abandon the letter before even reaching the end of the page is due partly to my complete inability to find the right tone, which always seems either too cool or too studiedly nonchalant. There's another reason too. I feel incapable of waiting – for a period of time which I imagine as being an eternity – for an answer to that ideal missive, should I ever manage to finish it to my own satisfaction, which is unlikely, given the present shifting nature of my criteria.

The advantages of a telephone conversation are indisputable: having an actual voice on the other end of the phone to give an immediate response to my proposal. When you want an answer to something, simultaneity counts for a lot, and tone of voice gives you a good idea of where you stand. I'm particularly sensitive to this kind of acoustic signal; I've always thought myself particularly gifted in interpreting what such signals might conceal, offer or presage. For that very reason, however, the mere idea of hearing Casilda Iriarte's voice also fills me with terror, blind terror; I will only have to hear her say "Hello" to feel that she has either opened the door to me or plunged a dagger in my heart. Yet, at the same time, that is also what I most want, the only possible solution if I am to break free of this infernal circle, a solution I keep in reserve, on hold. At the moment, I don't feel I would be agile enough to improvise sensible, ironic or ambiguous replies to her arguments. It is all a question of freeing myself from my own prejudices, if what I want from her – as I insistently tell myself – is that she should be interested in my offer. How could she not be? If the offer seems too low, let her impose her own conditions! I am prepared to accept them all, without discussion – don't you worry about that, it's not a problem; I won't bargain at all. I'll be quite frank with you, Señora Iriarte, I'm a very rich man. No, I can't say that. It would sound like boasting. I must be gentle, so that she doesn't feel pressurized. Anyway, let's take it in stages, we haven't even got that far yet. First, I have to be quite sure that this business of buying and selling is the main, indeed only, motive that impels me to telephone this person I'm so obsessed with. If I was sure of that, what would be so difficult about concealing, throughout a conversation with that abstract being, everything I have come to know about her life? Is it not, on the contrary, my desire to acquire new information which presents itself to me now like some diabolical pleasure that at once draws me on and drives me back?

Although bothered by such doubts, I remain clear-headed enough to understand that if, in one of my periods of delirium, I had given in to the temptation to phone the Quinta Blanca, it would have been a spasmodic decision, ruled by the impossibility of keeping to myself everything I already know; a bit like throwing up when you've eaten too much. It would bring out my worst instincts and possibly hers too, comparable to flinging open the windows on a night of hurricane-force winds when a terrible fire has just broken out inside the house.

What I'm experiencing is a fire, there's no doubt about it, a fire of love like the feelings described in the serials that my grandmother used to keep in a cupboard in the corridor, although none of those "shes" who stepped out of the novels in order to stroll through my youthful dreams was anywhere near as fantastical as Casilda Iriarte whom I burn to meet. Yes, why beat about the bush, I am madly in love with the lighthouse keeper's granddaughter, my father's girlfriend, who may, at this very moment, be inventing new lies to round out that long journey in her youth which transformed her into Silveria, an expert in meta-morphoses, a poet in Brazil, a witch and a lady from the sea; they are all simultaneously driving me wild, and I can't stand it any longer. Either none of them is real, or they all are. I need to know.

"But first you need something else, Leonardo. You need to sleep," says my grandmother. "First, have a long, therapeutic sleep, then do what you want. You've got great dark circles under your eyes and, in your worst moments, you look quite mad. You certainly can't get in touch with her in your present state, not even over the phone. Or do you think people can't tell from your voice when you're a wreck? We women are good at that. She'd have you for breakfast. No, I won't leave you alone. Take a sleeping pill, all right? And tomorrow is another day. 'Driving you wild', my foot. You do it to yourself, all that wallowing in literature, that's what poisons you, just as it poisons all men who closet themselves in their rooms with books. Just look at Don Quixote: all the statues may be of him, but the people I feel sorry for are his maid and his niece who had to put up with him. Come on, that's enough chit-chat; I'll sing you a lullaby and everything will be all right, you'll see. She always was mad that girl. Not that she's a bad person. Just don't let her get the better of you."

In my mother's bathroom cabinet there were various brands of tranquillizers. I've slept very well for two consecutive nights now and I've had very peaceful dreams, the sort you barely remember, but which leave you feeling slightly nostalgic when you wake from them, as you do when you've just said goodbye to someone you'll see again soon. Nearly all the dreams were filled with the kind of light you only get at the beach.

This afternoon I went out to buy some clothes, which I badly needed, especially shirts and sweaters. I wore two of my recent purchases straight from the shop, and that feeling of wearing something for the first time, always a revivifying experience, only intensified when I walked over to a litter bin in the street and dumped my old shirt and sweater in it. I had worn them a lot in prison.

It was cold but clear, and I set off along the Gran Vía, enjoying my walk, and my plan to phone the Quinta Blanca suddenly seemed like an exciting adventure. Why shouldn't it be? It all depends on you, you can make of it what you will, you just have to concentrate, to be alert to the information she gives you, to interpret that information and put it to use, because anything can be put to use. Or have you, from one day to the next, simply lost the power to trick and transform that is so closely bound up with your gifts as a storyteller? Use them to your own advantage. That's your strength, remember that, you inherit it from your grandmother; other people are always asking you to tell them a story, eager for some exotic tale that will awaken their desires – go on, don't stop – like that cellmate of yours, you had him hooked on stories. His name was Julián. How far away all that seems, as if a million years had passed; how could you bear it in there? Think what it would mean to be arrested again. Think how much broader your horizons would have seemed on one of those interminable evenings in prison if you had known only half of what you know now and had had a phone at your disposal. It's like something out of a novel, isn't it? Well, then, live that novel! It could be fun winning over Casilda

Iriarte, and not so very difficult. Going out into the street obviously bucks you up.

I paused by a few shop windows. I looked quite handsome, peering through the luxury goods into the mirror at the back, with a look of cool indifference on my face, like a foreigner visiting Madrid, strolling about, killing time, before keeping the most exciting appointment of his life.

And since when have you been frightened of women? Tell the truth, Leonardo, come on! You don't even have to try, you intrigue them, they find you interesting. You need look no further than Almu. Her interest in you dissolved because of her boyfriend or whatever, but as soon as she was sitting with her legs up on the sofa and looking at you, "you really freak me out, where have you sprung from?" Because you, you remember, were distracted, thinking about something else. That's important, you mustn't appear to be anxious, you must pretend to be thinking about something else. Of course, pretending to do that might just make it worse, even more so on the phone, when you can't see the other person's face. On the other hand, you have the advantage that your face remains in the shadows too.

I went down the sidestreets, in search of a barber who could give me a shave and a haircut, because my few furtive glances into the bronzed surfaces of those luxury shop windows had made me realize that, as regards my image, there was still room for improvement. If I could find one of those old-fashioned barber's shops, all the better, the sort where they massage your face with Floid, the shaving lotion that my father used when he was a young man. When you're going out on a date, you want to look impeccable. As I strolled along, going nowhere in particular, rubbing shoulders with other idle, mid-afternoon walkers, I began preparing ideal responses for the colloquium I was about to have with the lady of my thoughts. I imagined, too, deliberate pauses, disconcerting silences and perhaps the odd suggestion of a smile or a sigh. Above all, I must keep calm and keep control of my voice, whatever is said, however unforeseen, because that's bound to happen, of course. Yes, I need good reflexes, an eye for nuance, a good aim. Some phrase, which, when she least expects it, flies to its target and strikes home, transformed into a look of fire.

I continued elaborating these strategic fantasies with my eyes closed, abandoning myself to the hands of an old craftsman, who, luckily for me, was not a great talker, as his fellow artisans tend to be. I was sitting in a black leather chair with a metal frame and, reflected back at me from the mirror I saw my own face covered in shaving soap and wearing a distinctly conspiratorial look. There aren't many old barber's shops left in Madrid and that's why it took me a while to find one. In fact, I wasn't even looking, I was merely thinking that if one did appear, then I would accept it as a reward for finally breaking free of my awful enslavement to obsessions, which was just beginning to crack.

My walk thus meandered on, becoming a kind of slow, soothing zigzag taking me further and further away from the busy streets and leading me into the spiralling paths of my own inner labyrinth.

When I left the barber's, it was already dark and the shops had closed their doors or were about to do so.

I stood on the pavement, and the glow of the newly-lit street lamps provoked in me the confused feelings that always precede a moment of recognition. I was in a short street that led into a small square with a few rachitic trees growing in the middle. I walked towards the square. It formed a rough rectangle. The side facing me was occupied by a building site containing the ruins of a half-demolished house, a fence plastered with posters and an old house with iron balconies. The house had four storeys and in front of it, parked on the pavement, was a moped. It was Almu's house.

I approached slowly, the way you do when you're afraid of frightening away a butterfly. There was an eight above the door and to the right of the façade, which formed a corner with another street, was the name of the square, in white letters on blue enamel. I made a mental note of it. Mónica had written her surname in the front of *Essays on Vertigo*. Now I can write to her whenever I wish, and it will be for real this time; they'll forward the letter to her in Melbourne. A nice, long letter, I'm sure she'll like it, signed "The Farewell Angel". She'll smile to remember me; adapting to a new life is always hard and she wasn't sure that she'd done the right thing either. That night had been so unusual that it was easy to idealize it. "I've got so many things to tell you," I murmured gently, looking up. "I've a great deal to thank you for too. Meeting a friend like you is like a gift. We are accomplices. That's where it all happened, behind that wall. Everything. And a lot happened, you know." An unreal silence reigned and not a soul passed. A figure with his back to me was dangling from one of the balconies on the fourth floor. He was moving from one floor to the next with the nimbleness of a very peculiar bird – focused, silent and exact – alighting on the balustrades without once dishevelling his reddish hair or rumpling his green jacket. As soon as he set foot on the ground, a few yards away from me, he set off swiftly to his left and plunged into the ruined building – there was a gap over on the far side, the remains of a back door. It was Friedrich's traveller, the one looking out over the sea of mist.

As soon as he had disappeared, I too sneaked away, only in the opposite direction. Now I was sure that I would phone Casilda Iriarte.

I've waited until ten o'clock. My doubts now centre on the choice of setting. Finally, after a great deal of thought, I decide against the study and opt for the bedroom that used to belong to my mother whom, lately, I have taken to calling Gertrud, or simply Trud, as he did. That room is less burdened with memories and might help me in my attempt to appear detached. Besides, to the left of the bed there's a full-length mirror which will allow me to keep an eye on any untoward attitudes or gestures. I've also taken quite a lot of trouble over details of decor and lighting. The most important innovation consists in my having placed the photo of Sila jumping from the rocks in the tortoiseshell frame in which Trud used to keep a small photo of her father. They're more or less the same size. When I remove the photo of Walter Scribner it bends a little and cracks. I study it for a few moments and then tear it into four pieces, just enough time for me to see the look of cold disapproval in those pale, pale eyes. I throw the bits into the wastepaper bin. He was a bothersome witness.

I complete the transgression by lighting the candle in the silver candlestick and placing it next to the photo of Sila and the rocks.

I switch off the other lights, apart from a table lamp, and look for a classical music station on the radio. Mozart. Good. I lower the volume and go over to the mirror and peer at my diffuse reflection. I look good in light brown with just the collar of my white shirt visible. I stroke my hair, it's very soft to the touch. I will do my best to keep any harsh tones out of my voice too.

I lie down on the bed and pull the phone over on to the mattress. I stroke the phone voluptuously for a while. When I finally decide to dial the number of the Quinta Blanca, it's a quarter to eleven, perhaps a little late for a first incursion, but it's better like that, more exciting. My fingers are trembling. Exciting? Let's call a spade a spade here: what you feel is fear. No more subterfuges now; the bull is about to enter the ring. Now you are in actual contact with the Quinta Blanca. You can take it or leave it, as you choose.

The first three rings, echoing out beneath the high ceilings there, provoke such an intense feeling of emptiness in my stomach that it cancels out all my plans, all my bravado. Vertigo, yes, pure vertigo. I close my eyes and press my nails into the palm of my left hand. It is a childish fear of the starry vault: sometimes, however scientifically you try to explain it to yourself, it can be unleashed merely by the idea of that wire-less telephony. As a child, I found it frightening that voices from so far off could infiltrate the house. It was the same with the radio, although that had a different effect on me, because there the voices were not familiar ones. As soon as I heard the phone ring in the corridor, I would stand stock still, on alert, as if awaiting the colossal peal of thunder which, on stormy nights, unfailingly follows the scribble of lightning across the sky. It also brought news that could be bad or even worrying. My grandmother would hold out the black bakelite receiver, having talked into it for a while perfectly naturally, tracing little circles in the corridor as she did so; at the far end of corridor, my face would appear from behind the green curtain. "Yes, he's here with me now. I'll put him on. Come on, Leo, take it, don't just stand there. It's them, it's your parents." Apprehensively, I would take the receiver, still warm from my grandmother's cheek, and hold it to my own and be incapable of saying anything to those voices transmitted from such a long way away ("tele" = far, "phone" = voice or sound); I would lean against the wall, shy and mistrustful. "Leo, are you there?" my father would say impatiently. "Say something." I felt as if I were being duped, as if I were the victim of some enchantment. "I don't understand, I just can't understand, not with all that sea in between," I would say later, staring incredulously at the map. "I don't understand it very well either, but what can I say? You can't understand everything." "That's why I prefer fairy stories." "So do I! But look, enough of this nonsense; to each his own. Whenever I think of it, I say two prayers, one for that Mr Alexander Bell and one for the person who invented the bed, another very wise man, who is even more deserving of praise, since he didn't even leave a name behind him. They should erect a monument to him like the one to the unknown soldier."

There was no phone in the house until I was four years old, because the village was too remote, "the backside of the world" according to my father. The only switchboard was in the village shop attended by Benigna, the innkeeper's wife, and she was the one who passed on any messages. But grandmother, who had influential friends amongst the party leaders, immediately moved heaven and earth in order to get St Alexander Bell to bestow his favours on us, and thus a direct line reached our village before it reached any of the other neighbouring villages with much larger populations. "String-pulling," people said. "Doña Inés up to her old tricks again." I clearly remember some men in blue overalls coming to install the thing. It was one very hot August afternoon and they parked the lorry outside the gate. They fixed the phone very high up on the corridor wall, so high that I had to climb onto a stool to reach it. It was black and topped by two nickel-plated bells and, although, later on, two more phones were installed, the modern sort that stand on a table, the first one was never removed. "It would be like denying our own origins," my grandmother used to say, "that phone means more than all the others put together. It's the Father, the King. Everything has its symbol. And as long as I live, there it shall stay."

The worst thing is tentatively trying to imagine – as if I were engaged in a game of hide-and-seek – the place that is now echoing to the ring-ring that is digging this pit in my stomach, not daring with any certainty to assume that things are where they used to be, yet it's almost irresistible. The rings reverberate in ghostly fashion along the corridors of my body and of the Quinta Blanca; they ring out aimlessly like the tapping of a blindman's stick. That's six times it's rung. The house is big, I know, and she might have gone out for a moment in search of inspiration, although that would be odd because it's been terribly cold up north, they said so on the radio . . . seven . . . they echo in my kidneys, they trample on my heart, two more and I'll hang up . . . eight . . .

"Who is it?"

"Is Casilda Iriarte there?"

I breathe deeply and my wild pulse slows.

"Yes, but she's lying down. She's not feeling very well. May I ask who's calling?"

It's a man's voice. I seem to recognize it, but where from? And I focus all my powers of concentration on that new search.

"It doesn't matter. A friend. Don't bother her now. When would be a good time to phone her? Tomorrow?"

"Wait a moment. I'll go and see if she wants to take the call. She might fancy a chat. Just a moment. Don't hang up."

I caught his Portuguese accent then. Now I have it, it's Maurício. I mustn't let him escape.

"Hello, hello! Hey, Maurício!"

But he doesn't answer. He's gone. If the telephone is still in the corridor, he'll have left it hanging there in order to go and tell his mistress. "My mistress says that the sun rises on even the darkest night." Well, who would have thought it! So that was the woman he worked for. Perhaps he recognized my voice, as I did his. We talked for a long time that night. I find it very worrying that he may have gone to tell her, precisely because he did recognize my voice. There's no point getting sidetracked though. I may be wrong, but I like to think that I have a good ear. What I need now is patience and sang-froid.

Anyway, if it is Maurício how can I be sure that I'm not going to get myself entangled in the web of yet another fantasy? Maurício Brito was already a character in a novel, my own novel. To what extent will my narrative become snarled up with that of Casilda Iriarte? I feel suddenly indignant. So she wants to take over Maurício too? That really is the limit! Or are there two of them? And in that case, what relation does the Maurício in my novel have with the Maurício who has gone off with my message and is in no apparent hurry to come back? It doesn't take anyone that long to say: "There's a friend on the phone for you, Señora". He'll be saying other things to her too, talking about me, since he knows me. No, there can't be two of them, there can only be one, who is occasionally displaced by his ghost. And if the Maurício Brito of the Quinta Blanca is a ghost, everything that is about to happen from now on must be a lie too. I must be inventing it. Just keep calm, Leonardo, please, just wait and don't get all worked up; syllogisms have been your worst enemy ever since you were a little boy, they used to get completely out of hand, you even used to lose your appetite over them.

"Next, we will be listening to Symphony Number 2 in D Major by Brahms, played by the London Philharmonic and conducted by . . ."

I get up to switch off the radio, because it's beginning to get on my nerves. When I come back to the bed, I just can't get comfortable. And there's still no one on the other end of the line. I could simply hang up and get myself out of this hole. But I don't.

What are you complaining about, asks a submerged, warning voice. I thought you had accepted that the walls separating hallucination from wakefulness had been broken down? Did you think you would have repaired all the damage simply by taking a few sleeping pills, buying some new clothes and disguising yourself as a normal, healthy young man? You shouldn't trust that kind of miracle. What Gerda did was something else. She worked at it, she hurled herself on the world and brought all her faith to bear on the enterprise.

I shrug my shoulders. As well as my faith – not that I ever had much – I have lost every remnant of calm. My capacity to react to the unexpected is at an all-time low. It takes me a while to realize that, after a faint click, like someone picking up another receiver, someone has asked "Who is it?" in a voice that catches me at a moment when I'm too tense to let it enter my brain for analysis, although I don't register it as being Maurício's voice. I take even longer to connect that question with the suddenly vague reasons that brought me to the phone. I look at the black numbers on the white dial and at the coiled wire pretending to improbable connections. In the end, it would not be so very terrible if we did not exist, neither I nor the unknown owner of the Quinta Blanca who may also be the owner of the voice saying again – more loudly now, metallic and impatient, with a touch of authority – "Who is it?" No, nothing would change. The stars would still continue to shine at night and the dogs to howl mournfully, the spring would melt the most stubborn ice and new consignments of seagulls would circle the rocks beneath the lighthouse before swooping down to take their places on their ancestral isle.

My eyes rest on the photograph framed in tortoiseshell, on the photo of her leaping into the air, a white stain on a black background, very faint in the candlelight, and suddenly I am filled by a fear that I have gone too far. Enough! I need to ask for someone's help, the way you do when you suddenly emerge from a nightmare. I need to exorcise the void, to escape from this dream or to take control of it myself; I need to know what I mean when I say "I", to grab it by the lapels, that slippery, fast-fading "I" that is currently crashing against the walls of a strange house. Enough. I can bear it no longer.

"It's Leonardo!" I shout. "Leonardo! And who are you? What room are you in? What's Maurício doing there?"

I have achieved what I wanted – to wake up, for everything to be real, to provoke the biting response that will break the spell.

"I'm Casilda Iriarte, the person you were phoning, or so I believe," says a woman's voice that immediately takes possession of my senses. "And you're a very rude young man. What a way to introduce yourself! I don't owe you any explanations about the people who work for me. Honestly! Or am I supposed to ask someone's permission, yours for example, for Maurício to live with me?"

I like her voice, I like it a lot. I soften my own.

"No, of course not, I'm terribly sorry. It's just that . . . I'm terribly upset at the moment, but, please, don't hang up."

"Who said I was going to hang up? We're only just beginning, aren't we?"

I start breathing faster. That is the first unexpected phrase that treacherously finds its mark, like a look of fire. Except that she was the one to say it. It will be hard work overcoming that disadvantage. And besides she's addressing me as "tú", something I'm incapable of doing to her.

"It's just that it's been a bit of a shock dialling this number and having someone answer the phone. I was about to hang up, because, in my dreams, no one ever answers. And then it was Maurício who answered. I don't know, I just lost my head. It would be very difficult to explain in a way that you could understand."

"Why don't you try?" she asks.

"Because I don't understand it myself, it defies logic, and, besides, it's not the right time, and that isn't why I was phoning."

"The only questions that interest me," she says, "are those that defy logic, although it is harder to explain them, I agree with you there. Anyway, it's up to you."

"I can't say anything until you forgive my earlier outburst. I didn't mean to speak to you in that tone of voice, on the contrary. It's just that sometimes what you intend to do gets superimposed on and muddled up with other intentions, they whirl around, and you end up in a complete mess, especially if you've spent days alone at home, without talking to anyone, reading first one book and then another, moving from one daydream to the next. Well, that's what happens to me at any rate."

"To me too." It's as if she had held out a hand to help me up from the floor, but I sense that she still has her sword unsheathed. The fencing lesson is far from over.

"What a relief!" I say, giving a deep sigh. "So you forgive me, then?"

"Of course I do, don't be silly! But anyway, can you at least remember what it was you wanted to talk to me about and what tone of voice you were originally going to use? Because, before calling a stranger, I always draw up a kind of draft conversation, don't you?"

I'm flabbergasted. Can she perhaps see, from where she is, not only this room presided over by the photo of Sila, but also my father's study strewn with little balls of paper? I think she can.

"Or do I, in fact, know you?" she asks, given my silence.

"I'm sorry, you're quite right. I'm in such a state that I haven't even introduced myself yet. My name is Leonardo Villalba Scribner. You don't know me."

There is a brief, very tense pause.

"No, I don't know you," says a voice from the other end of the line, a voice so dense with emotion that I'm taken aback, as if I had suddenly found myself standing on the edge of a precipice.

I don't know what I should say to her now. The conversation is travelling along dangerous, muddy tracks, and she's holding the reins, that much is obvious. I'm losing my way, and my courage too. Especially my courage.

"Or to be more precise," she adds slowly, "let's just say that I've never actually seen you."

I lean towards the mirror in search of support and find there an indolent, attenuated figure about to disappear. I can't allow myself to be destroyed like this. Just because she has never seen me doesn't mean that I have to abandon my whole identity. I react by changing my posture. No more lying down. My grandmother used to say that in order to read or to talk to people you should have your back supported, so that it forms a right angle with the rest of the body. That way, she said, you understand things better and avoid the danger of going off at pointless tangents. Trud's padded headboard provides me with a good support for my back.

"I know what you mean. Obviously, my name must ring a bell with you, because some years ago you bought the Quinta Blanca from me, albeit through an intermediary. And that's exactly what I wanted to talk to you about, or rather, to discuss. Not right now, naturally, since you're not feeling well and it's much too late, but we need to have a longer conversation when we've got more time. I'll call you and make an appointment, whenever it's convenient for you. And it would be preferable if we could meet face to face. Do you ever come to Madrid?"

"Yes, sometimes. But wait a moment, let me just get this straight. What do you and I have to discuss about the Quinta Blanca? That's what I don't understand. I seem to remember that all the papers were in order, and if my memory serves me right, the notary who authorized the deed is called Octavio Andrade and he lives in Calle de Serrano. Why don't you go and ask him whatever it is you want to ask."

"I already have. He was the one who advised me to phone you."

"I don't understand!" she boils over. "Phone me about what? To discuss what? For my part, there's absolutely nothing to discuss."

I have just acquired a bit of first-hand information about this business, a fundamental bit of information which, although adverse, provokes in me a mixture of admiration and pride. Casilda Iriarte doesn't like discussing the Quinta Blanca. Quite apart from being the owner of the house, she feels that it is hers by right. Without even knowing what I'm about to propose, she has leapt to its defence like a lioness, just as Doña Inés Guitián would have done.

And suddenly I feel like bursting out laughing, the way you do when some eccentric but much-loved person has a sudden temper tantrum; I want to tell her that I can imagine her leaning over the balcony at the back, blunderbuss in hand, like Bette Davis in some film made in the Deep South; I feel like asking her what clothes she has on and how she wears her hair. Above all, I want to ask her not to be angry with me, that I don't want to cause her any trouble. After all, she's not that young any more, she has her own problems, she might be sad or tired. And I notice that my desire to dazzle her has given way to a feeling of tenderness, to a vehement desire to protect her.

"Don't get upset, please. I don't want to bother you any more at this hour. The important thing is that you get better. There's plenty of time. It's a delicate matter, one that needs to be dealt with unhurriedly."

"And who, may I ask, is in a hurry? I'm not in a hurry. I was reading a novel by Moritz, I almost always read at night, I'm more receptive then and that's how I tackle my insomnia too. So, please, don't tell me again how late it is, as if we were in an office and I were some kind of applicant. What door are you slamming in my face? Tell me. For whom is it too late? For me, as I said, this is the best time, because I adore the night; it's when I speak, read and think best, in fact, it's when I do everything best. And as for you, I hardly think it right and proper that you should grumble about the lateness of the hour when this is precisely the hour you have chosen to call me. Am I wrong?"

I look at the girl in black and white leaping off the rocks on the island of seagulls. I smile. It's the same girl. She still enjoys leaping. The image of a fifty-year-old woman, sad, tired and in need of protection, immediately dissolves.

"No, you're quite right. But you're making things difficult for me . . ."

"Don't worry, that's my particular speciality, the speciality of the house," she says. "Anything easy bores me."

There is a silence which, at last, I dare to break with a question. It feels like riding out from the rearguard.

"When you say 'of the house', do you mean that house?"

"Partly yes, but not only this house. I mean this place and this sea and the sky that covers it day and night. I've travelled quite a lot, but I've always known that the hardest thing would be to come back here. Not in search of my roots exactly, but in order – by pretending a calm I don't actually feel – to face up to all that's most difficult and shifting, the waves that bring everything and carry it all away. After you've studied the waves for a long time, they do eventually offer an explanation, but they require a lot of interpretative work. The sea is very mysterious. And the sea here, as I imagine you know, is unlike any other. You have to know its passwords."

I remain silent for a while. It could be the moment to ask her, playing the innocent, how it is that she feels so at home there, that perhaps she or some member of her family was born there. I'm incapable of such, hypocrisy though, incapable too – in direct opposition to that – of an outburst of frankness, based on the confession that I have read her letters. And yet I have to say something, something that won't upset this strange, exciting equilibrium, that will encourage her to go on talking about something, anything. Because, almost without realizing it, we are touching on an area of implied knowledge, of bittersweet complicity.

"You've no idea," I say, "how pleased I am that the person who bought the Quinta Blanca is someone who can speak of the landscape there as you have just done. Although, as far as my business with you is concerned, that makes things rather awkward."

I bite my lip. I'm convinced that what I've just said is irreparable. She'll start to ask me about the nature of the business I've just mentioned, and there'll be nothing I can do about it. But she doesn't.

"I'm pleased you phoned me, because that means that you're drawn to this place, that you're not one of those people who can just wipe the slate clean and start again."

"Well, I thought I was, but then I realized that I wasn't and also that you only appreciate things when you've lost them, that before you can appreciate them, there has to be a long period of separation and many pointless experiences. As a child, I lived there nearly all the time. And now I'm in some sort of radio communication with the sea that beats against the island of seagulls, in the very intense way with which one loves, misses and knows the things that are far away, or that one sees in dreams. I don't know if I'm explaining myself very well. There is a sort of strong but slender thread that binds me to the person I was as a child, and sometimes it fishes out submerged images and feelings, but there are always mysteries still to be resolved."

"You explain yourself very well. And it's such a coincidence too. Shortly before you phoned, I was reading something very similar to what you've just said. Do you know a writer called Karl Philipp Moritz?"

"No, who's he?"

"A German pre-Romantic. He died around the end of the eighteenth century. Do you mind if I read you a paragraph of his?"

"No, please do."

"Just wait a minute then."

There's a rustle of papers, the sound of something falling. She's probably making herself more comfortable or putting on her glasses. At her age, she probably needs them to read. I wait with pleasurable excitement, savouring my happiness, hoping she takes a while to find the quotation she's looking for.

"Right," she says at last. "Here it is. It's from the fragmentary diary of Andreas Hartknopf (I'm probably pronouncing it wrongly, I don't know German), a sort of alter ego of the author, who died young, by the way, like nearly all the poets of the time. It has a lot to do with what you were saying about the thread that binds us to our childhood. It's all so lovely, I'm not sure where to begin reading really."

"Please, read whatever you like. I'm not usually sleepy at night either and I'm tired of reading on my own, of talking to myself. I'd love to hear it."

"All right, for example, here – I'll go slowly because I'm translating from the Portuguese – 'He suddenly had the feeling that he had caught a glimpse behind a curtain that separated his present life from some unknown past existence. It evoked a state of mind entirely similar to this one and yet he could not link that memory with a time or a place. He remembered, then, that in his early childhood, when he had asked where he had come from, his mother had always shown him a well near the house as the first source of his existence. Ever since then, whenever he heard the words "well" or "fountain", what arose in his soul was that singular sensation that we usually experience when we recall some object from our remote childhood.' I can't seem to find the bit about the thread now."

"It doesn't matter, go on reading, please. It's wonderful."

"Here it is, listen. 'For Andreas, childhood was like the water of Lethe in which we drink the forgetting of our previous state. The thread that joins our present existence to another previous one is to be found there, he thought, so finely woven that the eye can barely see it. But if you look carefully, you can make out something, just as when you look intensely at the sky, you start to see stars, one by one, where, at first, you thought you saw only deep blue.' Well, I won't go on, otherwise I'll end up reading you the whole book."

"Just one more bit! I love listening to you. You have a beautiful voice, but I imagine lots of people have told you that."

"Some have, yes, but you're an unusually appreciative audience. Well, what shall I choose for dessert. He's talking about dreams here, would you like that?"

"Very much. I like everything. Where did you find the book?"

"I bought it in Brazil. Now don't interrupt. 'Look: as long as we have not entirely awoken from the dream of this life, we will always want to return to the beautiful dream that death interrupts. But once we have rubbed the sleep from our eyes, our gaze will look upon open spaces and then we will begin to be able to orient ourselves in the world of truth, just as when we wake up, we fix our eyes on a window or on a door and we look at all the objects surrounding us in order to persuade ourselves that we are not still dreaming.'"

She stops reading and the silence that follows sends a shiver through me. I look at all the objects around me, the lit candle, the photograph framed in tortoiseshell, the bundle of clothes on the armchair, the walls, the window, and I dare not speak. If I had only heard Casilda Iriarte's voice in dreams, where could I go to now? Who could I turn to?

"Casilda!" I cry. "Casilda! Are you there? Answer me, please, I beg you!"

"Of course I'm here, what's wrong?"

"I'm sorry. Blame the extracts that you read out to me. Sometimes the things that books say seem so true that I confuse it with what I'm actually seeing. I mean that literally, I'm not exaggerating. I forget who I am and such a close identification with a text frightens me. You probably think I'm mad."

"You were never mad, or at least what you had was the kind of madness I understand very well. Now, you'll think that I'm mad, talking about you without even having met you."

"Exactly. How did you know that I was going to ask you precisely that?"

At the other end of the line, the woman gives a soft laugh. Is she really laughing? Why? What's happening? And is this really happening, whatever it is? I need to make the dream mine, to control it. I look at myself in the mirror again, as if I wanted to shore up an identity that is once again beginning to crumble. It's time to make the situation a little more concrete. I say:

"I hope you don't think you know me because you knew my father. We're not at all alike."

"No, you're not. He would have got to the point ages ago. You're like me, someone who beats about the bush, and then immediately finds another bush to beat about. We'll either get on well or not at all. It depends how stubborn you are."

"I'm not stubborn."

"In that case, we won't get on at all."

Without realizing, I've started laughing. And answering me from far off, echoing beneath the high ceilings of the Quinta Blanca, comes a liberating peal of laughter that immediately makes us friends.

"We're obviously going to have to meet, don't you think? Everything we say suggests a thousand other conversations. One thing is sure, we won't be bored. Anyway, just to reassure you, I can be stubborn too. The fact is that there are very few things I care about now, and in order to struggle you need some stimulus. It's one thing running risks just for the sake of it – I'm no coward and I never back down – but when I feel no enthusiasm, then getting myself into dangerous or complicated situations is just another form of inertia; I would just be going through the motions. I've lost myself now. I've forgotten what it was I wanted to say to you. You say something."

Again that soft laugh.

"Which of the thousand conversations do you want me to reply to? It's certainly getting a bit confused. I think, like you, that this telephonic relationship has given us all it has to give. Anyway, I'd like to meet you too. What are you doing at Christmas for example?"

"Which Christmas?"

"This one. What a question! It's only two weeks until Christmas; didn't you realize?"

"No."

"Then there's no point my asking you what plans you've made."

"I haven't made any."

"Great. Why don't you come and spend Christmas here? It would be nice to read Moritz by the fireside."

"There? Christmas? How?"

"By train. Or by car if you've got one."

"I mean where will I stay? As you know, there's no boarding house or anything nearby."

"Don't be silly. When I invite you to spend Christmas with me, I'm inviting you to stay here, that's obvious, isn't it?"

I take a while to react. I'm drowning in emotion. I close my eyes and everything is spinning around me. Invited to my own house by a stranger. It seems inconceivable and yet it's also as tempting and attractive as the void itself. I excuse myself with a few stammered, disjointed phrases, until, pursued by her questions, I end up confessing that I would find it very hard to return to the Quinta Blanca and not find my room in the tower exactly as I left it. I beg her to understand. I ramble foolishly on in my evocation of that hiding place, recounting its treasures, how, on stormy nights, you could hear the sea far off, about my grandmother's tongue-twisters; I describe in detail furniture and objects, books, engravings, the great table-cum-desk with its top covered in green oilcloth. I talk non-stop; I myself find it strange. I even manage to bring in Hans Christian Andersen. She lets me say my piece and then comments in a calm voice, a voice like the high tide:

"Since you abandoned it so inconsiderately to its fate, you deserve to have the whole lot buried by a sandstorm. But for your peace of mind, I can tell you that it did not fall into enemy hands. Do you understand?"

"Not quite. Do you mean that my room still exists and is just the same? I can't believe it."

"Well, not exactly the same, no. It's much improved, because it's had a long overdue coat of paint, and I've had a new carpet fitted and double glazing put in. But, naturally, I haven't touched your things or rummaged around in them. I wouldn't dream of it. So the inappropriateness of staying here exists only in your imagination, which, I'm beginning to suspect, sometimes has a tendency to paint everything black."

There's a long silence. My words have frozen in my throat.

"Right," she says, "now I *am* beginning to feel a bit tired. You decide what you want to do and let me know. You just have to send a telegram. Not that I'm forcing you, of course. I don't want you to feel that you have to come either. Sleep on it. Goodnight, and thanks for calling."

"Casilda, please, one last question."

"Of course, but don't make it a difficult one. I'm feeling slightly faint."

"Why did you do that? I mean why did you keep my room as it was."

"I always assumed that you would come back," she says. "A simple question of faith. It would take me a long time to explain, a very long time."

"But we'll have time at Christmas, won't we?"

"I hope so, Leonardo. Goodnight."

PART THREE

I

Plus ultra

They found old Antonio Moura dead in his boat on an afternoon of
light winds and mean, fluctuating sun which, as it disappeared behind
marbled strips of cloud just before sunset, left in its wake a kind of icy
anteroom. There were no signs of an accident, because the boat was
tied up, as it usually was, to a sharp rock, with the anchor buried in the
sand; perhaps he had not even had time to set out to sea, assuming that
had been his intention when he got into the boat. This was not such
a wild conjecture as it might seem, if you bear in mind that he had
sometimes been seen rowing close to the rocks in far rougher weather
than that. And it would not have occurred to anyone to say that he
was gambling with his life, because for some time now old Moura had,
of his own volition, placed all his bets on that one card – the sea.
It was more like a pact, really. As he himself said, only someone who
believes that they will not lose their life sooner or later, someone
who resists destiny and therefore opposes it, can be said to be gambling
with his life.

He was found by Teófilo, a twelve-year-old boy with a stutter,
when he went over to ask him, on his grandmother's behalf, for some
ointment for her rheumatism. Given his tendency to fantasize, his
speech defect, and the excitement that any boy his age would feel at
being centre stage, Teófilo gave a very garbled account of things when
he arrived, out of breath, at the house of the priest, who was the first
to hear the news, since the church, in that remote village, served as
press office, police station, late-night chemist and funeral parlour.
Teófilo, a veteran reader of detective novels, kept insisting that he had
touched nothing. Seeing Señor Moura sitting in the boat, which he
always left on the little rocky beach in front of the hut where he lived,

he had called to him when he was still some way off, and only when he went over to him had he realized that he was dead, first, because he didn't answer, and then, because of the strange way he was looking up at the sky, his eyes wide open in the same frightening stare as the eyes of dead people in the movies. But he hadn't moved or touched anything, he would swear to it on his mother's grave. He hadn't even taken Don Antonio's pulse and he didn't see any blood.

It was already dark when he returned to the scene accompanied by the priest and by a couple of neighbours carrying a torch. Antonio still had his eyes open – as Don Ambrosio confirmed after closing them – and his book lay open too. That led Don Ambrosio to assume that when Antonio got into the boat it must still have been light, because otherwise, death could not have overtaken him while he was reading. His glasses had fallen off and were covered in sand.

"A leopard never changes its spots," remarked Don Ambrosio, after leafing through the book. "He must have had a heart attack. *Requiescat in pace*. He wouldn't have felt a thing."

The book was the third volume of Montaigne's essays, in a Spanish translation. It was open at the chapter entitled: "On Repentance".

"The world is in a perennial state of commotion. Everything in it is ceaselessly shaking – the earth, the sea, the rocks of the Caucasus, the pyramids of Egypt – both with the general commotion and with its own. Constancy itself is only a more languid form of that ceaseless trembling. I cannot keep my goal in sight. It moves ahead of me, dim and faltering, by its very nature drunk . . . If my soul could find a firm footing, I would write no more essays, I would be decisive, but my soul is always on probation, still serving its apprenticeship."

He was given a pauper's funeral the following day, a day that dawned very cold; few people attended. That great solitary figure had scarcely any friends and scarcely any enemies either, since, before his death, he had been closer to the world of myths and ghosts than that of everyday concerns. Almost all those who attended were boys the age of Teófilo, who had often visited old Moura's modest dwelling and whom he had taught how to mend nets, how to distinguish the songs of different birds, how to make baskets, how to caulk a boat. He had also read poetry to them and told them fantastic stories about shipwrecks, sailors captivated by siren songs and of cities submerged beneath the sea. There must have been about a dozen boys altogether. They stood in a circle around the niche in the wall where the coffin was placed, their eyes serious, on their best behaviour, as if they were members of the family.

As Don Ambrosio was saying the last prayer for the dead, Teófilo gave the boy to his right a nudge in the ribs, whispered something and indicated the gate to the little cemetery. His whispering alerted the others and soon everyone was looking in that direction, their eyes filled with mingled respect and amazement. A tall woman, wearing a woollen beret and dark glasses, and swathed in a long raincoat, was walking slowly towards the place where they were gathered. She was carrying a bunch of chrysanthemums in her arms. Everyone knew her. It was the lady from the Quinta Blanca.

Although the reason for her visit to the cemetery seemed indisputable, she stopped a few feet short of the group and thus, set slightly apart, she remained until the whispering of prayers had ended and Don Antonio's friends had begun to disperse. Some spontaneously bowed their head to her as they passed, in such a way that, although no one had done so on purpose, since everyone else was moving and she was still, it looked as if she had come there in order to receive the condolences of the other people present. When, at last, the others had left, she stepped forward and stood silently for a while before the anonymous stone. Then she stood on tiptoe to place the flowers that she had brought in an iron ring, apart from two white flowers which she separated out from the bunch. Some glanced furtively at her and thought they could see her moving her lips, perhaps reciting some prayer, despite the fact that she had never been seen in church.

She was there for nearly ten minutes, motionless and enigmatic behind the mask of her dark glasses. Gradually, everyone else left.

"Either she's got sore eyes or she doesn't want us to see her crying," reasoned one of the boys as they were walking back down to the village, "because no one would wear dark glasses on a day like this."

"And she n-n-never wears them ever," stuttered Teófilo.

The sky looked like snow and an ice-cold, brackish wind was blowing. When the sound of voices and straggling footsteps had gone, the lady from the Quinta Blanca started strolling slowly amongst the tombs until she reached one that was more lavish than the rest, in the north-east corner of the cemetery, presided over by a life-size angel carved in black marble. Its wings rose up above the wall like those of a giant bird poised on the boundary between two worlds, listening for the sea, in order to bear the sound of its lullaby to the dead. The woman stooped to place the two white chrysanthemums next to the name of Inés Guitián, and just as she was standing up, she noticed someone behind her. She turned round. It was Don Ambrosio. They looked at each other without speaking and, after a few moments, they left the grave together. She went ahead of him, but before going out through the gate, she stopped.

"I suppose you want to tell me something. If you do, please do so before we go out into the road. Forgive my being so direct," she said, looking at him.

"There's nothing to forgive," he replied. "On the contrary, I hate hypocrisy".

"So, what can I do for you?"

"It's about our old friend. Yesterday, when I was helping to prepare him for burial, I found amongst his books an envelope with a wax seal; on it was written: "For the lady of the Quinta Blanca". I decided to take it with me, although I had my doubts. Not any more though. I was thinking of coming to see you."

"Doesn't he mean the former owner?" she asked.

"That's what I thought at first, because I noticed that the first page of some of his books bore the ex-libris of Doña Inés Guitián. I imagine she lent them to him at one time."

The lady shrugged her shoulders.

"I don't know what to say."

"But, judging by the shaky writing, this envelope seems to have been written recently. And besides, since Antonio knew perfectly well that Doña Inés died years ago (I remember he was at her funeral), it doesn't seem logical that he should hang on to something for so long, something which, anyway, he could have sent to her son, don't you think?"

Without waiting for a reply, which was not forthcoming, Don Ambrosio removed from amongst the folds of his cassock a bulky envelope which he held out to the woman.

"As I said," he added, "I was thinking of coming to see you this very afternoon, so you've saved me a walk. When I saw you appear a while ago, I had no further doubts about who the envelope was addressed to. You've no idea what a relief it was to me, this proof that you and Antonio knew each other."

The lady from the Quinta Blanca took the envelope that the priest was holding out to her. It was a large brown envelope and seemed to contain various objects of different sizes.

"Well," she said, looking down at the ground. "I did know him a little. We sometimes met on one of my walks around the lighthouse, and we started talking because I discovered that, like myself, he was addicted to literature. It seemed to me that he spent too much time on his own and needed someone to exchange ideas with, an extremely common complaint, by the way, amongst people of a certain age and with refined tastes when they gradually lose those friends who once shared and nurtured their enthusiasms. What else remains to them when they reach that point, can you tell me that, apart from the refuge of dreams?"

Don Ambrosio had listened to her thoughtfully.

"Well, what Antonio had, apart from his love of literature, and apart from his dreams, was his faith," he said in a firm voice. "Not your average-man-in-the-street's faith perhaps, but a special faith, very much his own, but he had it. He was filled, as few people are, by a sense of the beyond, the *plus ultra*, as he preferred to call it. And that is what saved him."

There was a silence and the priest's serene eyes collided with the dark glasses protecting hers. Her voice had lost the controlled, impersonal tone she had used before and she replied gently:

"I didn't know that. And it consoles me greatly to know it, it really does. Thank you for telling me."

They said goodbye on the road, because they were heading in opposite directions. The wind snatched at their clothes.

"If you don't mind," he said, as he shook her hand, "I'll come by one afternoon and bring you the books that came from Doña Inés Guitián's library. I took those too. I feel they should be returned to the library they belonged to, even if they were a loan or a gift. That's the best place for them, don't you think?"

"Of course. Where else? Things always find their place sooner or later, although sometimes they have a long, strange journey before they finally settle down. But nothing happens by chance. Anyway, Father, I'll leave you now, it's starting to sleet and I've got a cold I can't seem to shake off. Come and see me whenever you like."

"I will indeed. It's been a great pleasure. And take care of yourself. There's some very nasty flu about this winter."

II

Visit to the Tower

That night, Maurício Brito simply couldn't get to sleep. Twice he had put on the light, got out of bed and stretched out on the floor to do some exercises. Raising his legs, keeping them absolutely straight, he began describing wide circles with them, his eyes fixed on a damp patch which had been growing larger since the beginning of December, and had spread across the ceiling like some troubling rain cloud, until, finally, it had reached the door.

The whole right wing of the second floor was more dilapidated than the rest of the house and needed, amongst other things, a new roof. Built in brick and shoddily fitted out for various, successive uses, in contrast to the stone solidity of the façade, it always looked like a some-what anachronistic addition – a caprice, so people said, of the late Leonardo Villalba, before he died of drink. People also said that, for a long time, his widow, Doña Inés Guitián, had kept those rooms locked up, the rooms where he had sought refuge in the latter part of his life. She had never dared to have them demolished, however, despite her hatred of them, because she would have considered that an attack on the memory of her husband and because she felt the stirrings of a slightly uneasy conscience. That north-facing part of the house known as the attic, which formed an angle with the corridor and was separated from it by a flight of eight steps, was more exposed to the elements than the left wing, which was protected by the mansards and the terrace roofs adjoining the tower.

"It's cold," Maurício said to himself as he got back into bed for the third time. "And, as she remarked the other day, that leak is like a Stealth bomber about to drop its bombs. She does come out with some funny things sometimes!"

And he smiled but left the light on. He was still wide awake.

She herself had been insisting for a month or more on the urgency of re-roofing the attic, ever since Maurício had moved in there, for his arrival had coincided with a prolonged period of heavy rain and strong winds.

Before, when he had first moved in to the Quinta Blanca, after she had written to him asking him to fly over from Brazil, he had slept in a room in the basement, because the house was in the throes of being refurbished and, having a room near the hall made it much easier for him to keep an eye on the workmen and to give orders about transporting materials and removing rubble; he could even jump on his motorbike and go into town to protest loudly about delays, botched jobs or astronomical bills.

"You're always standing up for me, Maurício. You're my feet and my hands," she said to him sometimes.

And since she was little given to praise, her words were like celestial music to his ears.

He had, in fact, performed the job of foreman. He didn't mind where he slept, because he dropped into bed like a stone. The refurbishment took more than a year, which was understandable, given the magnitude of the job as well as the difficulty they had in persuading local craftsmen – who were naturally lazy anyway – to drive out to such a remote place, especially when all the carpentry, painting, plumbing and electrical work had to be done to such a high, not to say, finicky standard. There was also the fact that his mistress often shut herself up in her room to write and then she forgot about everything. Maurício loved her dearly, but, in the end, he got distinctly fed up. She spoke to him in quite a different tone now.

"I want your room to be really lovely, the prettiest room you've ever had," she had said to him when she took him up to the attic. "You can choose whichever of these three rooms you want, and you can take whatever bits of furniture you like from the others. I think the last room's the nicest, the one near the bathroom, don't you think?"

"I don't really mind."

"Well, we'll say no more about it, but tomorrow morning you

must call the roofers and the heating engineers too, because none of the radiators in this part of the house work properly. You've got the numbers for those people, haven't you?"

"Possibly, but it's not an immediate problem, Señora. I'm up to my eyes in work on the other part of the house. There's no hurry."

"Yes, Maurício, there is. Winter's nearly upon us."

Oddly enough, though, now that winter really was upon them, she had spent several days absorbed in her thoughts, immured in an almost hostile silence, indifferent to any questions of a practical nature.

After almost twenty years' acquaintance, Maurício was no longer surprised by his mistress's sudden abstractions which erupted periodically, with no warning symptoms; a state of galloping agitation wrenched her from this world and carried her off to another known only to her. And yet from those unknown regions – whatever they were – she continued giving off light and transmitting signals which, little by little, he had learned to interpret.

This time it was different. She wasn't writing. She didn't even glance out of the window and she rarely changed her clothes. She spent the empty hours lying on her bed, surrounded by books that she would open and close again without bothering to put on her glasses. The lines around her mouth had grown more marked. She ate, barely opening her mouth, with the inexpressiveness of someone chewing gum. She had become opaque, ordinary. It was as if she had grown suddenly old, and, although he hoped it would be only a passing phase, this change made Maurício's heart contract.

He got out of bed yet again, alerted this time by a sharp sound repeated at more or less regular intervals and which he could not quite locate. This time he got dressed, picked up the torch, opened the door and stood for a few moments, listening. It must be a shutter that had come unfastened and was beating against the wall of the house, flailed by the wind. Perhaps he should go out into the garden. He went down the stairs from the attic and stopped at the top of the great double staircase that led to the rooms on the main floor. No, the noise wasn't coming from there. It wasn't coming from the second floor either, but from above. He switched off the torch and continued walking in the dark towards the left. He peered into the distance. No light came from beneath the last door on the corridor, the one that led to her private rooms. Just as well. Tonight, it seemed, she had managed to get to sleep. He walked a short way across the carpet, pressed a switch just before he got to the bedrooms, and a soft light illuminated a spiral staircase with a modernist bannister that led up to the tower.

The delicate light grew gradually fainter as the stairs descended until, at the bottom, it was only a vague halo that made you doubt the reality of that stairway to the heavens. The cubist decorations, woven into the wrought-iron bannister, projected a tenuous, phantasmagorical shadow on the wall. The light grew more intense as the stairs rose, just as she had intended.

Maurício put one foot on the first step. Whenever he went up there at night, the same words always sprang to mind – why, he didn't know – words that he liked to recite by way of a prayer, because he knew them by heart. They came from Valle-Inclán's *The Marvellous Lamp* – a paragraph from which his mistress had copied out for him, at his request, when they were in Brazil.

"It seems as if the divine, exemplary shadows of all the images we have glimpsed along the way have left those images in order to accompany us, and they seem to lean over to peer into the pools of the soul, as willows lean over clear springs."

It was a pleasure to go up those stairs and watch as those "divine, exemplary shadows" gradually faded to nothing. It was very clever. His mistress had taken special care over the lighting there; it had to be changed several times, because the different electricians who came couldn't get exactly the effect that she wanted, although, to be fair, that was far from easy. The detailed explanations that she gave – although never intransigent or authoritarian – may have been startling in their linguistic precision, but they were better suited to poetic than to technical discourse. She compared the increase in light to the slow affirmation of a hesitant belief, she spoke of the invention of non-existent spaces, of the way certain steep stairs suggested a road to perfection, but she never got angry when they didn't understand her. She would simply shrug her shoulders with a weary smile.

"You have to respect what you don't understand," she would conclude.

Finally, an architect from Madrid managed to achieve what she wanted. He was engaged on some work on an expensive state *parador*, a hotel some thirty miles from there, and he was a friend of Eugenio Villalba's, as Maurício learned later on, when he saw the architect one afternoon at the house of the Villalba Scribners when he first went to work there. Maurício found that meeting, however brief, rather embarrassing, because he realized at once that the lady in Madrid knew nothing of the other lady's existence. The situation was saved by the young architect's aplomb – he was accompanied, incidentally, by a woman who appeared to be his wife – for when Maurício came in to serve the tea, the architect looked at him as if he had never seen him before in his life, despite having had frequent conversations with him about the lighting in the tower and about various other matters on which his mistress required his advice during the visits which he began to make to the Quinta Blanca from then on. Those visits gave rise to new consultations and those new consultations to new visits. Their initial understanding about the difficult juxtaposition of light and space, a problem that went far beyond the merely domestic, gradually revealed unexpected affinities between two solitary souls eager to expand, especially as evening fell. The tower was like a little island that had to be conquered through the light of fantasy, a symbol of absence, of a land that vanishes the moment you sight it. It provided the opportunity to become embroiled in long conversations that ranged from avant-garde art to Plato's *Dialogues*. Casilda Iriarte's sense of humour always prevailed in those subtle talks, she being an expert at the kind of tangential remark that somehow lets a breath of fresh air into any situation threatening to become too serious. She had never been able to tolerate the idea that a man might feel bored in her company and she knew how to prevent that from happening. Indeed, Maurício often heard them laughing together. That was how Maurício knew that she was attracted to the architect, long before she confessed as much to him herself.

"He's the funniest, most sensitive person I've met in ages," she said one day. "He's so stimulating. He's taken years off me. Thank God for the tower."

The architect's name was Sebastián Ortigosa; he was tall and in his early forties, and he dressed with a kind of rumpled elegance that accorded well with both his awkward gestures and the easy way he would fling his raincoat over an armchair. He was extremely attractive and he knew it, just as he knew that his greatest attraction lay in pretending that he didn't. Maurício wondered if his highly intelligent employer, Casilda Iriarte, could possibly have failed to notice that detail.

As long as the work on the hotel lasted, he visited her with almost excessive frequency. Then, suddenly, the visits stopped. Sometimes, they used to sit in the large living room until late at night and, on more than one occasion, when dawn was breaking, and shortly before the workmen arrived, Maurício had heard from his basement room the sound of Sebastián Ortigosa's black Citroën leaving the Quinta Blanca. On those days his mistress would sleep until very late and when she came down for lunch she would be ravenously hungry and her face would be glowing. In the afternoon, she would be unusually active and able to laugh off tedious problems which, on other days, she didn't even want to talk about. And she would speak to Maurício in Portuguese, as if she wanted to create a special intimacy between them. These were unequivocal clues to anyone who knew about other similar affairs she had had. She only started an affair when it seemed irresistible. She didn't seek affairs out or allow herself to be enslaved by them. They simply came to a natural end, much as one season gives way to another. Perhaps it was some implicit pact, because Maurício thought her incapable of deceiving anyone. He was almost sure, for example, that both José Maria, her former husband, and Eugenio Villalba had, willingly or not, accepted that degree of liberty, because they must have known that, otherwise, they would have lost her. And losing her would mean not having her there, not having her words or her smile, all because of a blundering, pointless desire to rummage around in her secret territories. It would mean destroying the bridge of that consoling "See you" with which she always said goodbye, even to the dead.

Sebastián Ortigosa's absence was followed by a rather melancholy period during which she took refuge in her writing, a symptom with which Maurício was also familiar, but for a long time, up until he left her in order to go to Madrid, her eyes continued to shine with a special intensity. That was the light that he missed now when he looked at her.

"I may have been madly jealous of him, but I wish another handsome architect would turn up!" sighed Maurício as he reached the top of that complicated spiral. "But, as we know, the sun rises on even the darkest night."

Once he had reached the top step, there was another switch on the wall to the right which, if you turned it slowly, left the stairs in darkness whilst lighting up the hexagonal room known as the tower, although that name also included other adjoining buildings. Maurício strode across it, leaving the light on the dimmer switch. It was clear now that the noise was coming from the window facing north.

He opened it and a great gust of wind bearing huge snowflakes burst into the room. He leaned right out to grab the metal panel of the shutter that had come loose. He managed to grasp it with both hands and tried to grapple it back into its support, struggling against the icy air that whistled round the cuffs of his jacket. It resisted his attempts.

The figure of Maurício, framed against that wintry backdrop, whilst, in the foreground, the tenuous light in the room spilled over furniture and objects alike, was reminiscent of an illustration in one of those serialized novels, in black and white and with a caption underneath it, for example: ". . . battling against the wild winds, heedless of the risk to his own life" or something of the sort. There were a lot of such novels in that very room. Fabulous stories, full of adventures, that had fired Leonardo Villalba's imagination as a child, adventures with heroes who were always intrepid, with shipwreck victims, pirates, explorers, errant princesses, bandits with hearts of gold, prisoners sentenced unjustly, saints and sea captains. The shelves groaned with books, because not even schoolbooks had been thrown away. And hidden amongst the others, slept a small volume bound in hard covers, with a silk ribbon to mark the page and gilt lettering along its grey spine that read: "Hans Christian Andersen. *The Snow Queen*." There it was, to the right of the window.

His task completed, Maurício closed the window again and drew the velvet curtains, his hair and shoulders thickly flecked with white. He brushed the snowflakes off, took a deep breath and leaned back against the wall. He glanced round at the different corners of the welcoming room, as if seeking shelter. It was obvious, however, that any attempt at rest that night was to be systematically frustrated.

"What are *you* doing here, Señora?" he exclaimed, startled.

He had just seen the figure of a woman stretched out on the divan bed at the far end of the tower. She was fully clothed and lay with one arm covering her face. Her other arm was resting on the pillow, the hand dangling loose. Scattered over the bedspread, in total disorder, were various papers, drawings and photographs. Her immobility and her silence were so complete that Maurício almost ran to her side, like someone hurrying to deal with an imminent catastrophe. When he got there, he took her by the shoulders and started unceremoniously to shake her.

"For pity's sake, Señora, say something! What's wrong?"

"Nothing," she replied in a dull voice, still keeping her face covered, "why should anything be wrong with me? As you see, I'm just having a bit of a lie-down. Don't shake me, Maurício. Goodness, how you love a tragedy!"

Maurício slid down on to the carpet and sat there, staring resentfully at the wall. He sighed.

"It's just that sometimes you give me such terrible frights," he said. "I didn't see you there. I came in because one of the shutters was banging and I couldn't sleep."

"No, nor me, but I felt too lazy to get up. I did hear you come up the stairs and come in. I haven't suddenly gone deaf."

"But the room was in darkness. Were you thinking of staying the night here?"

"I wasn't thinking anything. I had a terrible headache. It occurred to me to come up here because there's something about the tower that draws me, that helps me unwind, that's all. You know I'm not one for making plans. Or do you really still not know me?"

She took a while to remove her arm from her face, and before she did so, she surreptitiously wiped her eyes on the sleeve of her dress, though not furtively enough to escape Maurício's eyes. She had been crying, he could see it, although he only dared risk a glance at her out of the corner of his eye. And when he saw the traces of recent tears on her weary face, he had to clench his jaw hard in order to restrain any tender impulse that might reveal his concern for her.

"Does your head still ache?" he asked solicitously.

"A little bit."

Her voice opened up a crack of hope. Perhaps the bridge of communication between them, impassable for some days now, was beginning to be rebuilt. He watched her sleepily picking up the papers scattered on the bedspread and putting them back in a large brown envelope.

"They're the papers and other things that the priest gave me," she said softly, without looking at him.

Although those whispered words might contain the germ of some interesting story, they were followed by an abrupt silence, and could just as easily be interpreted as an almost imperceptible sign of the perpetual, submarine monologue in which she lived immersed and which she only allowed to surface from time to time, like the silhouette of some strange periscope. Maurício had learned to ignore the confusion of her darker moments and to try to interpret whatever he could pick up, just as he had when he first began watching films in English knowing only a few isolated words. Gradually, he began to make sense of it and to become used to the music. The worst thing you could do was to get impatient or get stuck on a word, because then there was no way you could get back into the rhythm. "It's through her music that I understand her too," he thought, as he shot her another sideways glance.

He saw that she was absorbed in the contemplation of a modestly framed watercolour. It was a seascape in which the figure of a woman appeared, although you couldn't see it very well upside down. Besides, he didn't want to seem too curious. He looked away. What did the priest have to do with all this? Outside, the blizzard howled.

"Would you rather I left you alone?" asked Maurício.

And her immediate response was like a rainbow triumphing over storm clouds.

"No, please don't go. I don't want to be alone tonight. A while ago, I nearly got up and called you. I was thinking of those endless nights in São Paulo, when poor José Maria was dying and you stayed up with me and made me curação cocktails. You were such good company. You used to tell me stories about the sailor Pedro Álvares de Cabral and about the customs of the natives of the lower Amazon Basin at the time of the Conquest. That was when I learned that, amongst the Guaraní Indians, the word they use for being born means "to drop", do you remember? And I told you lots of things as well, especially about birth. I see from your face that you remember too. Tonight, I need to talk, Maurício."

"Well, I'd never have known it," he replied in a hurt voice. "Before, when you came in from the cemetery, you didn't even look at me. And when I asked why you were so late and if you wanted some supper, you just grunted."

"That's why I didn't dare call you just now. I don't know how you put up with me, really I don't. But you must forgive me, Maurício; I haven't been feeling at all well these last few days."

"How can you expect to feel well if you don't look after yourself? For example, when did you have your last ECG?"

"I think it was when I went to Madrid to see my publisher. That's less than a year ago I think."

"Well, I do remember, because we had lunch together. You invited me to a restaurant in Calle Huertas. It was February, St Valentine's Day to be precise. And then you went to the doctor."

"Oh, what does it matter? Honestly, you have the memory of an elephant."

"Did you keep it? The ECG I mean."

"Maybe, but I don't know where I put it. Why do you ask?"

"Because you've started getting palpitations again, or did you think I wouldn't notice? We should get the doctor to call here really, although I know you hate the idea. Or better still, go and see him. Call him tomorrow, ask him for an appointment, and take all your X-rays with you. I could drive you there. Fifty miles is nothing."

She didn't even bother to protest, she didn't even seem annoyed. She had switched off and was sitting on the divan now, hugging herself, as if trying to get warm; she had her arms around her knees, her eyes fixed on the window. You could hear the furious whistling of the wind. She shivered.

"It's not something a doctor could treat," she said, at last, in a voice heavy with emotion. "I'm not feeling well inside, that's what it is, you know what I mean."

"Not inside or outside!" Maurício said angrily. "Aren't you always saying that body and soul are one and the same? Well, try applying that to yourself. Look, you're trembling. You've probably got a fever."

He held out one brown hand and delicately picked up his mistress' left wrist. She unclenched her fingers and allowed him to feel her pulse, although she didn't seem to care either way.

"Your pulse is very fast, it sounds like a samba, and you're missing some beats. Fancy staying here all this time, with a blizzard raging outside and not even a blanket for your knees. Even worse, you haven't had a thing to eat since breakfast as far as I know. Did you eat anything when you were out?"

"Oh, Maurício, don't check up on me, please! I'll have supper later. Stop treating me like a little girl."

"I don't know what you were like as a little girl," he said. "but I bet you got spanked a fair few times. Quite right too."

She burst out laughing. She seemed suddenly animated, as always happened when any kind of controversy arose.

"Me? You must be joking. When I was a girl there was no one who could tame me, less then than now. I wasn't going to put up with any lectures. My grandfather knew that and had given me up as impossible. Anyway, he was just the same. I never complained of the cold or the heat, of having too much to eat or too little, nor when I'd hurt myself, which I often did. I would just dab on a bit of alcohol and that was that. I didn't give my grandfather much trouble, and I earned my living from early on, I'll have you know, making necklaces out of shells and painting watercolours, because painting was my first vocation. In the summer I'd walk miles to the most crowded beaches to sell my wares to the tourists. I used to read people's palms sometimes too. I gave any money I made to my grandfather, I didn't leave it to burn a hole in my pocket. I remember he used to say to me: 'You look at money as if it was going to bite you.' Well, that was my grandfather for you; a fine figure of a man."

She again emptied onto the bedspread the things she had started putting back into the brown envelope and looked for one small photo amongst them. She held it out to Maurício. It was a snapshot in black and white with a serrated edge. It was slightly bent and there were four holes in the corners, evidence that it had spent some time pinned up on a wall somewhere. It showed a tall, smiling man, standing in front of a lighthouse.

"He's younger there, of course, it's long before I was born. I never knew my mother. I've told you that, haven't I, and about the English sea captain? I told you that in São Paulo too, during one of those late-night talks that last summer; I bet you even remember the date. What I remember is the heat, how I could feel death fluttering about us, and the taste of those curação cocktails. Look, look, this is me! It's a wonderful photograph. I look like I'm flying, don't I? Eugenio took it. He would have made a wonderful film director, if his mother hadn't pushed him into business. And all to get him away from me, and all to no avail. It was taken on the rocks, I must have been about fifteen. It used to amaze him the way I would leap off the rocks like that, but he managed to capture that one moment. I twisted my ankle when I fell. Dear God, all that life behind me!"

Maurício felt it imprudent to make any further comment. After looking at them, he returned the photos to her and he noticed with a mixture of satisfaction and alarm the feverish light that was shining in her green eyes now. There was no help for it. They were in for a night of confidences.

"Look, Señora, forgive me interrupting you," he said. "If you want us to go on talking, let me go and light the fire downstairs in the living room, because it's terribly cold up here. I'm not sleepy either. You can tell me what you like about your grandfather and the English sea captain and the late Dom José Maria and about Eugenio and his mother, may they all rest in peace. You could even read me bits from the *Iliad*, if you wanted. But I would like us to be nice and cosy first and for you to have some supper, all right? I can lay down conditions too, can't I, because the person doing the listening doesn't belong to the realm of the shades or of the dead, those poor souls have neither voice nor vote. So, is it a deal?"

She smiled and held out her hand to him. It was very cold. Maurício squeezed it and held it for a moment in his.

"You are a bossy boots! All right. You go on down, and I'll pick up these papers."

"OK, but don't spend too long looking at them; I know you," he said as he walked towards the stairs. "I'll just go out and get some wood from the woodshed, and then I'll warm you up a bit of soup. See you in a minute. I don't want to have to come up here again."

When his foot was on the first step, he thought he heard her call him and he turned round to look at her from there.

"Maurício," she said in a voice that was suddenly weak.

"What's wrong? Tell me."

She took a while to reply. He saw her glancing round at the walls and the shelves, with eyes that were dull and frightened again. Her gaze rested on a desk that stood against the opposite wall; it had lots of large, solid drawers and the top was covered in green oilcloth. In the centre was a Chinese vase full of recently cut laurel branches.

"Do you think he'll come, Maurício?" she asked at last. "He phoned ten days ago and I've heard nothing since. I'm afraid."

"Afraid that he'll come or afraid that he won't?"

"Both."

III

Confidences

". . . All I'm saying is what other force moves the spheres and makes us oscillate within time if not the threat or the hope of what has not yet happened? We hone our wits in order to avoid the claws of fate or seek out places where we can shelter from the elements, all in order to keep alive the bonfire of hope, which, when you think about it, needs very little fuel, sometimes a few eucalyptus leaves will do. Those are the only two poles of reference, Maurício. As long as we are moving towards something or fleeing from something, however fanciful our goal may seem, at least we are alive. The alternative is to vegetate.

"Ever since I was very small, I've accustomed myself to living amongst chimaeras and to transforming whatever happened to me into something else. I was much more inclined to believe in something that hadn't yet happened or might perhaps never happen than in something that you took for granted simply because you could touch it. I learned a lot from butterflies. Were they mine because I had touched their wings and seen them flutter for a few moments between my fingers stained with gold dust, or afterwards when they took flight again? Afterwards, of course. And I picked them up merely in order to prove that, because the relief I felt at letting them go made me one with all the twists and turns of their flight, with the sprigs of heather they chose to alight on and even with the sky, the air and the smell of sea; they taught me to breathe better, to take the long way round in order not to bump up against the dangers of reality, and to feed the fire of my fantasy. I never found out where they settled to sleep, they symbolized 'the other', the intangible, everything as yet untouched by certainties and laws.

"The boy from the house with the tower used to come with his butterfly net and prowl around the hill on which the lighthouse stood, because that was where you found the best butterflies; they must like the smell and spread the news to others, so that each spring new species arrive, iridescent, yellow and blue, stamped with lines and dots; they fly about there freely, confidently, alongside the grasshoppers and the dragonflies. The boy from the house with the tower would creep up on tiptoe, he would watch their bodies tremble as they alighted and then he would throw the net over them; his aim wasn't always particularly good. I'd seen him there several times and he'd seen me too, but it took quite a while before we spoke to each other. 'He has come to my territory,' I thought rather proudly. After all, he lived in the most beautiful house in the whole area and must have been at least five years older than me; later, I found out he was seven years older. I would study him as he crouched on a rock and I would pretend to be keeping watch on the intruder's manoeuvres from one of the turrets of my castle. It began to annoy me that he didn't seem to notice and, at last, one afternoon, I went over to him and dared to speak to him. It was the 7th May; I found it written down here in a little notebook, amongst the papers that Antonio Moura must have inherited from my grandfather, '7th May: I spoke to the boy from the house with the tower,' and there's a star drawn above it. I was almost right next to him before he looked up, and he did so rather angrily, because my arrival frightened off an orange butterfly with black markings that he was about to catch in his net.

"'Haven't you got any butterflies in your own garden?' I asked gravely, sounding like an offended queen, which seemed to me the tone of voice best suited to the occasion. And he looked at me astonished. He had very lovely dark eyes; Eugenio's most attractive features were always his eyes and his hands. 'In my garden? Yes, there are some, but the ones here are much prettier.' Then I said to him that I would never think of going into his orchard to steal fruit, although I'd heard that they had some delicious pears, so many, in fact, that they rotted on the tree and had to be thrown away, instead of being sold off cheap or given away, but even so, I would never dream of going into his orchard. He didn't know what to say, he didn't understand, he obviously wasn't used to being addressed in that impudent manner by an eight-year-girl in battered sandals. 'What's that got to do with it?' he said, at last, embarrassed. 'This isn't your garden, it's not your orchard either.' 'What do you mean it isn't mine? Do you think it isn't mine just because I haven't put a fence around it? Well, I'll tell you something, not having a fence around it makes it even more mine, much more, no doubt about it.' And you see, Maurício, that was the first time in my life that I had put into words all those intricate ideas about the rights of ownership that had been boiling in my head almost since I began to think for myself which, according to my grandfather, was very early on. Things belong to the person who can look at them and know how to appreciate and understand them and even speak to them, so the hill with the lighthouse on it was mine, just as the sea was, along with all the clouds and stars that bloom above it and all the butterflies and seagulls that plough the air and land wherever they fancy, and in order to make those things mine I had no need to take them home with me. 'Look,' I said, 'do you see that white tower? Well, I live there, and you couldn't fit the sea in that tiny space, for example; it wouldn't fit in your house either, however big it is. And if you must know, we don't need it to either, because my grandfather controls both the sea and the ships from a distance, he doesn't need to touch them, and if it wasn't for him they would all be smashed to smithereens.' Later, Eugenio would some-times say to me that on that seventh day of May, he realized that he was falling helplessly in love with me, but pay no attention, at other times, he said that he first realized it when I proposed we make a blood pact, or when I wrote him my first letter, or when he saw me jump off the rocks on the island of seagulls or when he went to the city to study law or when he came back here married to another woman and found me gone. He would say a different date depending on the image that surfaced in his memory, so if you were to believe him, he had spent his whole life beginning to fall in love with me, whether I was actually there before him or not. That is the advantage of not marrying someone, of course, they idealize you. But, anyway, to get back to what I was saying about butterflies; it was because of them that we started talking on that May afternoon and it was what made us want to go on talking, and I found out that he was in the fifth year at school and had been told to put together a collection of insects. We ended up sitting down together on the clifftop, and by the time the sun had set, we had exchanged a substantial amount of information about the lives of insects. The fact is that he knew more than I did or, at least, different sorts of things, the sorts of things that books tell you. And I was envious. I will be eternally grateful to him even if only for the enormous quantity of books that he began to lend me from then on. Some were very good, for example, encyclopaedias with colour plates, which he had to sneak out of the library behind his mother's back; others were simple text books or school books; I devoured them all and when I gave them back, I immediately asked for more. He thought it odd that I could finish them so quickly and, sometimes, to prove that I wasn't just tricking him, he would make me summarize them. The odd thing is that, later on, I was the one who made him recite his lessons to me, and he used to say that I helped him a lot, because I clarified things which he had only learned parrot-fashion, without really understanding them. 'You're so quick!' he would say, astonished. 'You learn things much faster than I do and it all goes in.' And I would say that was because I didn't have any fences in my mind either and that I was determined never to take any exams. Some of those books are still there, upstairs, in Leonardo's room; I recognize them by their shape, by the coloured plates showing the human body and geological strata and the lives of Indians or of dinosaurs, even the book I learned English from, imagine that; it made my heart turn over. It's extraordinary, we learned things from the same books; he obviously inherited them from his father. What is even more amazing to the girl that I once was, is that I had to come and re-find that treasure in the tower, which is the part that always fascinated me most about this house then, seen from outside. I still remember how I imagined the house would be before I'd ever been inside it, and if I dream about it now, what I see is what I imagined then, with the same odd arrangement of corridors and stairs; I even invented a smell for it. Sometimes that smell suddenly resurfaces – it happened earlier on upstairs – and it superimposes itself on and dissipates everything around it; it's a smell that has been incubating in those books, the smell of lost time.

"Eugenio never managed to persuade me to come here, although later he sometimes invited me. 'If you're embarrassed about my mother, we can wait until she goes away,' he used to say to me. 'Look, leave it, I don't want to, but it isn't because I'm embarrassed or ashamed.' 'Why then? You'd love it, it's beautiful. The garden . . . the garden is fantastic!' I would shrug my shoulders. What I felt was a confused idea that resisted the pressure of his inquisitive eyes. It had something to do, though, with the apprehension you feel when you sense danger ahead, that fear before you enter a forbidden place, it's usually a castle, where the hero in fairy tales is tempted to go in – an attractive place – but he draws back or hides until the right moment, because he senses disquieting presences and camouflaged traps. And I, as fond of risks as I was of explaining things, could not confess my fear without specifying the cause, still less attempt to explain it by saying, for example: 'You see, I'm afraid I might cease to be free, that's what it is, that I might start to become like you.' I didn't want to hurt him, so how could I tell him that? I would lower my eyes and fall silent, but in the silence that followed, the house with the tower interposed itself, separating us.

"Eugenio had visited the lighthouse and met my grandfather, but he wasn't received as some kind of special visitor nor did his presence cause any kind of upset; my grandfather spoke to him while he went on working, as he did with everyone; he asked him if he wanted to have tea with us and, when he left, he sent his regards to Eugenio's mother. Why was the opposite so difficult to imagine? Having dismissed my feebler reasons for not going, I finally found where that difference lay. I didn't care what he thought of the lighthouse, of my grandfather and of our way of dealing with company, leaving other people in peace; I liked living the way we lived and I wasn't afraid of anyone else's view of us. The same thing wasn't true of him. He always wanted my approval and the poor man died never knowing if he had ever completely had it. Above all, though, he never really did what he wanted to do. He was full of talk, but it never really came to anything. He wasn't happy studying, or marrying, he didn't really enjoy his son and thus he reached the end. It seems he was doomed to die in a car crash on a motorway in the back of beyond, bound to someone who made his life unbearable. Although, perhaps he was driving the car; perhaps, in that case, he had simply got to a point where he said: 'This is where I stop, and I'll take her with me, just for the hell of it.' We'll never know.

"The fact is that, at first, I found it odd that the boy from the tower, who was, indeed, almost a man, found it more difficult than I did getting out to visit the cliffs at night, the place which, tacitly, became our trysting place. He came to see if he would find me there, but he took a long time to admit it; instead he would pretend to be surprised ('What are you doing here? You frightened me!'), when, in fact, what was odd was that he should be invading alien territory at that late hour, not that I should know its every crevice like the back of my hand and happen be hiding in one of them. 'Doesn't your grandfather mind you wandering around here alone at night?' Honestly, Maurício, I've lost track of the number of times he asked me that, when I was small because I was small, when I was older because I was older. In the end, I just ignored him. And long before there was any mischief in those meetings, at least on my part, I began to realize that he envied me precisely for the reason I mentioned before: I did things because I wanted to, not in order to make a statement or as some act of revenge. I threw myself into the arms of night because I would hear it calling to me when I couldn't sleep, because I liked to breathe in the cool air and watch my shadow on the rocks if there was moonlight and recognize the stars and hear the sound of the waves beating down below and think: 'Even the birds have gone to sleep now and all the creatures of the countryside; I alone am awake and watching. They have lit up the sky just for me. How wonderful!' I went out in search of the night because I chose to, not in order to defy my grandfather or because I felt the walls of the lighthouse pressing in on me. He, on the other hand, was running away not just from a place, but from the person who owned that place — because there are some things that are inseparable. His mother's tentacles lay hidden in the long shadow that the house cast over that unsuspecting explorer of my territory, a shadow that came between us sometimes like a barrier. Eugenio was always two people: the one he imagined his mother saw in him, even when they were apart, and the one that awoke from the depths of that concave mirror as our friendship grew and I allowed him to enter through a tiny, secret door to share some of my dreams, and showed him how to weave other realities: a landscape without senses or walls where we would sometimes escape together on a day trip. He was always afraid, though, keeping an eye on the time when he would have to go back. You could tell from what he said and what he didn't say, in the look of sudden sadness on his face, in the harassed way he would keep consulting his watch. 'But, Sila, are you sure your grandfather won't be worried? It's getting awfully late.' One night, I'd had enough, because he had interrupted a dialogue worthy of Plato himself, and I jumped up, unable to control myself. 'Look, does Doña Inés tell you off if you get home late? What time do you have to be back?' 'I don't like you calling her Doña Inés.' 'All right, your mother then, does she tell you off?' And he shrugged his shoulders, visibly embarrassed. 'It depends where I go,' he replied. 'Ah, so she always knows where you go. That means she knows that you're here with me now, and she doesn't much like it. Is that what you're saying? Well, say it straight out, and don't keep going on about my grandfather, he doesn't keep a check on me!' He got extremely angry, in a very peculiar way, and he came out with something which I wasn't expecting at all. 'You don't love her!' he shouted, as if accusing me of some crime. 'Why? Why don't you love her? Why don't you, she's never done anything to you!' I think it was the first time that I had ever seen him so angry, but that complete lack of logic almost made me laugh. 'She hasn't done anything to me, are you mad? Nothing. I only know her by sight and she never speaks to me or looks at me. To know whether or not you love someone you have to talk to them, they have to smile at you or stroke you or insult you, but at least do something. Don't you see that? She just ignores me, so I don't love her and I don't not love her.' In fact, I did love her in the end, Maurício, but many years had to pass, many years, and a lot of really terrible things had to happen. So that night, which was the first time that the name of the Quinta Blanca's owner was mentioned between us, was also the first time that we quarrelled. His main reproach was that I never asked after his mother or his house, which, after all, even appeared in tourist brochures; I had offended them both with my indifference, and that was when I understood that his mother and the house formed a kind of symbiosis, although I never realized quite to what extent. He got even angrier when he saw that I wasn't intimidated and that I was even smirking a little. 'If you must know, you would have to be the one to take the first step!' he blurted out at last. I looked at him as if he were some creature from outer space. 'What step? What step and where? You're sick in the head, you know! Just leave me alone.' He got up, and he looked so angry, I thought he might hit me. When he left, he said that he intended to do exactly that, to leave me alone, who did I think I was anyway. And for some time he didn't come back.

"My grandfather and I had often talked about how intelligent animals are, much more than we are in some ways. He had pointed out to me how they get their children used to making their own lives as soon as they are physically separate from them; as the Guaraní Indians would say, they just drop them. Off you go then, fly; I've given you your life, haven't I, well, now you have the whole world to explore and you can even take the wrong road if you want to, the choice of adventure is yours. Man, on the other hand, is so domineering and proud that he even tries to tame animals and put them in cages, as if he wanted to teach them a lesson; it isn't enough just to make each other's lives hell. Ever since I was a child, my grandfather had put me on guard not only against becoming too attached to things but also to people. Human beings get in each other's way when they grow too close, he used to say, just like trees when they are planted too close together – they don't let the light through. 'You can die of asphyxiation if you love someone too much, just as you can be enslaved by objects if you take ownership too seriously.' My grandfather used to come out with some wonderful things. Earlier on, I was remembering a poem he used to recite: 'Why let greed make of you a slave and a drudge/when, come the final day, it will rise up to be your judge?' Well, there was a bit more after that, but I can't remember the rest.

"How things change, Maurício. If my grandfather were to raise his head tonight and find out that I was the owner of the large house he used to see in the distance from the top of the lighthouse, the mistress, according to the deeds, of this garden and all this furniture, that's what he would say: How things change. I've been thinking about that for several days now, especially since Leonardo phoned. What I will say, Maurício, is that then, when I used to call it the house with the tower and I had never yet set foot in it, it seemed more real to me than it does now. Don't ask me why.

"I used to think about reality a lot. In fact, my favourite game was trying to catch reality out, by lifting the lid on its brainpan and leaning in to see what could not be seen and had not yet happened. I would start a battle between plenitude and the void, a battle that the latter seemed all set to lose; and I enjoyed watching that ghostly army lay traps for the other and gradually snatch victory from them, slipping out of enemy hands and adorning the parapet at the entrance to its hiding place with invisible trophies. I fought on the side of the void, its shadowy ranks peopled nevertheless by both presence and word. That empty space was much more real than reality itself; it was 'the other thing', what had not yet happened nor been described. It was a bit frightening, but if you lowered yourself down into that region you could enter mysterious labyrinths that you only began to understand better as you travelled through them.

"So, for example, when I finally found out more about my origins, I had already had more than enough contact with my mother in the galleries of that subterranean kingdom, and I felt that I knew her much better and loved her far more than other girls in the village loved their mothers; they were so used to the sight of each other that they barely gave each other a second glance. My relationship with her has lasted ever since, it keeps me alive. My grandfather had said to me when I was very small: 'The sea brought you': and I liked that explanation so much that, for a long time, I didn't want to ask anyone any further questions; in order to believe it, I had only to watch the tide rising up the rocks and to feel its attraction. The sea was my compass. It seemed quite possible to me that, one day, it might, in one of its capricious moods, return my mother to me, but rather than waiting for that to happen, I would go out to the rocks and talk to her, tell her my dreams and ask her for things that she almost always gave me. I imagined her as a mermaid and, on many nights, her voice would mingle with the song of the wind and the waves, like a lullaby. I would go to sleep listening to that chorus and she would float up to the surface of the waters to brush my hair with a coral comb, to look at me hard and to kiss my hands. She would hum a tune to me, but she could not speak. She was always in a hurry. I think she had to visit me secretly, concealing her visits from some marine monsters who had fallen in love with her and who kept her captive in a palace at the bottom of the sea, along with the wrecks of sunken ships. It was built out of polyhedrons of glass or, at least, that's how I drew it, often, very often – there are sketches of it here on the pieces of paper that the priest gave me – and the passing shoals of fish would press their snouts against the walls to watch her sleeping. But she was only pretending to be asleep, she was waiting until she was alone, and that's when she would escape and come up and see me. I don't know how she escaped; she probably had some accomplice."

Maurício kneels down by the fireplace and uses the tongs to reposition the unburned wood in the centre of the fire. Then he picks up two large logs from the basket to the right and throws them onto the newly kindled flames.

"What I don't understand, Señora, is why you don't write all these stories down," he says, still with his back to her, "just the way you're telling them to me tonight. It's wrong that I should be the only one to hear them. I'm saying this for your own sake too, because now you're getting it off your chest, I agree, but it might just be a case of feast or famine, it's happened before. You could wake up and find that far from talking your way out of this malaise of the soul you're speaking of now, you have merely provoked an even more virulent attack. I don't know, I feel happier when you're writing. Listening to you talk is great, and even though you hardly speak to me once you do go into your room and all I can hear is the sound of the typewriter, nevertheless, that's what suits you best. I can tell from your face when you look at things, it's not just some kind of drunken outburst, the effect lasts longer, much longer. And there's no need to ask where you would get the plots from, you don't even have to invent them, what with all the things that have happened to you in your life – as well as the things you keep quiet about, because you do keep quiet about a lot of things – I mean it, Señora, you've got enough there to begin and never end; set to it. Even estimating on the low side, you've got enough material there for ten novels."

Once the fire has revived and orange flames are once again licking the logs, Maurício sits down again in an armchair, opposite the sofa where she is lying with a plaid rug over her knees. He looks at her now, across the low table on which lie the remains of supper, as if wanting to see the effect his words are having, or perhaps even slightly regretting having said them. She too glances away from the fire, fixes her eyes on him and notices with a look of pleasure that he has just stretched out his legs and settled back expectantly in his seat. He shows no sign of impatience, but neither does he seem to be bored with hearing stories or anxious to get to bed. The pendulum clock has just struck two, but there is no echoing response in the expression on Maurício's face, no change in his relaxed posture. It is his way of saying to her: "Go on, then!" although he won't actually ask her to, and she, who knows him well, smiles and takes note.

"It's odd," she says, staring into space again, after a brief pause, "the last time that Eugenio came here he said something rather similar. I'd been reading him bits from my book, before sending it off to the publisher, and it isn't that he didn't like it, he liked it a lot, but suddenly, without a word of explanation, he went very quiet, as if he felt sad. It was an abrupt, rather incomprehensible squealing of brakes, like when someone stops in mid-sentence and the person hearing that ellipsis glances over at the door to see if someone has come in or at the window to see if a car has arrived or if the wind is getting up. It was sorrow rather than curiosity or surprise that was reflected on Eugenio's face. We were sitting on this very sofa; I had my glasses on and had the typescript on my lap; night had fallen and he'd just switched on the light. When I think that that was the last night he spent here, in the Quinta Blanca, I say to myself: 'Could it have been a premonition?', but how could I think that, it's the kind of thing that we go over and over afterwards, because of that blind passion of ours for interpreting the gestures or behaviour of other people, as the road where we once walked in company with others gradually becomes scattered with more and more corpses that we can never call as witnesses. I can't get it out of my head, the anxious way he looked around him as if the walls and the furniture were telling him something he did not dare confess. I hate having to ask anyone: 'What's wrong? Why are you sad?', just as I can't bear people asking that of me, but, in the end, I had no option, because the silence was becoming unbearable and, as I said, there was no reason for it. I tried to put some humour in the question: 'May one know, paying whatever the going rate might be, what God-forsaken place you are lost in, sir?' I was kneeling on the sofa by then, sitting closer to him, and I began drawing lines across his forehead, like roads on a map, to make clear what kind of inner journey I was referring to. He snatched up my hand in one of his and squeezed it hard, whilst with the other he described a broad circle indicating the room. 'Here, Sila, here,' he said, 'I can't escape from here. This is what traps me, all this. And you. It's especially since you arrived to make it rise from its ashes, since you fanned the dying embers, and here you are like a fish in water, oblivious to the past. I know you have a perfect right to feel like that, and perhaps what I'm feeling is morbid, but it gives me vertigo, like the vertigo you're writing about in the abstract, and if you're capable of abstraction that means that you have already tamed it and it no longer harms you; I feel it here in my guts, that vertigo, it stirs inside me every time I find you here or I phone you, or I simply think of you calmly living here, immune to its ghosts; I know it's unfair, but it makes me angry just to think of it, I can't free myself from all those accumulated errors, from all those nightmares, all those unpaid debts.' He had grown obsessive with the years, he'd have these moods which were a mixture of envy and bad conscience, I don't know, I think he just wanted to meddle in my life, to give a good shaking to the 'impassive warrior' so loath to display her wounds, 'if you have any', as he said to me that evening, 'because, I'll have you know, I have given up all attempts to understand you; you drive me mad.' And he looked at me keenly, expecting a violent response. He hadn't given up trying to understand me; if only he had, 'then maybe you would leave me in peace', I said to him, 'that's where all our ills come from, from the fact that you have never been able to leave me in peace. I can feel your curiosity from a thousand miles away, even those times when we've said: That's it, it's over. So don't give me that. Anyway, who has done most to blow things up out of all proportion this evening? You. Firstly, because you have no idea what relationship I may or may not have with the ghosts of this house, unless, of course, they've been sending you telegrams, and, secondly, because something's come over you, don't deny it. You were talking about my book in a perfectly normal tone of voice, saying that it doesn't sound as if it were written by someone my age, that young people immersed in their own personal hells will love it. Then what happened? Because something must have happened, was it when you mentioned hell?'

"That was when he revealed the unexpected cause of his unease: what I should do was write my memoirs. I looked at him, shocked – memoirs? Yes, but taking in everything, lighting a bonfire with my memories and his and those of Leonardo and those of Doña Inés – he'd even thought of a title: *The House with the Tower Speaks* – reveal the truth and tell everything. That's what he would do if he had my amazing talent for words. Tell everything, and leave nothing out. So, I thought to myself, yet another version, one of many, of his desire to move into my soul, his youthful dream that had never come true. There was something more, though, and he was quick to tell me. When I was reading him extracts from my essay, he said that he had closed his eyes for an instant and it had seemed that it wasn't my voice he was hearing, but that the person talking to him from afar was the young Leonardo, 'that guest in hell' as he called him, a stranger with whom he used to discuss literature – making do with the invisible feelings and emotions that barely surface in that kind of arm's-length conversation – until Leonardo disappeared for ever. That was what my book was like too. Distant. It held out a hand, but when you went to grasp it, you bumped headfirst into a kind of thick, glass wall, 'just like those fish prowling round the underwater palace of your mother the mermaid'. And it touched me that he should remember that and mention it again. Sometimes, often, he was absolutely right. That is precisely what literature is, a glass prison. But I didn't say that to him. I'm saying it now to you."

There is a silence which looks likely to be a long one, and Maurício holds his breath. All you can hear is the crackling of the fire. He doesn't dare move. Whenever his mistress is in confiding mood, he is invaded by the same feeling of unreality, of something miraculous. He is not entirely sure that he is doing the listening; it seems so odd to be listening to a conversation that took place in exactly the same place and provoked by a similar remark, that they inevitably became confused one with the other. "I too asked her why she didn't stop inventing stories and just write the novel of her life; she obviously prefers to tell it rather than write it, and I can't say I'm surprised, because there would be an awful lot to write down. She writes it down in fragments as she talks to one person and then another, as she lives her life, that's the way she is; I don't know who will sew all the pieces together afterwards, they'd certainly have their work cut out, but she doesn't seem to care; I won't interrupt her again, or perhaps she's sleepy and wants to leave it for another day." He half-closes his eyes and sees her blurred and distant, inside her glass palace, surrounded by grotesque fish, amongst them Don Eugenio opening and closing his mouth, entirely given over to speaking and to peering in at what he didn't understand. "I understand it all better," thinks Maurício, "because she's telling it to me like a story; when you live through things, you don't notice what's going on, you have to get some distance, you have to let time pass; that's what must have happened to her with that book on vertigo." And he feels a need to close his eyes completely, because what he's heard, along with his own thoughts on the matter, have gone round and round in his head so often that now what is turning round and round is the room, the room he's in tonight or the room she and Eugenio were in on that other night, he doesn't know; the silence buzzes and he too is feeling the beginnings of vertigo.

"Are you asleep, Maurício?"

"No, Señora."

"You closed your eyes and I thought . . ."

"It was just so that I could think better while you were quiet. To allow you to think more clearly too, or to rest, if you prefer. It must be exhausting rummaging around in that crowded attic of a head of yours and choosing which things to leave and which to bring out, because some things will inevitably draw others along with them, I imagine, or, rather, I see, because I can see that that is what's happening."

"Exactly, Maurício, you understand things so well," she sighs. "That's what I said to Eugenio, I asked him if he thought it would be an easy matter setting myself up as the chronicler of a house like this and then simply interleave my own story too – can you believe it? – because that was his ideal book; he wanted my story incorporated into the other; what could be simpler?"

She sits up a little on the sofa and again falls silent, but Maurício is no longer afraid that she will fall silent for good. Leaning back, she looks across at the stone border round the large fireplace. On it, framed in silver, are two portraits turned slightly so that they seem to be looking at each other. The one on the right is of a lady of about sixty with thick wavy hair caught back in a bun on top of her head: Doña Inés Guitián. In the other, an extremely handsome man in uniform and with a thick moustache smiles rather smugly out at her: the English sea captain.

"He said I should let the house speak, can you imagine?" his mistress goes on. "Why else had I come here, otherwise? The house was begging me to write the book; couldn't I hear it? He could. He was terribly upset, his eyes blazing; he couldn't bear the fact that everything that these walls had witnessed, everything that was kept in these drawers and that sat crouched in the corners of the garden should be lost for ever. He spoke to me almost with the urgency of someone making a deathbed request: I was the best person for the job because I knew everything, I knew about now and about before I came here, when I used to call the Quinta the house with the tower. And he kept broadening out the scope of the book he was proposing, like a madman; it had to contain the story of our turbulent love affair from start to finish, as well as all the stories I had ever told him, about the lighthouse, the butterflies, my dead mother, my decision to run away and the actual event itself, because, like it or not, those memories had become fused for ever with those of Inés Guitián. 'Like it or not, mother, like it or not!', he repeated, addressing her portrait. 'Everything's all tangled up now, all part of the same mess', and then he started talking directly to his mother in a slightly crazed way, getting the truth all out of kilter in a series of aggressive reproaches that absolved him from all charges of egotism and cowardice, and even managing to blame her for a marriage that the poor woman never wanted in the first place. I stopped him right there and said that either I left the room while the two of them settled their scores alone or he must allow me to intervene as a witness for the prosecution, because things weren't like that with his mother; he mustn't forget how well she treated me afterwards, in the second part of the novel, and besides, as regards the first part, he was painting things the way he wanted them to be; he had his own reasons for bringing the lady from Chicago back with him, that was his business, but I wanted to make it quite clear that the lighthouse keeper's grand-daughter had never once considered marrying the boy from the house with the tower; the fault did not lie only with his mother, he really should try to remember things more clearly. That only gave him more arguments: 'You see? You're the only one who can tell the story,' it was true, his psychiatrist said the same, he said that Eugenio tended not to be objective enough and to offload his guilt on to other people, it was a symptom of immaturity. 'He doesn't miss a thing your psychiatrist, does he?' I said. And he was annoyed that I was trying to change the subject, which I was, of course, but I did my best to be patient, because he's impossible when he's like that. As well as having a bad memory and lacking a writer's skill, he was lacking in objectivity; he recognized that. That was why I was the person for the job. 'Things don't affect you so much, you know how to keep a distance.' He was contradicting himself now by praising the glass walls of the underwater palace which, shortly before, he had condemned. He got muddled up and embarrassed when he saw that I was enjoying myself. 'Really, Sila, this is a serious commission,' he said, excitedly. 'Listen, you just sum it up, I can take notes if you like.' What he was commissioning from me was an account of our love affair, since I had perhaps understood it better or been more in control. If I liked, I could conclude it with my journey 'in search of the Father', that's how he put it, in Freudian terms. And then he stopped talking, as if he were beginning to feel ashamed of having started the whole business solely to dictate to me the index of a book that still only existed in the mind of God. I waited a little for him to calm down and I looked at him mockingly. I was almost sure that when he mentioned my trip to England, which coincided more or less with his trip to Chicago, he had experienced a slight feeling of vertigo. 'Is that all? Before you said "from start to finish". Are you sure that's where you want the book to end.' He couldn't hold my gaze, he knew that we were entering an area of shifting sands. 'I don't know, that would be up to you,' he said in a voice that had grown suddenly faint, as if he wanted to abandon that whole byzantine discussion. But he had aroused my baser instincts and I was now the one who wanted to get to the bottom of things. 'Fine,' I said in mock-solemn tones, 'End of Part One. Don't you think the second part would be of interest to the public? I find it the most exciting part myself, although it is, perhaps, a little shocking. When shall we call in the censor's scissors? When we find out that your lovely wife is infertile or a little later?"'

There is a silence, like the silence at the end of a chapter. But there's no music playing. Maurício and the lady from the Quinta Blanca exchange a brief but intense look. Only a few seconds are needed for that flash of complicity by which a friend understands what their companion is alluding to and makes it clear that they have understood, a look that always carries with it a faint "Do you remember?" Yes, Maurício did remember. It was the night when Dom José Maria went into a coma, when Maurício, seeing how sad his mistress was, had asked her if she had no family left. That was the first time that Maurício heard Leonardo's name ('I had a son when I was in Spain; I gave him up immediately after he was born; that was the agreement'), the first time that he had seen her cry real tears and had taken her in his arms to console her, how could he forget it. "You've got me, Señora, you've got me," he had said. He gives a slight nod, the scene comes to life again between them, and that allows her to continue, though not before she has smiled sweetly at him, at Maurício Brito, with no ghosts interposed between them. And suddenly, the fire flares up.

"... Then he looked down very nervously and he said, almost stammering, that, yes, I should include the second part too. 'Everything that happened after that, Sila, everything that happened when you went back to England and I went in search of you and asked you that favour,' he repeated, taking my hands, 'something that only you could give me, when my mother asked you too. Surely I don't need to remind you of what happened? Everything ... up until your departure to Brazil with the old widowed diplomat – like a character out of a play by Moratín – you can leave that out, that's just a parenthesis in your life that simply doesn't exist for me.' I got angry at that point and said who was he to tell me how I should write my memoirs, should I ever decide to do so; that really was the limit; the writer is the one who selects and orders the events in a book. And the fact that my time in Brazil didn't exist for him was largely because I have enough good taste not to mix the men in my life nor to talk about them one with the other, and then he asked me if I had ever told José Maria about Leonardo. 'What has that got to do with you? Have I ever asked you if she knows or if she still believes that Leonardo was abandoned one night in a bundle at the door of the Quinta Blanca? That's what really gets you, the fact that I never ask you anything,' because it's true, Maurício, you're the only person I've ever asked about her; and I told him too that I had more respect for the man who was not only dead but had treated me better than anyone else in this world, who had nurtured not only my vocation but also my will, he backed me to the hilt, you know that, Maurício, he was one in a million, if he hadn't been, how else could I have married him? So, I lost my rag, which is what he wanted deep down, and I hauled out some dirty washing that he had waved under my nose hundreds of times before. But it was wrong of me to get angry, I recognize that. After all, hadn't his affair with Miss Scribner been tantamount to throwing a hangman's noose about his own neck – all very noble; they weren't even particularly fond of each other and then it turned out that she had an immature womb and she hadn't told him; they spent thirty years making each other's lives hell, that's all Eugenio ever went on about in his conversations with me and in his letters, accusing himself of cowardice, looking for a way of making amends that no one was asking him to make. 'I'm sick and tired,' I said, 'of being your rubbish bin.' And we ended up having a bitter quarrel, as we always did when our respective marriages were mentioned. It was our last quarrel.

"When we said goodbye the following morning, we had made peace again.

"It was very early, because he had to get back to Madrid before lunch, but I wanted to get up with him and make his breakfast. I don't usually do that, because at that time, as you know, I like to sleep. I don't know what came over me. And I even took extra care over how I looked. In the kitchen, while we were having breakfast, he suddenly said: 'Sila, I can't believe how stupid I am not to have understood, even after knowing you all these years, that I won't get anywhere trying to meddle in your affairs. And forgive me for comparing José Maria, may he rest in peace, with a husband out of a play by Moratín. As you know, I envy him, because he, at least, was able to make you happy.' I was on the point of saying that I couldn't say the same about his wife, but it seemed too cruel. Instead I said: 'Believe me, no one's happy. Do you want some more coffee?'

"Then, when we were standing at the front door, I went to fetch a jacket and asked him to drive me as far as the lighthouse, because I wanted to make the most of being awake at that hour in order to watch the sunrise. When we arrived, it was still dark, more or less; he glanced at his watch and he got out of the car too, saying that he still had time to walk with me a while. We went up the hill, holding hands, not speaking, and it was very cold, even though it was spring, last spring. But how good the sea smelled in the early morning. He left me there alone, on the cliff, with the waves crashing on the island of seagulls, when the sun was just about to come up. It was a long time since we'd been up there together. 'I'd like to stay here with you for ever – and that's the truthful part of me speaking – you do know that, don't you?' I nodded and we kissed. I was afraid that he might get too solemn. 'Do you remember,' he asked, 'when you proposed making a blood pact, on this very spot?' 'Of course I do, I remember everything. Don't worry,

I'll put that in my memoirs too, when I finally get round to writing them. But I don't feel like dissecting butterflies just yet.'

"Then he began running his index finger across my forehead, as I had done to him the previous evening, and he asked me if all the butterflies were still flying about inside there, if none of them had died yet. I shrugged. 'Well, look after them,' he said, 'you know how fragile they are.' He left me then and I watched him walk briskly down to the foot of the hill, and, before he got in his car, he turned to wave goodbye."

For a moment, Maurício doesn't know what to do or say. Finally, he gets up and slowly crosses the space separating his armchair from the sofa. He stops close by his mistress, now hunched into a ball. His knees almost brush the plaid rug covering hers, but she doesn't seem to notice. She has covered her face with her hands and, from the moment her voice faltered over the word "goodbye", interrupting the flow of words, her body, shaken by a sudden fit of shivering, provides the first indication that she is losing control. She doesn't seem to want to avoid it or to attempt to disguise it. Maurício knows her; she has given up the struggle. And yet she doesn't cry, that is what she finds hardest. She's like a tree shaken by a harsh, dry wind, reaching out imploringly with her branches for the first few drops of rain to fall.

Taking advantage of the fact that she is no longer lying down, Maurício sits silently by her side, expectant, motionless, his eyes fixed on the glowing embers of the logs in the fireplace. He is not sure whether to put any more on or not. It's very late and his mistress, who has run the whole gamut of emotions today, would do best to drink some herb tea with orange flower water in it, and go to sleep. But now is not the moment to give her advice about her health, that would merely trigger protests; now it is a time for silence, to help those pent-up tears leap the barrier of words; that was the best first-aid he could possibly offer. He looks at her out of the corner of his eye, moves a little closer and, after a moment's hesitation, he finally dares to put an arm about her shoulders.

"Poor thing," he murmurs, "poor thing. Come on, try and have a cry, it will do you good. Just a little cry."

Her immediate response is to rest her head on Maurício's chest;

she clings to him and unleashes a stream of incoherent words, drowned
in tears.

"... I thought I would be able to bear it, but I can't, Maurício, I
can't ... I've just walked into the lion's den all alone, his father was
right, too many butterflies have died ... know your own strength ...
and I just laughed, I know what I'm doing, I know, I know, I know ...
always betting on the most unlikely card, defying vertigo ... but not
now, Maurício, not now, this is the end ... this is one leap I can't
make ..."

Maurício feels his mistress' faltering breath, her body shaken by
sobs, the warm breath on his chest of words half-muffled by his check
cotton shirt; he can barely understand what she's saying.

"Quiet now, Señora, calm down a bit. You'll do it, you'll see," he
says in a persuasive voice, although he's not even sure what leap she's
referring to. "Your heart's big enough to bear anything, as long as we
look after it a little, that's all we can do. You see, you feel better for
having a cry, don't you? You've been talking too much, that's what it
is, you've had a touch of verbal colic. Just be quiet for a while now,
please, just let it pass. Talking and crying don't mix, you know, they
cancel each other out, neutralize each other, but you know that, you
said as much in your poem 'Time for tears', it's your own words I'm
trying to console you with, you see, they've become mine now. Would
you like a cup of herb tea?"

She shakes her head, still buried in his shirt, and gives a deep sigh.
She remains for a while huddled in that position, until her body gradually stops trembling and her breathing becomes regular and easy, as if
she had just got over a fright. She kisses one of Maurício's protecting
hands, moves delicately away from him and leans her head on the back
of the sofa, murmuring "Thank you" and looking totally exhausted.
The occasional belated tear still leaks out from beneath her closed
eyelids. She slowly opens them, as if in search of something. Maurício
gets up and gives her her handbag, they look at each other, she nods
with an almost imperceptible smile that seems to augur a return to
near-normality. He watches as she opens the zip and takes out a handkerchief. It's the handbag that her husband gave to her the Christmas

before he died, nine years ago now; dates too are like preserved butterflies. The pendulum clock strikes three.

Maurício sits down on the carpet, facing the dying fire. He prefers not to look at her. He rehearses mentally how to say to her, without it sounding like a lie, that he's utterly exhausted and about to go up to bed, to see if he can convince her to do the same; it's the kind of trick you would use on a frightened child unable to sleep after waking from the unfathomable terror of some nightmare. She referred to a leap, "I can't make it", she said, nightmares are always full of leaps into the void, a premonition of the abyss, of the vertigo that she knows so well. What will she be thinking about now? He doesn't want to look at her.

"It was very rash of me to ask him to come, Maurício," she says, after drying her tears, "very rash indeed. I don't know how many letters I've started to write to him these last few days, the number of bits of paper I've looked at, from his father and his grandmother, that might serve to document the story, and I still haven't decided whether or not to tell him, far less how or where; it's as you said before, it's like going into an attic and asking: 'Now what shall I take out and what shall I leave?', because not even Faulkner or Cervantes or anyone could do what Eugenio wanted me to do, to set out everything from start to finish; at some stage, the novelist has to choose a starting point, which may or may not be the starting point, it depends on how you look at it. You can't tell the whole of a story, Maurício, because no story is complete, not even for the person who has lived through it. Stories don't end with death either. That's a mistake we pay for dearly, not taking into account the traces left by the dead, forgetting that the dark tunnel beginning to be dug beneath the feet of those apparently left alive is always another beginning. And as if that were not enough, I now have the legacy left by Don Antonio, the photo of my grandfather, Leonardo's great-grandfather, and I will have to say to Leonardo: 'This is your great-grandfather, kindly make room for him in your attic too' – more butterflies to collect. And I just can't, I just end up bruising them, I regret catching them, I let them go and they just flutter about unable to leave the ground, unable to take flight again, it's awful to see them like that, caught between two worlds, neither one thing nor the other.

The fire's going out, Maurício, why don't you put more wood on?"

"Certainly not. The fire gets you all worked up. You've got to go to bed and give your mind a rest. The same goes for me, because I'm tired too."

"Yes, you must be. You go up, if you like. I'm feeling better, much better, really I am. You're such a good listener, Maurício, you have such patience. I don't know what was in that fire tonight, did you throw some potion on it? My husband died nine years ago and I haven't cried as I did tonight since; you were there as well and I was crying for the same reason. Although it wasn't the same, at the time I wasn't worried about papers; my soul was papered with memories, it's true, but I just had to find my way through that inner topography, to know where each thing was, just walk through there to remind myself, not thinking that one day I would have to give an account of all this to someone else, to hand it on. Now I notice that the paper is peeling off some of the walls and that some of the objects are getting rather rickety, that I no longer walk with any pleasure through my secret garden; I'm just not in the mood to put things in order, to air the rooms, as you do when you're about to receive an important visitor."

"Of course," says Maurício, "that's exactly what's happening, you're expecting an important visitor. But, forgive me for saying so, you don't seem yourself; I've never seen you so excited, so off-balance, and I imagine you want to make a good impression on him. That's the main thing. It doesn't matter what bits of paper or whatever you show him, the important thing is that he should know you as you are, not in this obsessive mode. Do you know what you should do? You should carry on as if nothing had happened, as if it had all been a dream, assume that he probably won't come."

He's still sitting on the carpet, looking into the dull embers of the fire. He stretches out his legs to make himself more comfortable. He's not going up to bed until she does and, besides, it doesn't look as if this conversation is about to end just yet. He feels her hands on his shoulders; he turns round and sees an anxious, tense look on her face.

"What's wrong? Are you feeling worse?"

"What makes you say that he won't come? Has he phoned you and you haven't dared give me the news? Is that it?"

"And you say that I enjoy making a drama out of everything! What news do you think I'm hiding from you now? I'm just saying it to calm you down, because I don't know what's wrong with you tonight, you seem in a sort of daze. When he comes, he'll come and that's that. But please, don't wander around all day like a lost soul."

"Yes, you're right, I am like a lost soul, and do you know why? Because I start thinking about what he might be thinking, and a very odd thing happens, you'll probably laugh: I can *see* him thinking. After the phone conversation we had, I can't help it, I can see him thinking, I know him, Maurício, he's like me. He'll be going over and over what I said to him, just as I am. On the one hand, I provoked his curiosity, but, on the other, he'll want to surprise me; there's something going on, I'm sure of it; that's what has me on tenterhooks, on a knife-edge; something's going on. And whatever's going on and whatever game it is he's about to play all depends on what attitude I take. This delay is all in order to disconcert me; he's throwing down some kind of challenge, although it's similar to the one I proposed to him; neither of us knows quite how to approach the other's territory, do you follow me?"

Maurício burst out laughing.

"I've followed you through all the years I've known you and because I'm hooked on crosswords, the harder the better, otherwise, who else would have sat with you all these hours tonight, because your head, Señora, is in a complete and utter mess."

She's laughing a little now too. The pressure of her hands eases and before withdrawing them, she strokes Maurício's curly head affectionately.

"Of course," she says, "it's just that I'm not used to anyone keeping me on tenterhooks. Eugenio told me as much a thousand times: 'Perhaps one day you'll find out what it's like to be utterly dependent on someone else, and be unable to sleep because he can't sleep, and want to put his brain under a microscope to know exactly what he's thinking; until someone teaches you that, Sila, for all your intelligence, you've still got things to learn'; his son had to be the one to teach me that, you see. I'm as afraid of being controlled by him as I am of wanting that to happen and not knowing how to handle it. In short, I'm not free. I've spent thirty years calling to him across the sea, just as I used to call to my mother, and sometimes he would come and at others he would go again, thirty years writing to him, dreaming of him. I knew that one day I would see him, because he hadn't died as my mother had, but I wasn't in a hurry. I was sure that on some beach in the world he would pick up my coded messages inside a bottle, but they weren't dated and didn't arrive in any particular order – my usual relationship with the imaginary, with what has not yet happened. Now it's different, now he's actually going to come. And I'm afraid because I know him, because he's like me, that he may do something unexpected. Besides, don't forget, Maurício, I have a story to tell him, a long story, and I don't want to put a foot wrong."

Maurício stands up, goes over to the fire and uses the tongs to pick up the half-burned logs and arrange them carefully on the ashes. Then he turns round and starts to collect together the remains of supper.

"Look, Señora, you're worried about this story and about where you should start and about the letters from his grandmother and his father that explain how he was born and when and whatever. I'll tell you something, you won't need any of those bits of paper. So you can sleep easy. Understood?"

She looks at him, surprised, trying to decipher the enigmatic smile flickering on her friend's lips.

"No, I don't understand, I don't understand anything, and I don't know why you're smiling either."

"It's very simple really. Stop worrying your head about how the story ends and begins. It starts with you seeing each other, doesn't it? There's no doubt about that, is there?"

"Fine, we're going to see other, if he comes, that is. So what?"

"You won't have to tell him anything. Believe me. He'll just have to see you. You're forgetting that I've met him."

The woman's face lights up with a smile that is halfway between amazement and pure pleasure.

"You never told me that. Are we so very alike?"

Before answering, Maurício carefully studies the woman's face. His expert eye looks with a lover's satisfaction at her prominent cheekbones, straight, slender nose, the dimple that softens her determined chin, the soft fold of her lips, the widow's peak of her hair, the arch of her eyebrows, her green, mysterious eyes, lit now by curiosity.

"As like as two peas in a pod, Señora," he assures her. "And now, I don't know about you, but I'm going upstairs, because it's nearly four o'clock in the morning and I need some sleep."

IV

The splinter of glass

Leonardo Villalba woke up with a start an hour before the train was due to reach its destination, and he sat on the edge of the bunk amongst crumpled newspapers and tangled clothes. He switched on the light. The heating was on much too high.

He had just been dreaming that he was travelling at high speed in a gigantic steamroller built like an aircraft carrier that razed to the ground all the woods and houses in its path. He was observing the destruction that he himself was causing from a sort of lofty control cabin shielded by glass, and he was incapable of stopping the machine or of getting out of it, although he kept feeling desperately for a door or a crack in those hermetic walls. He noticed too that it was getting colder and colder. His anxiety increased when he spotted the Quinta Blanca in the distance, complete with hexagonal tower, and saw that the unmistakeable outlines of the building were approaching at vertiginous speed; instead of growing larger, though, it was growing smaller. How easy it would be to crush it, how inevitable! It looked like one of those fragile cardboard castles carefully constructed by the hand of a child after patient hours of labour with scissors and glue. He woke up at the point when the infernal machine, captained by himself, was about to reach the gates, but he just had time to glimpse the tiny figure of a woman standing in the middle of the garden waving her arms. The train had suddenly stopped.

He got up to look for a bottle of mineral water in the cabinet above the built-in washbasin, and he drank nearly all of it. Then he lifted the curtain covering the window. They hadn't stopped at a station; they were on the edge of a maize field with a scattering of small houses in the distance. He lowered the window and leaned out to breathe in a

lungful of morning air. The sun had just come up. It was quite cold, but
not a scrap of cloud spoiled the uniform, pale blue of the sky, quite an
unusual phenomenon in that area. Although his stomach still knotted
whenever he thought about his imminent arrival, Leonardo felt that the
novelty of a clear sky was a good omen. During the last few days, there
had been heavy snow over the whole of northern Spain, and he had
spent a great deal of time keeping an eye on the weather reports, on
graphics and hypothetical figures, trying to make a decision. Now,
with his eyes fixed on the overwhelmingly real sight of a passing maize-
field, he felt strange. Did the lack of snow mean something? Those
forecasts of bad weather, which, a few days earlier, had coincided with
his indecision about whether or not to make the journey, had become
an excuse that was as abstract as it was fallacious: "I can't go because
it's snowing", instead of confessing the truth: "I haven't reached a
decision yet because I'm afraid." Afraid of what? Of having his doubts
resolved, of breathing differently? Then one morning, the real crux
of the matter had been suddenly laid bare, as so often before, via the
providential intervention of literature. He remembered Gerda and that
was when the scales fell from his eyes. Had she given any thought to
possible changes in temperature before setting off on the complicated
journey that she had to undertake in order to decipher her own hieroglyphs and to return Kay's memory to him. Had her adventure not been
marked by periods of shadow and sunshine, day and night, wind and
snow? He stopped buying newspapers and listening to the radio. He
ordered a ticket over the phone and sent a telegram to the Quinta
Blanca. "Arriving tomorrow on the night train. With best wishes.
Leonardo Villalba." Now, watching the first light of morning spread
over a landscape full of familiar echoes, he wondered what his story
really had to do with that of Gerda galloping off on the back of a reindeer. Naturally, it had something to do with it, but he almost preferred
not to know precisely what, to give himself a rest from investigation
and interpretation, "You'll go mad with all that searching in books for
the philosopher's stone; go out and take a walk." His grandmother was
right. On the other hand, she was the one who set him endless riddles
even after her death, indeed perhaps even more so. Smiling, he closed

the window. The train slowly moved off. He began brushing his teeth.

Once he was washed and dressed, he left the compartment; the corridor was empty. He leaned against the window and watched as the trees, houses, roads, bridges, rivers and telegraph poles sped past and were gone, while the light ripened, rescuing from the shadows those newborn images of a young December morning, a gift for the absorbed, melancholy child who has finally decided to take his grandmother's advice and leave his books and go out for a walk. It's inevitable, though, that the words trapped in books should have such resonance; with them we build the very bridge that carries us across to that landscape glimpsed from the battlements of the fortress. He thought of the Cavafy poem that had one night served as a viaticum for someone else's journey and which he kept remembering, when he least expected it, as if it were the catchy chorus to a song. Mónica, the sleeping girl, came and went in an equally sporadic manner, and her appearance in his memory only increased Leonardo's nostalgia for what he had not got. He left her dreaming on the platform of an uncertain journey; what end would her adventure have had?

> When you start on your journey to Ithaca,
> then pray that the road is long.
> To arrive there is your ultimate goal,
> but do not hurry the journey at all.

After complicated discussions with himself, having Ithaca as his destination had, in the end, prevailed over the charm of what he had not got. Hurrying the journey meant going back over all the ups and downs of an inner schism, blindly anticipating improbable behaviour, no longer seeking shelter in the glow of the moment, in the privilege of breathing; in short, immersing himself in the paralysis that drives away the miracle. He had to forget the text of all the conversations he had rehearsed and perfected alone, of all the imagined questions, to think only that he was going on a journey in a comfortable train and not on board some infernal steamroller, that he had escaped from places where the air was beginning to smell of death, that he was thirty years old and that the day had dawned with a cloudless sky.

The guard in charge of the wagon-lit appeared at the far end of the corridor and started walking along it knocking at the doors of the different compartments to wake up the travellers. Leonardo asked him if he had time to have a coffee and was told that, yes, he had half an hour.

While he was having breakfast in the buffet car, he learned, from fragments of conversation overheard between waiters on the other side of the bar, that it was Christmas Eve.

*　*　*

He saw her at once, even before he set foot on the platform, when the train had just come to a halt and he, having spent ten minutes waiting in readiness, had picked up his suitcase and glanced casually over in that direction from the running board. He saw her, despite the fact that she was a long way off, despite the fact that he neither knew what she looked like nor expected her to be waiting for him. He hadn't glanced in that direction in order to look for her or for anyone, since his telegram gave no indication, at least not intentionally, of any need for a lift to the Quinta Blanca. Why would he? He had given the date and the time of the train he was catching in Madrid because he didn't want just to turn up at someone else's house, he wanted to allow them some margin for preparation and to allow himself time too. Of course, in his case it wasn't a room or a meal he had to prepare, he had to prepare his mind; but perhaps his hostess would be going through the same process, who knows how she would be feeling about taking into her house someone who had lived there for years and years and who was, more to the point, the son of her girlhood lover? It was bound to be the cause of some turmoil, even without knowing that he had read her letters and her book and the draft of her novel. Reading her ideas, particularly her ideas on vertigo, you did not get a sense of a person with the utter equanimity of one who has known no storms.

He, at any rate, needed that breathing space. He could arrive there in time for lunch or even, perhaps, mid-afternoon, take a taxi or a bus, even hitch a lift, depending on the weather, his mood and how tired he was; what he absolutely didn't need was a chaperone. In fact, while he was having breakfast in the buffet on the train, and since there was still not a sign of a cloud in the sky, an alternative had begun to take shape in his mind, had almost become a firm decision: he would go for a stroll about the town, lunch quietly in some small bar he happened upon and postpone his trip to the Quinta Blanca until the afternoon. What he wouldn't do, on the other hand, was give in to the parallel temptation of composing in his mind the script of a possible telephone conversation warning of that delay, and setting a time to do so; he would just wait and see, he would leave it to chance. It was best not to pile up useless anxieties beforehand, and hearing Casilda's voice again without seeing her face could provoke such anxieties. "It's not a good idea, Leonardo, you're on dangerous ground there, because afterwards things don't turn out as you planned them at all; that mania of yours for always putting the cart before the horse, you were like that even as a small boy. Don't worry, let her do the worrying." And the suspicion that his delay in coming might have sown a seed of disquiet in the mind of the Quinta Blanca's new owner excited him. He had to find some comfort in that, as well as in the thought that she had been the one to invite him; he had simply asked for an appointment without specifying a time or a place. It's true that the initial aim of that meeting – suggested by the notary – had foundered completely and now belonged to the underwater world. What was happening now was equally irrelevant. He had come unarmed, with no script prepared, to celebrate Christmas with a strange woman, under her roof. It was a question of trying to enjoy the adventure and have a good time. He smiled at the waiter – who, when he picked up the tip, had just wished him a happy Christmas – then went to collect his suitcase. He stood on the running board feeling at peace with himself, ready for anything except what awaited him when the train stopped.

Taking a taxi to the Quinta Blanca (this option had definitively replaced all the others) was the most pleasurable chapter in the whole plot, and Leonardo had assumed that he would do so alone. That road – sometimes following the meanders of the coastline, sometimes moving inland – was etched in fire on his memory. The idea of travelling that road again, after all these years of opaque, complicated adventures, was like a kind of beneficent truce before he finally glimpsed Ithaca, his goal, on the horizon. To arrive there is your ultimate goal, he muttered to himself while he ate his breakfast, gazing up at the cloudless sky, but do not hurry the journey at all. Exactly; he would take Cavafy's advice and savour the journey without hurrying it, without hurrying himself, submitting to the vivid images which, during that final stage of the journey, were becoming superimposed over the equivocal design of a tired, old story, perhaps – why not? – in order to correct that story using some clue hidden in the folds of the countryside itself, which is yet another text that requires deciphering – a bearer of riddles. Perhaps, on the way, he would find the key in the landscape, fifty miles offered up to the perspicacious eye that neither prejudges nor dismisses anything, eager just to look. He would open the window of the taxi and he would abandon himself to the salt air, the best medicine for sweeping the soul clean of ghosts, fifty miles with his pores open to the vivifying energy of the sea, open to its absence when, though hidden, you can still smell it, and to its exploding presence when it reappears around the next bend speaking a different language. "Please," he would say, "can you drive slowly." He hoped he didn't get a talkative driver.

Now, suddenly, the circumstances and the significance of that final stage of the journey had been ruined, because he wasn't going to be travelling alone. He knew it as soon as he saw her at the far end of the platform, standing under the sign saying Exit, and to the left of the newspaper stand. He immediately adjusted to this change that was spoiling his plans, however, with the same naturalness with which he accepted that she had come to take him to her house where she had invited him to spend Christmas, as if he did not know how to get there alone or as if it would not have been more logical, in any case, to have sent Maurício, since they already knew each other, a fact that would have eased the first meeting. Leonardo Villalba had not said in his telegram from Madrid: "I am tall, have green eyes and will probably be wearing a black raincoat." He had simply said: "With best wishes."

The strangest thing of all was that he and that woman, though they had never met before, unequivocally recognized each other. Or was it stranger still to realize that fact without feeling any particular sense of shock? He thought these things vaguely – along with other ideas that came into life and fluttered about – as he walked straight towards the woman, with the same mixture of incredulity and certainty he felt when his grandmother or his father appeared to him in dreams, and he was dragged along by a mysterious force that did not stem from his will exactly, or at least not from the type of will that comes and goes when one is awake. It was a dream (if that is what it was) from which fear and sorrow were happily absent. Slipping from one perception to another is not that unusual for someone used to taking drugs, but these were not concentric whirlpools that mutually excluded and strangled each other as they narrowed into one, like water running down a drain. No, it wasn't like a funnel at all, it was like an infinite opening out, a harmonious parade of thoughts that had all agreed to tear down walls and fling open windows – an open-air hallucination. "I hope it lasts," Leonardo said to himself, slowing his step, "I don't want to wake up. I hope it lasts a long time. Perhaps when I reach the end of the platform, she'll just disappear and my supply of optimism will have been used up. It often happens in dreams." As also happens in dreams, he had a suspicion that the person was only visible to his eyes. If not, why did nobody stop, why did nobody look at her? How was it possible to walk by, brush past her even, without noticing her?

Sometimes he lost her from view, either because he was shoved out of the way by other travellers who were walking more quickly, or because his view was blocked by endless ranks of bobbing heads, or by the need to step to one side to make way for carts laden with luggage. And when that motionless figure, wrapped in a pearl-grey overcoat with the collar up, reappeared in the distance – as if between the folds of a half-drawn curtain – he would breathe a sigh of relief and again watch the rhythm of his steps, saying sometimes: "I hope that woman in grey I can see is Casilda Iriarte," and at others: "It is her, I'm sure, it must be." A "she" who plunged into his soul, leapt from stone to stone, and whose splashing stirred the ancient well left by those adolescent dreams, eternally unsatisfied, regardless of all his travelling or of the various affairs he had had. It was "she", the "she" in novels; she had stepped out of the books that his grandmother kept in the cupboard in the corridor, out of romantic engravings where her figure was silhouetted against a backdrop of stormy seas (perhaps with a ship going down in the distance), of the romantic stories he had written alone and in secret. Whole years spent dreaming of her in the tower, on the cliff, during the torment of those family lunches, in the voice of Patsy Cline or Teresa de Noronha, during dawns shared with various rootless girls, on exotic beaches, in a prison cell, and always in order to achieve the same object, to make the barren loveless wastes more bearable. She was emerging now from the S of sleep and of secret, the S of Sila, the S in *flor de lís*, and from a series of letters addressed to the young Eugenio Villalba and read later on by his son; it was her, the lighthouse keeper's granddaughter, a character straight out of a novel who had just been made flesh.

She didn't move or come to meet him, but when Leonardo had covered half the distance separating them, a gap opened up between two people who before had been clasped in an embrace, and he could make out not only her whole figure, from the small felt hat pulled down over her eyes to the little boots with heels, he could see that she was smiling and moving her right hand back and forth in front of her face as if trying to clear a misted window, and there was no doubt then: it was a sign intended for him. He did not, however, dare to reply to that strange greeting with a sign of his own, for fear of being unceremoniously expelled from the troubling land of doubt. He felt a wave of heat flush his face; he averted his eyes and decided not to look at Casilda Iriarte again until he was by her side, and to delay that meeting as long as possible. He was not used to such strong emotions.

The odd thing is that when he finally reached the newspaper stand and looked up, having kept his eyes fixed firmly on the ground as he approached at a tortoise-like pace, Casilda Iriarte was no longer there. He stopped, disconcerted, put his suitcase down on the ground and looked anxiously about him, and, for the first time in many years, he felt a forgotten emotion. It wasn't the anxiety of knowing himself watched or pursued or of feeling trapped by bloodsucking companions, but the sense of having lost something precious and irreplaceable that had evaporated without warning – like his grandmother – a saline drip keeping him alive. It was like noticing suddenly that the water had been turned off at the mains. He stood there for a moment, in the grip of indecision, not wanting to leave the place where he had seen or thought he had seen that woman, craning his neck in all directions, looking lost, and letting himself be buffeted by the hurrying, gesticulating people heading for the exit.

Finally, he noticed that the woman selling newspapers was eyeing him curiously and so he spoke to her.

"Excuse me, did you see a lady in grey standing here?"

The stallholder was a rather plump, confident-looking woman of about forty. She looked at him scornfully.

"What do you mean in grey?"

"I mean in grey, she was tall and she was wearing a grey overcoat."

"Well, dear, you can easily miss a colour like grey. Haven't you any more clues?"

"Yes, she was tall, like I said, and she was wearing a hat."

"Was the hat grey too?"

"I didn't notice."

"What do you mean you didn't notice? You did see her, didn't you?"

Cast down, Leonardo shrugged his shoulders.

"I think I did," he muttered, still scrutinizing the people passing by.

There wasn't a sign of the woman in grey. He pretended to be looking at the books on one of those revolving display units, because he was suddenly conscious that he must cut a rather ridiculous figure. He didn't know what to do. Whilst still attending to her other customers, the saleswoman was watching him, amused.

"Hey you," she said smiling, while she was giving change to someone buying *Hello* magazine, "if you're a stranger, and you look like one to me, I'd better warn you about something: people often see ghosts around here."

He looked at her, stunned, about to tell her that he had never felt more of a stranger than he had at that moment, exiled from paradise, completely out of his depth. The only other time he had perhaps felt something similar was on that snowy morning when he read the letter from his grandmother, brought to him by Trud, dressed entirely in white, and in which he hoped to find the key to all his grandmother's hieroglyphs. Naturally, he said nothing. He looked so helpless, though, that the newspaper seller took pity on him and suggested that he find the station master and have them broadcast a message for the person on the public address system.

"I assume you know her name," she concluded. "Or don't you know that either?"

"Yes I do, but, don't worry, I'll find her. Thanks very much. I think I'll have a look outside. Could I have a copy of *El País*?"

He wasn't going to stay there all morning. He had to make a decision, and calling for Casilda Iriarte over the loudspeakers seemed to him absurd. How could he be sure that she really had come?

"You know best, dear. Good luck, though. Hey, come back, you've forgotten your change."

When he left the newspaper stand, the platform was already much emptier. As he walked hesitantly towards the exit, following the last groups of travellers, he was trying to give himself sensible instructions that would exorcise the feeling of sudden exhaustion that was also rather spell-like in its effects. After all, what had happened? Nothing. A woman dressed in grey, who might or might not have been Casilda Iriarte, had disappeared amongst the crowds and he had allowed her to escape. She might not have left alone, she might have left with the recipient of the strange wave that Leonardo had believed to be directed at him. He had given them plenty of time to meet and disappear together, more than enough time; he had taken so long to cover the last stretch of platform! And that person would have embraced the woman in grey and called her by her name, a name that need not necessarily have been Casilda Iriarte, however tempted he was to call her that, and they would have gone out into the morning sun with their arms about each other's waists. Although there was also a possibility that it might have been a woman friend or a distant relative, there was no reason why it had to be a lover. He felt an urgent desire to find out. If he hurried, he might catch up with them in the cafeteria or at the taxi rank. He reproached himself for his ineptitude in losing track of that story out of pure cowardice, just because he had been incapable of holding someone's gaze, because he had deliberately held back, half-hiding himself, from the moment that she had given him that slow wave. Or perhaps it had all been an hallucination. The woman selling newspapers was right, it was a place of ghosts.

Nothing irreparable had happened. "Don't get things out of proportion, Leonardo, you have to adapt to unforeseen changes, that means not hurrying your journey and not letting yourself be taken in by mirages or by siren songs," he kept repeating to himself with no conviction whatsoever. "It's still nice weather, isn't it? Well, go back to the plans you were hatching over breakfast: take a stroll about the city, have a bit of lunch and then, this afternoon, you can calmly take a taxi out to the Quinta Blanca by the coast road." These plans, however, had lost their glow, and he went over them in his mind as if they were a tedious maths lesson.

He was standing in the station lobby, looking out, absorbed, listless. Suddenly he saw a row of telephone booths to his left and realized that his priorities had changed. The most urgent thing was to phone the Quinta Blanca to find out if Casilda Iriarte was there or not. It was the only reasonable thing to do. Why hadn't he thought of it before? Her voice would unblock the log jam once and for all; that voice would just have to say, for example: "Is that you, Leonardo? Did you have a good journey?" in order to extract him from his mental mire. And, of course, now he wouldn't play any games, he wouldn't beat about the bush or play it cool. "I'll come at once if you like," he would say, "you gave me such a fright, I'm so looking forward to seeing you, I dreamt that I'd lost you. Would you mind very much dressing in grey?" It was bound to come out like that.

He had just put the coins in and was dialling the first number of the code that he knew by heart, when he felt someone tap him on the shoulder. He turned round, startled, and it was her, in person, the lady in grey. She was smiling and carrying a suitcase. She placed it on the floor, removed the glove from her right hand and held it out to him in the void, because Leonardo was so confused at seeing her that he was incapable of reacting. Finally, he dropped the phone, which swung like a pendulum, almost touching the floor, and shook the hand that the lady in grey was holding out to him. He was staring at her with a look of radiant incredulity on his face. She was even more interesting seen close to. She reminded him very much of someone else, perhaps some actress in an old film. The penny did not yet drop.

"You need to have your head screwed on a bit tighter, young man," she said, pointing to the suitcase that she had deposited on the floor, a black leather suitcase. "It is yours, isn't it?"

Leonardo nodded, although it was of little interest to him; it seemed a foolish addition to the plot, something added to throw them off the track.

"Well, if it wasn't for me, it might have disappeared."

"It would have been worse if you had disappeared," said Leonardo, eager to get to the crux of the matter. "Where did you get to? I was just about to phone you."

It seemed natural to him to address her as "tú". As for giving her explanations or demanding them from her about how and why they had recognized each other, it didn't even occur to him. It was just another red herring. She didn't seem concerned to seek enlightenment on that accessory matter either, because no one, for example, finds it illogical that Gerda should arrive mounted on a reindeer in the final part of *The Snow Queen*; what difference does it make if it's a reindeer or a winged horse, the important thing is that she finds Kay and gives him a kiss. They still have their hands clasped.

"You were going to phone me at the Quinta Blanca?" she asked. "That's a bit daft, isn't it? I haven't got wings."

"Are you sure?" he ventured.

Casilda Iriarte withdrew her hand and replaced her grey kid glove. She seemed slightly embarrassed.

"Sometimes I think I do," she said in a low voice, not looking at him, "that's the worst thing; then you come down to earth with a bump. Look, hang up the phone and let's go."

Leonardo put the phone back on the hook and picked up his suitcase. They started walking. She went on ahead at a brisk pace. At the door, they stopped. It was cold, but very sunny. Leonardo was apprehensive about the silence that might begin to thicken between them, although he still wasn't quite over his shock. He needed to make certain that he wasn't a stranger to her, to hear her say his name; she still hadn't done so. He grasped her elbow.

"Why did you hide? You still haven't answered my question."

She didn't look at him.

"Well, you can't always explain everything. I don't know, I just fancied spying on you."

She had spoken in a tone that attempted to be light, but instead sounded almost artificial.

"Spying on me?" he asked, rather uneasily.

"Yes, it's just a game like any other. I wanted to spy on you for a while before speaking to you. Don't you enjoy seeing how people behave and what they do when they think no one's looking at them? I hid behind the newspaper stand, and it made me laugh when you couldn't see me, we were so close, and you looked so lost too. Then when I saw that you'd left your suitcase behind, without even a backward glance, I thought: 'He's just like me', and so I followed you. Come on, let's cross. My car's over there, the black one."

She let go of his arm and crossed nimbly to the other side of the small square. Leonardo's heart turned over. At first he didn't know why, but then he realized. He had just remembered the redhaired girl who came to pick him up outside the prison. "My car's over there." It had been the same afternoon that he found out about the death of his parents, in her car, a rather battered 2CV. He made a mental calculation as to how much time had passed between that journey and the one he was about to undertake now with the lady in grey. Barely two months. It gave him vertigo just to think of it. Vertigo has a lot to do with the way time passes. Everything was so strange that morning.

Casilda Iriarte had opened the boot and placed the suitcase inside. It was quite heavy. Since he had packed his suitcase, Leonardo had forgotten that he'd put all his notebooks in it and he realized that to have lost it would have meant losing track of the last few months and of all the time slumbering in the frozen lake of memory. Although it would perhaps also have meant dropping a bit of ballast.

"What's up? Aren't you getting in?"

That was what the other woman had said, or something similar,

Ángela her name was; later he'd found out she'd had a miscarriage, poor girl, she didn't seem very happy, and he had never really found out the cause of her suffering, only that she was trying to take him with her to a house where others were waiting for him; he was well off out of that. He shook his head; mammoths, they're always ready to leap out at you, the waiter was quite right about that. But today was today, a different day; he was escaping from another prison and Casilda Iriarte was going to help him. It was marvellous letting himself be carried along by her. He couldn't allow any mammoths to cast a shadow over today's sun.

He was so immersed in his own thoughts that he hadn't noticed they had already been driving for a while and were now on the outskirts of the city. They hadn't said another word. The car drew up at some traffic lights. Beyond, between the buildings, you could see the sea.

"I imagine you'd like to take the coast road," she said, "here is where you have to decide."

"I would prefer the coast, yes."

"Do you want any breakfast first?"

"No thanks, I had breakfast on the train."

"Well, fasten your seat-belt then. Are you feeling all right?"

"Yes, fine, I was just thinking what a strange time this is."

"Extremely. I don't know what a beautiful day like this is doing at the end of December. I was just saying so to Maurício this morning. Only two days ago, it was snowing here."

"Yes, it snowed a bit in Madrid too. But I meant time in general, the passage of time; you never know whether it's going to race past or tiptoe by."

"Ah," she said, "I could give you a seminar on that, but let's leave it for later, if you don't mind. I have to concentrate when I drive."

"Don't worry, so do I, even when I'm not driving."

They were on the coast road now. The landscape was so lovely that there was no need to say anything, nor any desire to. Leonardo lowered the window on his side, taking a deep breath and letting the cold wind ruffle his hair, delighting in the rainbow reflections from the sea on his half-closed eyes. And the lady in grey, who had turned out to be Casilda

Iriarte after all, had not got lost. He had recovered from his fright; he felt her presence next to him, although, so as not to distract her, he only looked at her out of the corner of his eye. She was driving slowly, without talking, concentrating on the bends in the road, each one of which had a new marvel to reveal. It was just as he had dreamed, no one was hurrying the journey, there was still not a single cloud in the sky and he hadn't got stuck with a talkative driver. On the contrary: she was perhaps even too impenetrable. From time to time, without turning towards him, she would merely raise her index finger to point out a promontory, an island in the distance, a boat, a seagull – slow, somnambular gestures that seemed more like an expression of her unfathomable inner world than a sign to another person.

When they had been driving for about half an hour, Leonardo began to feel uneasy and, above all, intrigued. What would she be thinking? He looked at her surreptitiously and beneath the apparent impassivity of her profile he seemed to see traces of melancholy. Or even a certain tension. The ebullient self-confidence of the woman who had spoken to him on the phone had made him feel inhibited. This woman seemed different, more vulnerable, sadder. Even though he didn't know the underlying reasons, Leonardo felt touched by that sadness, the way one can sometimes be infected by a rare fever. The suspicion that he had something to do with that virus brought a lump to his throat; he would give anything to analyse the virus under a microscope. But he was incapable of rummaging around in anyone's soul, of asking "What are your symptoms?", "What are you thinking about?" Besides, few people, perhaps no one, had ever awoken in him that burning curiosity. He usually awoke it in others; now the opposite was happening, and it infuriated him to think that someone else might be the protagonist of the thoughts that were making that sad, absorbed face even more beautiful. What could she be remembering? Who? What could be the reason for her suffering?

As they approached their destination and the bends in the road became ones which Leonardo knew well, the silence in which they were wrapped became thick with sparks: an electric charge that came neither from the past nor from other stories, but from the friction of the silence between them. The line of Casilda's lips had grown harder and Leonardo understood that the secret lay there, in that gesture, not in any corner of the landscape nor in any images of childhood that looking at that landscape might revive. He stopped looking out of the window. Something extraordinary was happening or about to happen inside the car and at that very moment. He was afraid to say anything. He was equally afraid to remain silent. Both things had their dangers.

"It's odd," he finally blurted out, "the last time I was on my own in a car with a woman, all I wanted was for her to be quiet."

He paused. He realized how nervous he was, that he was about to get in a muddle. She didn't help him, she merely waited.

"And I told her so," he went on, "in no uncertain terms actually; she just wouldn't let me think, she was one of those people who end every sentence with a question. And I needed peace and quiet. I need it now too, but you don't disturb my peace deliberately, not even by talking to me, it's something else completely different; I'm only comparing the two occasions because I haven't been in a car with a woman since, or with anyone else. Travelling with someone else gives me claustrophobia, well, we weren't really travelling, I'd just got out of prison – it seems incredible, it's only two months ago – and the girl didn't really interest me at all, I don't even know where I met her."

"You're explaining everything in a rather confused manner," she broke in, "wouldn't you say?"

Was he making her feel slightly queasy, as the redhaired girl had made him feel on that other afternoon? But there was no hint of impatience or reproach in her voice, only sweetness. As if she were talking to a child.

"Yes, I know. It's just that things do come out in a rather confused way when you want to tell someone about something, doesn't that ever happen to you? When you say something, it becomes suddenly murky, it changes, and it's worse with things that you thought you had understood when on your own, with the things that gleam like a flash in the dark – those are the hardest things to make other people understand. I admit that I don't usually care much if people understand me or not; I've lived in a kind of cave, especially since my grandmother died;

I tend to do without other people quite a lot. That's why, frankly, what's happening to me today is so odd; I mean, thinking to myself isn't enough. Frankly, Casilda," he said, summing up after a brief pause, "I want to know what you're thinking, I need to know."

He was surprised by his own boldness, by the firmness of his voice. At last, he had been the one to make the first move.

She had slowed down and the car stopped at the top of a hill. Leonardo didn't need to know why they had stopped or where they were. He had lost all interest in the outside world, he was dependent exclusively on her reaction. He was looking at her pleadingly, searching her face. But Casilda still did not turn to look at him. Her breathing had grown faster, and she bent her head, pretending to concentrate on stopping the car.

"What is it you need to know about what I'm thinking, Leonardo?" she asked rather bitterly. "Thinking about what? Because I have so many things going round and round in my head all day, so many, you can't imagine. And I too see them much more clearly when I don't have to explain them."

"What do you think about me, for example, about the fact that I've come to see you. You seem suddenly quite indifferent, and I can't bear it. Forgive me for saying so, but, to be honest, I don't understand why you've invited me. Please, Casilda, look at me, why don't you look at me?"

Before doing so, she placed a hand on his knee. She gave a deep sigh and her nostrils trembled.

"No, Leonardo," she said at last, turning towards him, "I'm far from indifferent to your visit, you can be quite sure of that. And I too have things to tell you, a lot of things, it's just that I don't quite know where to begin. They'll emerge gradually anyway. We have plenty of time ahead of us. But if you pester me like this on the first day, we won't get anywhere, you've got to help me. Just relax, all right?"

She was speaking in a voice that seemed to emerge from a very deep well, grave and helpless. Above all, though, she was looking at him when she spoke; they were looking at each other full on for the first time, and Leonardo couldn't believe what he was seeing. Because he was seeing his own face. It wasn't an hallucination, it was real: it was like looking at himself in the mirror. For a while now, he had been trying to think who Casilda reminded him of, trying to fathom her mystery, and now it turned out that the clue to the riddle was hidden somewhere he would never have dreamed of looking, in the features of the face he had looked at so often, routinely, while he was shaving, in the knowing look she was now giving back to him, like a reflection of his own eyes. A sea-green reflection. He had lost the power of speech. He merely placed his hand over the smaller hand resting on his knee. Even their hands were alike. And he nodded in silence, astonished.

Casilda Iriarte changed position, undid her seat-belt and opened the car door. She didn't pull away from Leonardo brusquely, but after a friendly, albeit weary smile, as if she were asking him permission to remove her hand.

"Right," she said, "I think we could both do with getting out and stretching our legs and having a bit of fresh air before we go home. I don't know if you recognize where we are, but I love this place. I used to come here with your father."

Leonardo tore his eyes away from his own hand abandoned on his knee and saw, through the back window, the white tower of the light-house, with the cliffs to the right. Through the door, which had been left open, there came the violent smell of boundless sea and the eternal noise of the waves tirelessly rising and breaking. By the time he got out of the car, she had started walking up the hill and the wind was catching at the long scarf she had around her neck, the scarf she had just taken out of the large handbag that she wore slung across her shoulders. He stood for a while watching her from behind, indifferent to everything, and then he slowly followed her. He was in no hurry to reach her, on the contrary. The indolent gait of that grey figure ahead of him, her easy step, was another piece in the puzzle, and he liked to keep the requisite distance in order to understand it and to enjoy simply contemplating it. Framed by that wild landscape, alone and deep in thought, she looked like a character out of a painting by Friedrich.

He only caught up with her when they were almost at the top of the steep hill that leads to the lighthouse. She did not turn her head when she felt him put an arm around her shoulder, but she responded by moving slightly closer to him. Although she was quite tall, she only came up to his chin. Leonardo was aware of the smell of her hair, mingled with that of the sea. He had never felt so comfortable walking along with another person, unhurried, unembarrassed, feeling no obligation to say anything. They walked round the lighthouse and stood with their arms about each other, battered by the wind, watching the waves breaking on the island of seagulls and then dissolving in jets of foam in the brilliant morning light.

"On one of those rocks down there," Casilda said, pointing towards the cliffs, "I once made a pact with your father. We promised that we would always have a secret that would bind us together, even if life should separate us. It was my idea. I was very young, almost a child; in the village they used to say I was a fortune teller. Your father was afraid of that oath because he didn't understand it properly, and he always wanted to understand everything, and the idea of sealing that mysterious alliance with blood frightened him even more. Deep down he was afraid of his mother; he said: 'God will punish us', but I said he was a coward and got out my penknife. After a few years, he was the one who came to ask me to keep my promise. Or rather, he didn't come here, he looked for me in other lands. I didn't come back here until six years ago, when I bought the Quinta Blanca from you. Through an intermediary," she said, smiling, "as you yourself put it the other day. Some intermediary, eh?"

Leonardo moved away and looked at her. He realized that the lump in his throat was growing. Despite all the years that had passed, he recognized that unmistakeable warning sign, like recognizing the voice of a person who once used to visit our house and who now approaches and calls to us from outside. But he still had not opened the door. He swallowed hard.

"And the secret?" he asked in a murmur.

She opened her arms wide, indicating the immensity of the sea. She looked like a bird about to take flight.

"It's lost out there. I don't know, it went and hid in underwater palaces, in storms that don't break, in bottles from shipwrecks, who knows, perhaps it's in a letter from Doña Inés Guitián lost in some corner of the tower."

"Did my grandmother know about this?" said Leonardo, very excited. "Did you know my grandmother? I'm sorry, Casilda, what's wrong? Don't you feel well?"

She didn't answer. She had stumbled slightly and was leaning against the wall of the lighthouse. She was very pale and had closed her eyes.

"It's nothing," she said in a voice so feeble he could barely hear it. "It's just a touch of vertigo."

Leonardo took off his black raincoat, folded it up and placed it on the ground for her to sit on. She meekly let him do so. He knelt at her side and noted the comings and goings of that faltering breath whose waves upset his own. It was like the sharp drop in blood pressure you get when you've smoked a lot of hash. He knew all too well that, in such cases, the important thing was to remain calm.

"Breathe deeply and lean your head back," he said. "Does it happen often? No, don't talk."

Her only response was to half-open her eyes and point to her handbag; it had slipped off when she sat down. Leonardo handed it to her and she opened it. It was filled with a clutter of disparate objects that she blindly rummaged around in. She finally found a small tube of pills. She opened it, took one out and placed it under her tongue. She closed her eyes again. She already seemed to be feeling better. She communicated this to him with a slow movement of her hand, as if recommending complete calm. Leonardo read the directions inside the tube. Then he took her pulse and it was as if, through those arrhythmic beats gradually returning to normal, he received the same relief that he was trying to give to her, like a fluid in communicating vessels exchanging passion and hope.

"I'm all right now," she said, after a while, opening her eyes. "It doesn't usually last very long. I'm sorry if I frightened you."

"It was my fault for pestering you with questions. I didn't know you had a heart problem. Well, how would I? You've still got so many things to tell me, but we need to take it slowly. The main thing is that you look after yourself. You shouldn't have come to meet me at the station."

"That's what Maurício said. We spent yesterday evening arguing. He didn't want me to come at all, but I'm very stubborn."

She paused and smiled. All the light of the sea seemed to have returned to her green eyes. But now she was talking more slowly.

"It's just too many emotions all at once," she went on. "I've been sleeping very badly lately and I'm overexcited; I'm in no condition for somersaults any more. Maurício's going to take me to the doctor after Christmas. We argue a lot, but I don't know what would become of me if it wasn't for him. We've known each other for twenty years, imagine that."

She was gazing off into the distance, serious, absorbed. But her face lit up when Leonardo, still kneeling by her side, took her two hands and squeezed them hard.

"Now, you've got me, Casilda, I'll take you to the doctor or wherever. I'll be your chauffeur, your secretary, your barman, your typist, your dancing partner, and we'll go on journeys together and play games, and we'll laugh, and I won't leave your side until you send me away. But, please, don't send me away, it's been so long since anyone loved me."

Emotion drowned his words and his eyes glinted like the sea about to dissolve into foam. Casilda stretched out her legs and made a place for him on her lap, telling him to rest his head there.

"Don't worry, I'm feeling much better now. Just be quiet for a moment, you have a rest too. We've only been here ten minutes and we've already created a proper little melodrama for ourselves! I don't know which of us is crazier. Just relax. It will do you good."

And then, as she stroked his dishevelled hair and noticed how he was trembling, she said softly, as if she were singing.

"You're trembling, my dear, see if you can have a cry. It's difficult, I know, it's hard for me too, but it does you good, especially if there's someone there to collect your tears. It clears the blocked soul, and you're born into another life, you emerge from the fire into the water. As a child, whenever I felt something burning inside me, I would invent stories with unhappy endings so that I could come up here and cry, looking out at the waves. Crying is like a breaking of the waters.

Babies always cry when they're born. Would you rather be alone?"

He looked up from her lap and shook his head fiercely. Then, kneeling again by her side, he gazed at her fervently, wildly, as if at a miraculous apparition.

"At last you've come, Gerda. You've taken so long to arrive. Kiss me," he begged, his voice choked with emotion.

Casilda sat up, leaned forward and started kissing him slowly on his forehead, his cheeks, his eyelids. Then, when she saw that the moment had come, she put her hands together and placed them beneath Leonardo's chin, like a cup, to collect the tears which were sliding gently down his cheeks, overflowing from eyes incapable of containing them any longer.

Inside the first tear she noticed a sort of glass needle that pricked the palm of her left hand as it fell. She picked it up between two fingers of her right hand and looked at it against the light. It was the splinter of glass.

Ex Libris